THE POLITICS OF GERMAN REGULATION

The Politics of German Regulation

Edited by
KENNETH DYSON
University of Bradford

Dartmouth

Aldershot • Brookfield USA • Hong Kong • Singapore • Sydney

Published by
Dartmouth Publishing Company Limited
Gower House
Croft Road
Aldershot
Hants GU11 3HR
England

Dartmouth Publishing Company
Old Post Road
Brookfield
Vermont 05036
USA

A CIP catalogue record for this book is available from the British Library and the US Library of Congress

Printed and Bound in Great Britain by
Hartnolls Limited, Bodmin, Cornwall.

ISBN 1 85521 273 0

Contents

List of Tables and Figures

Tables

Figures

List of Contributors

Simon Bulmer, Senior Lecturer in Politics, Department of Government, University of Manchester.

Kenneth Dyson, Professor of European Studies, Department of European Studies, University of Bradford.

Peter Humphreys, Lecturer in Politics, Department of Government, University of Manchester.

Karl Koch, Senior Lecturer, Department of Linguistic and International Studies, University of Surrey.

Gerhard Lehmbruch, Professor of State Theory, Faculty of Administrative Science, University of Konstanz.

Michael Moran, Professor of Politics, Department of Government, University of Manchester.

Stephen Padgett, Senior Lecturer in Politics, Department of Politics, University of Essex.

Albert Weale, Professor of Politics, School of Economic and Social Studies, University of East Anglia.

Douglas Webber, Lecturer in Management, European Institute of Business Administration, Fontainebleau.

Series Foreword

The Association for the Study of German Politics (ASGP) was established to encourage teaching and research in the politics and society of the German-speaking countries: the Federal Republic of Germany, the German Democratic Republic, Austria and Switzerland. Since it was founded in 1974, the ASGP has brought together academics from a variety of disciplines – politics, languages, history, economics and other social sciences – who, along with others with practical and personal interests, are concerned with contemporary developments. The ASGP, through holding numerous conferences and seminars, has proved to be an invaluable forum for discussion and research. The launching of this series, based on the work of specialized study groups, represents a significant extension of the Association's research activities. The publications committee of the ASGP believes that, in drawing upon a wide range of expertise, the volumes in this series will be of value to a wider public – teachers, students, and those involved with policy and research – who otherwise may lack readily accessible information on current issues.

Simon Bulmer, Manchester
William Paterson, Edinburgh
Gordon Smith, London School of Economics

Preface

The decade of the 1980s witnessed a new period of fierce controversies about regulation in the Federal Republic of Germany. New ideas came to inform the debate about regulation, notably in broadcasting and environmental policy. Particularly with the Single European Market and German unification the cast of actors on the regulatory stage was enlarged. Professional economists with a commitment to the model of the competitive market sought to augment their influence, as in other countries (see Lehmbruch's chapter). Regulatory agencies attempted to expand their sphere of jurisdiction, for reasons of institutional philosophy and self-interest. Meanwhile, actors already part of the regulatory process began to redefine their institutional self-interests, sensing new opportunities or threats from economic and technological changes and particularly from the internationalization of policy sectors. As we shall see in this volume, this new politicization of regulation was manifested in changed policy agendas and in new forms of coalition activity within and around the regulatory process. The result was a challenge, or rather compound of challenges, to the policy inheritance of the Federal Republic and to traditional views about German public policy.

In seeking to address the domestic debate about regulation in Germany, its consequences and the issues raised, this volume is both timely and important. New pressures for regulatory change have been unleashed by major changes in the international arena. In addition to the pervasive effects of technological innovations, three sources of change are particularly important: the international pressures consequent on American 'deregulation'; the implications of the European Community's Single European Market programme ('1992'); and German unification. Singly and together, these new forces represent a major transformation in the economic and political context of German regulation, as the chapters by Bulmer, Dyson, Humphreys, Lehmbruch and Moran emphasize. Liberalization or 'deregulation' is one dimension of regulatory change unleashed by these pressures. In the name of competitive advantage regulatory barriers to competition are abolished, modified or circumvented. As this volume reveals, however, liberalization

xiii

by no means adequately characterizes the regulatory changes at work. Another dimension of change has been represented by state intervention in the name of increased legal codification and control: a process visible not just in nuclear and environmental regulation but also in financial services. The third dimension of regulatory change – harmonization of national regulatory regimes, notably though EC action – has sometimes promoted liberalization, as in broadcasting and road haulage, and sometimes fostered increased legal codification and control, as in insider trading. It is important to try understand what effects these complex and often contradictory pressures have had on German attitudes to, and use of, regulation in public policy. Is it correct to speak of a radical change in the assumptions underlying German public policy?

Whilst the 1980s saw a growth in the literature on German public policy, the literature on the Federal Republic of Germany lacks a systematic analysis of the role of regulation in public policy. This neglect is somewhat surprising. German public policy has traditionally accorded a central role to regulation as the expression of basic political and cultural concerns and purposes. More specifically, regulation has articulated key and distinctive characteristics of the legal culture and the industrial culture of the country, summed up in the term *Ordnungspolitik*. It reflects the importance attached in political ideology and practice to the 'social dimension', to 'public-interest' arguments and to such values as predictability and calculability in social, economic and political relationships. In analysing the specific characteristics of regulation in Germany this volume is also addressing a gap in the existing literature.

The volume is also a contribution to the literature on regulation. Whilst this literature has grown rapidly during the 1980s, its bias has been towards the United States and the United Kingdom, as the pioneers of 'deregulation'. Germany has tended to be neglected, despite the fact that it remains the foremost European economy and one of the world's top two traders. An innovative feature of recent writing on regulation has been the attempt to 'bring culture back in' as an explanatory variable. A systematic analysis of Germany offers an opportunity to test the value of this type of explanation.

The underlying thesis of this volume is that, whilst regulation is caught up in an ever more complex web of interdependence, international and domestic, German regulation continues to be shaped by two dominant factors: by the cultural and institutional characteristics of domestic policy processes; and by the coalition dynamics of specific policy sectors. At the same time, Germany's pervasive regulatory culture and powerful regulatory paradigms at the sectoral level are undoubtedly caught up in new and complex economic and political pressures. These pressures are mediated through international markets (in particular, the role of multinational firms) and institutions (like the EC) and are reinforced by the new challenges created by German unification. Together, they have unleashed a new contest for power within German regulation. An accurate assessment of the changing role of regulation in German public policy must embrace the complex interplay of these factors and weigh their importance in relation to specific policy areas and issues. It is important to be sensitive to the possibility of variations as well as similarities in German regulation and in the nature of regulatory change. Accordingly, the volume focuses on the nature of regulatory policies and processes in different sectors and on how and why these have changed in the 1980s. Sectoral experience serves as a basis for generalizations about the distinctiveness and/or diversity of West German regulation in the 1980s.

In addressing these general questions, each chapter examines a specific policy sector and asks:

(1) given that regulation is a contest for power, who is pressing for regulatory change, why and how, and with what success?
(2) how has regulation changed within the sector? Has the agenda of regulation changed? Have the methods of regulation changed?
(3) how can one best characterize and explain regulatory culture within the sector (that is, attitudes towards the role of regulation)? How greatly have these attitudes changed?
(4) what are the implications and impacts of the EC's role, especially in relation to completing the internal market by the end of 1992?
(5) what are the implications of German unification?

This volume is based on a workshop of the public policy working group of the Association for the Study of German Politics (ASGP), held at the University of Bradford. Particular thanks are due to the German Academic Exchange Service (DAAD) for generously supporting the workshop and, of course, to the contributors who have had to deal not only with numerous editorial demands but with the difficulties of integrating German unification into their analyses. It remains, of course, the case that assessments of the implications of German unification must remain tentative and provisional.

Kenneth Dyson
Bradford
November 1991

1 Theories of Regulation and the Case of Germany: A Model of Regulatory Change

Kenneth Dyson

Regulation is a pervasive and widely accepted phenomenon in advanced industrialized societies. As a general proposition few would deny that it is desirable to place constraints, in the form of the imposition of rules, on the exercise of discretion by those with market or institutional power. Where they would be more prone to disagree is about the precise scope, objectives and methods of regulation. Neo-liberals and social democrats might accept regulation in principle. Yet regulation remains highly contested, both in theory and in practice. To what extent is liberalization or 'deregulation' desirable? To what degree and in what manner should the harmonization of different national regulatory regimes be promoted? In what circumstances is increased legal codification and control justified?

These remarks apply not least to the Federal Republic of Germany. There, regulation is so deeply ingrained as a social and political phenomenon that it is possible to identify one of Germany's distinctive characteristics as its 'regulatory culture'. German attitudes towards regulation appear notably supportive. Regulatory action enjoys a high degree of legitimacy. Yet, the German economy is ever more enmeshed in a fast-changing international economy which, notably since the mid-1970s, has been signalling the need for radical changes in national regulatory frameworks. Liberalization or 'deregulation' emerged as a major international political and economic phenomenon, challenging the inherited ideas about the organization of markets in Germany. This conjunction of a pronounced 'regulatory culture' with a 'deregulatory' international environment makes a reappraisal of German public policy both timely and important. Such a reappraisal, as offered in this volume, can shed fresh light on two areas: the directions of change in German regulation; and the appropriate theoretical approaches to understanding regulatory change. In the process, it is possible to contribute to both the literature on German policy and politics and the more general literature on regulatory policy and politics.

1.   The Nature of Regulation and Approaches to Understanding Regulation

Regulation is a complex phenomenon that can only be properly understood in terms of its four main interrelated characteristics. In the first instance, it is a cultural phenomenon, expressing particular and perhaps changing and contested views about the role of the state in economy and society. Reference to Germany as possessing a regulatory culture draws attention to the importance attached to rules as a means of encouraging or enforcing 'public-regarding' behaviour. 'Deregulation', by contrast, signals an attempt to justify a new and more delimited role for the state by abolishing, modifying or circumventing barriers to competition. Fundamentally, then, regulatory ideas are socially constructed.

From a second perspective, regulation is a very formal and technical mechanism for exercising and controlling power. In the words of Stone (1982), regulation is 'an activity in which the discretion of individuals and institutions is restricted by the imposition of rules'. A general characteristic of regulation is that it is a knowledge-intensive and highly technical process in which power readily gravitates to officials and high-placed experts operating in institutional contexts. As we shall see, this factor, plus the strength and character of the regulatory culture, has traditionally made for the presence of powerful, coherent regulatory paradigms at the sectoral level in Germany and reinforced the autonomy of regulatory action at this level. At the same time, from a third perspective, regulation is pre-eminently a political process involving power relations (Bernstein, 1955). It is a dynamic process of adjustment of interests, public and private, and operates in a context wider than that of the parties directly involved. Power relations in regulation result from the way in which actors develop and apply regulatory ideas within formal institutional contexts that do not exclusively define their interests. The characteristics of regulation as a political process are, accordingly, not just shaped by its formal nature. Its outcomes are not determined in advance. They are the product of the characteristics of complex policy networks and coalition activities which reflect the ability of policy actors to formulate and choose regulatory actions and to make use of ideas to guide the development of regulation.

This emphasis on the dynamic, coalition-based, processes of adjustment in regulation leads on to its fourth characteristic. Regulation is a learning process – above all from past experiences of policy, including policy failures, but also taking account of new information (Heclo, 1974). It is a learning process about the goals of regulation, about the kind of regulatory instruments that are appropriate to achieve these goals, about precisely how to cast rules, about how to constrain regulators and regulated within these rules, and about how to reconcile the fact of change with the creation and maintenance of rule-governed institutions. Goals and instruments of regulation, as well as specific rules, are deliberately generated and adjusted in a complex, multi-tiered process of learning and in a complex interplay of current contingencies and historical legacies. This learning process may be confined to a narrow network of highly professional actors (in the case of changing regulatory instruments and specific rules); or, where the problems and goals of regulation are being reconsidered, the process will involve a wider process of social learning through public debate and conflict, electoral competition and the displacement of authority over regulation (Hall, 1989). Ultimately, however, the essential nature of regulation cannot be captured unless one retains a sense of its four-fold character: as a cultural phenomenon; as a formal, institution-based mechanism; as a political and coalition-based process; and as a learning process.

This view of the nature of regulation informs the theoretical perspective of this volume. Underlying the different chapters is an attempt to caution against attaching too much explanatory weight to a single concept of regulation or approach to regulation. In the case of the analysis of public policy in general, and Germany in particular, attention has tended to focus, sometimes in a very selective and one-dimensional manner, on specific variables and the way in which they have become embedded in the policy process. In relation to Germany attention has been drawn in this way to the importance of the concept of the 'social market economy'; to the legal framework of the *Rechtsstaat*; to the institutional order of federalism; to the degree of 'self organization' within German capitalism; and to 'social partnership'. These traditional dimensions of political analysis are undeniably important. However, in the context of deep-seated changes in the international economy, a re-evaluation of their importance is overdue. That re-evaluation will contribute towards our understanding not just of Germany but also of the appropriate conceptual framework within which to study government–industry relations and, in particular, regulation.

This introduction reviews a set of interrelated factors that shape the nature and dynamics of regulation and that condition and limit the reception and adoption of new regulatory ideas: the role of the international political economy, of culture and of institutions, and of coalitions and policy networks. They are labelled respectively the 'international-centred', the 'culture-centred', the 'institution-centred' and the 'coalition-centred' approaches. Whilst each of these approaches has its own emphasis, they are appropriately seen as complementary. The task is to specify the links amongst them by means of empirical analysis. In this spirit the contributors to this volume seek to document the impact of deregulatory ideas on German public policy by reference to the international, cultural, institutional and political forces that facilitate or hinder their reception.

This chapter argues that a systematic account of German regulation must pay special attention to macro-political institutions and cultural characteristics, notably legal and industrial cultures. They provide more than just the context within which regulatory change takes place. Many of the key ideas that inform debate derive from the cultural and institutional inheritance and

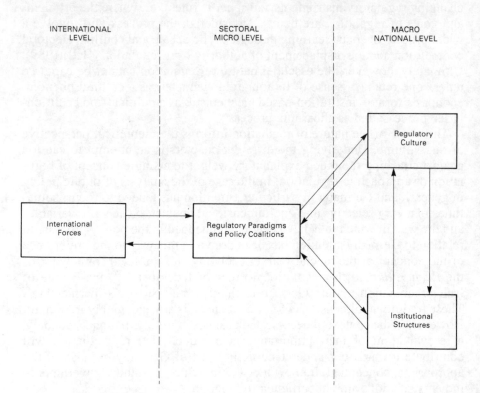

Figure 1.1   A Model of Regulatory Change

the bias that the latter imparts to regulatory responses. At the same time regulatory culture and institutional arrangements are far from being timeless monoliths; they are part of processes of change and cannot independently account fully for regulatory change. Analysis must become more attuned to the impact of changes in the coalition dynamics of particular sectors and in the international political economy. In particular, the combination of international market change with a more assertive role of international institutions, like the European Community, in promoting regulatory harmonization is changing both the operating context and the internal dynamics of the German political economy, not least in regulation. The conclusions suggest the main themes that should inform the analysis of regulation. In particular, they underline the importance of studying the dynamics of coalition change at the sectoral level and their connection, on the one hand, to the general regulatory culture and, on the other, to the international political economy.

2. The 'International-Centred' Approach

From one perspective regulation is inextricably bound together with the character of, and processes of change under way in, the international political economy. Regulation reflects the imperative of international competitiveness, particularly in a context of rapid technological change, and of the emergence of new competitor economies. From this perspective the nature and direction of regulatory change is seen as universalistic, applying in the same way to Germany as to the United States and Britain. The key question becomes where Germany lies in the cycle of regulatory change, not how it differs substantially from other states.

Since the 1970s there has been an upsurge of interest in analysis of the international political economy. This interest has reflected a deepening sense that the state is becoming increasingly less viable and relevant as an economic and industrial entity. A state like Germany cannot sustain its economic and industrial sovereignty in the face of such developments as increased reliance on international trade, the proliferation of huge multinational business companies engaged in international acquisitions, mergers and joint ventures, and the inadequacy of national markets to stimulate profitable investment in ever more expensive research and development. These very same factors act to legitimize the ceding of authority to the European Community, represented most clearly in the form of the Single European Market programme (see the chapter by Bulmer). Regulation of particular sectors becomes, as a consequence, integrated into the international economy. In the process the possibility of controlling the development of regulation is ever more severely limited. Domestic regulatory processes

exhibit symptoms of becoming overburdened by ever more complex interdependence and internationalization. In this context regulation appears to
evolve towards a more pragmatic form of 'brokerage' between the rewards
of tailoring policy towards the needs of international competitiveness and
recognition of, and adjustment to, powerful domestic electoral and political
interests. Albeit in different ways, the chapters on regulation of broadcasting
(Dyson), financial services (Moran) and telecommunications (Humphreys)
underline this impact of international market change. In each of these areas
interdependence has been accompanied by a mounting recognition of the
importance of developing international regimes – new institutions, procedures and rules at the international level. Within that context the EC has
become increasingly significant for a widening range of German policy
sectors. With their focus on domestic institutions and cultures, political
scientists have been disposed to underestimate the changes at work in
German regulation as sectors become more internationalized. Actors in
such sectors as broadcasting, financial services and telecommunications
have become more orientated to the international market and, correspondingly, more interested in developing economic, financial and political links
with overseas actors. This process has enormous implications for regulation.

Pressures from international markets manifest themselves in a variety of
ways. Most obviously, domestic interests use changes in international markets to legitimate regulatory change as imperative for competitiveness,
wealth creation and jobs. They also use their acquisition of a detailed
knowledge of international markets and their high level of technical and
scientific expertise to press for a changed, reduced role for domestic regulation. Additionally, domestic interests can reveal a willingness to divert
their investment abroad to 'regulatory havens' in which operating costs
will be lower. This process can unleash a process of 'international gamesmanship' in regulation as governments seek to use changes in regulatory
provisions as a means of attracting or maintaining investment. In such
'gamesmanship' a particular advantage is held by powerful economies with
high levels of overseas investment. Pressures for regulatory change can
then be seen to reflect asymmetries in the distribution of international
power, perhaps even the hegemonic power of a single state like the United
States. In some of the sectors covered in this volume these factors have
been clearly at work during the 1980s, notably broadcasting, financial
services and telecommunications. The result is that German regulation has
become more interactive with regulation elsewhere. This process has involved new pressures to assimilate regulatory policy changes made elsewhere. It has also drawn attention to opportunities for resolving regulatory
problems at the supra-national level. In short, national autonomy of regula-

tion has been eroded. The consequence is that explanations of regulatory change must be sought outside the national context.

The relationship between regulatory change in Germany and the international political economy has been complex. On the one hand, German policy seems particularly susceptible to changes at the international level. Foreign trade accounts for a high proportion of Gross National Product, with a tendency for many sectors to be heavily export orientated and dependent. On the other hand, Germany has enjoyed a very high trade surplus, notably with the other members of the EC (which represents by far its largest market). This trading success does not act as a stimulant to radically reconsider domestic regulation. Germany's position as such a high-performing trading nation within the international economy might be said to deter radical 'deregulation'. Looked at in a longer historical setting, perhaps no advanced industrialized society can claim to be quite so completely a product of the international system as the Federal Republic of Germany. This observation relates not just to the circumstances of its political birth in 1949 but also to the impact of the 'Americanization' of the German economy after 1945 (Berghahn, 1986). German firms were integrated into an American-dominated international economic order; American managerial ideologies became more influential; and the old cartel structure of industry was modified by imported American anti-trust doctrines. And yet this immediate post-war impact was qualified by two factors: the high quality of Germany's inherited capital stock, and the match between the huge post-war international demand for capital goods and the manufacturing strengths of the German economy. For these reasons the pressure for a radical overhaul of traditional German ideas about the role of regulation was reduced in the 1950s. With German unification in 1990, however, and the erosion of Germany's trade surplus and mounting inflation, the scope for perceptions of policy failure to unleash more radical ideas for deregulation was enhanced.

3. 'Institution-Centred' and 'Culture-Centred' Approaches: The Impact of Historical Legacies

Attention to institutions and culture makes the student of public policy above all sensitive to the *qualitative* differences between German regulation and regulation in other countries, not least the United States and Britain. This perspective, following the intellectual footsteps of Max Weber, points to the importance of historical variations in the role of government and in the cultural and institutional legacy of economic development. The specific characteristics of German historical development have provided Germany with a distinctive normative underpinning to its regulatory policies and processes. In this account, accordingly, the emphasis is on the peculiarities of German responses to market and technological change. Regulation embodies a framework of order and 'normative underpinnings' that is specific to Germany.

During the 1980s this approach has been reinvigorated by the development of the 'new institutionalism' in political science (for example: March and Olsen, 1984; Hall, 1986; and Scott, 1987). The consequence has been a new self-confidence in the political-science contribution to political economy and to regulation. Essentially, institutions are seen as important because they create a framework of duties and obligations. They function not just as constraints; they also channel and shape interactions within the regulatory process. The key characteristic of institutions is that they provide structures and the ideas that inform and legitimate these structures. In other words, they bring together a formal patterning of behaviour with norms that guide that behaviour. As Hall (1986, p. 19) argues, institutions shape behaviour through a combination of formal rules, compliance procedures and standard operating practices. Regulation is, accordingly, more than the sum of countervailing pressures from social and economic groups. It is shaped by an institutional logic. And, in turn, this institutional logic embodies the legacy of history, especially in the form of the ideas that underpin regulation. An additional characteristic of the 'new institutionalism' is that it does not imply a 'state-centric' view of regulation. Indeed, it draws attention to forces outside the state in the wider political realm (including interest intermediaries and political parties) and to their potentially important impact on regulatory policy. The approach ranges more widely to consider the role of institutions located within society and the economy.

Ideas form the linkage between institutions and culture, which are to be seen as two separate but closely related concepts. Cultural analysis draws attention to the importance of beliefs, feelings and values as influences on behaviour. It also argues that the development of specific cultural patterns in particular countries is explained by reference to particular historical experiences, like National Socialism and total defeat in the Second World War and post-war division in the case of Germany (Almond and Verba, 1980). The 1980s also saw an upsurge of interest in cultural analysis within political economy (Dyson, 1983; Wilks, 1989). Examples of this approach include the emphasis on 'policy style' (on Germany see Dyson, 1982) and the concept of 'industrial culture' (Dyson, 1983). These two types of analysis focused respectively on attitudes towards the use of public authority and attitudes towards government intervention in industry. In addition, a feature of the literature on regulation in the 1980s has been the attempt to 'bring culture back in' as an explanatory variable (Vogel, 1986). Hancher and

Moran (1989) seek to achieve this by an emphasis on the nature of the surrounding legal culture and on the 'culture of capitalism'. Whatever the specific organizing device selected, cultural analysis emphasized the importance of values and norms. The importance of values and norms is strengthened when they become embedded in institutions which reflect, articulate and give momentum to them. In this respect institutional and cultural analyses are complementary.

Observers are quick to notice the strength, durability and distinctiveness of German institutional life. German institutions, and the culture within which they are embedded, appear to possess considerable integrative properties. One main source of these institutional qualities seems to be the state tradition. This state tradition makes the character of German institutions different from that of institutions in the Anglo–Saxon world. As Dyson (1980) has argued, the state tradition involves the idea of a set of moral ideas existing apart from the conflicts of interest of social and political life. At the root of this attitude towards public authority is a sense of the importance of unity and order in national life. It expresses itself in the effort to create conditions which seek to encourage individuals and groups to pursue their self-interests in ways that are consistent with the public interest. This effort is manifested most notably in the willingness of the state to specify the organizational parameters of institutional life in a range of areas outside the public sector, for instance chambers of commerce and chambers of crafts as well as the 'constitution' of the firm (Streeck, 1984, p. 145). The result is a widespread sense of 'public-regarding' obligations, possibly the most distinctive cultural hallmark of Germany

Nowhere does the state tradition manifest its significance more obviously than in the strength and distinctiveness of German legal culture. Central to German legal culture is the idea of the *Rechtsstaat,* of a state governed by law. Law provides the architecture of institutional life. It also provides the language in terms of which policy debate tends to be couched. Policy debate tends to be rapidly translated into arguments about the application and interpretation of constitutional principles. Here we are reminded that the post-war state has adapted to living with the legacy of Hitler and the Third Reich by embracing a markedly activist conception of the central role of law in social, economic and political life. Two main consequences flow for public policy, and for regulation in particular. Procedure matters and tends to be elaborate with, for instance, ready recourse to administrative law. Law also matters in a material sense: it involves constitutional rights and the possibility of judicial review. In such a context actors are disposed to mobilize and use law and to frame their arguments in its terms. A 'juridification' of policy takes place. Policy is bound up within a framework of constitutional rulings, based on the Federal Constitutional Court, and of specialized administrative courts, for instance for labour relations. Perhaps even more importantly, law is internalized within discrete policy sectors. It is built into the working world of policy. This formal, legalistic approach to policy is central to the regulatory culture of Germany.

The state tradition and legalism provide an initial opportunity to grasp the essential nature of Germany's regulatory culture. This regulatory culture combines two elements. On the one hand, there is the preoccupation with order, the *Ordnungspolitik* that is so central to German public policy. Regulation reflects the importance attached to such values as predictability, reliability and 'public-regarding' behaviour. On the other hand, legalism enshrines the primacy of legal rights and procedure. Regulation is a manifestation of a pronounced constitutionalism that infects contemporary debates about the proper relations of government and industry but whose roots are in the political trauma induced by National Socialism. In other words, Germany's regulatory culture can be seen as shaped first and foremost by political concerns and purposes that transcend contemporary market realities. It illustrates the extent to which politics matters and cannot ultimately be subordinated to markets.

Germany's regulatory culture is also to be understood as something that came into being during modern Germany's formative phases of historical development. In effect, it represents an earlier process of institutional learning about how to cope with challenges of state-building and international change. The lessons learnt then became dissociated from these earlier historical circumstances and became self-sustaining through institutional momentum (Lehmbruch, 1990). In nineteenth-century Prussia *Ordnungspolitik* was driven by a notion of the special mission of the bureaucracy as the autonomous guardian of the public interest. This ideology, and cultural legacy, reflected the attempt to reassert Prussian power after defeat by Napoleon Bonaparte and a view of the bureaucracy as the only integrating element in a state lacking religious, ethnic, legal and geographic unity (Koselleck 1967). With the later drive towards an industrial society this ideology was further developed to incorporate the idea of a bureaucracy of social reform, notably influential under Bismarck's welfare policy innovations. An aspect of this Hegelian vision was the idea of a civil society integrated by a modernized guild system, under state tutelage, and thereby ensuring the representation of the 'estates' and the honour and recognition that comes with being a member of an 'estate'. In effect, this idea took practical form in the establishment of the system of chamber organization that still plays so central a role in German economic and industrial life. Whilst the position of the bureaucracy has altered, particularly after 1945, the early idea of a 'state-orientated' regulatory culture tended, in the words of Lehmbruch (1990, p. 20), 'to petrify into ideological sediments that guide much of the interpretation of later crises and structural adaptation'. The manner in which interests interact in the regulatory process remains deeply affected by inherited ideas about the legitimacy of public action.

At the same time it is not enough to argue that institutions and culture are important; that the state tradition and legalism have powerfully affected German regulation; and that Germany has a distinctive regulatory culture. These general ideas need to be unpacked and refined for the purpose of analysis. Regulatory policies and processes in Germany operate against a background of coexisting and often competing institutional and cultural complexes. At the sectoral level the way in which regulation is made and applied is shaped by the intricate specifics of how these different complexes interact. In short, there is too much institutional and cultural variety within Germany to allow us to speak of a single, simple regulatory system. More accurately, five institutional complexes can be identified: the legal frame- work; federalism; party politics; the public bureaucracy; and 'self-organi zation' within the private sector. Correspondingly, it is possible to isolate five specific cultural complexes: the legal culture; the federalist culture; the 'party state' and coalition culture; the bureaucratic culture; and the industrial culture. One point needs to be underlined: the fact that these institutional and cultural complexes interact so closely with each other produces appar ently paradoxical effects. One effect is to introduce further internal com- plexity. Thus, for instance, federalism, party politics and bureaucracy com- plicate each other's operation. On the other hand, with the exception of the legal and federalist cultures, the industrial culture of Germany is relatively autonomous of other cultural complexes. A second effect is that these different institutional and cultural complexes can reinforce each other's internal characteristics. As examples, 'cooperative' federalism and the coa- lition-minded and 'party-state' outlook of the party system facilitate each other; the degree of 'self-organization' within German capitalism protects the public bureaucracy from demands that it play an assertive managerial or interventionist role.

In order to properly understand these institutional and cultural com- plexes that form the political basis of German regulatory policies it is necessary to ask some common questions about their historical origins and development. How and why were they formed and perpetuated? To what extent have they changed? From this analysis it is possible to identify the historical effects of specific events and periods; the role of specific interests and coalitions of interest in creating specific institutional and cultural com- plexes; and the way in which their development has been shaped by the dynamics of the interaction of interests. In the very brief analysis that follows of the five major institutional and cultural complexes it will be readily apparent that certain events and periods have had an exceptional impact on Germany: the impact of Napoleon Bonaparte's defeat of Prussia in 1806; German unification, both pre- and post-1870–1; the Great Depression and the legacy of National Socialism (1933–45); and the impact of total defeat, Allied occupation (1945–9) and division of Germany (formalized in 1949). Taken together, this analysis underlines the importance of seeing German institutional and cultural patterns in a longer-term perspective than that of the post-war period. Use of the phrase *Stunde Null* (zero hour) to describe the end of the Second World War may be useful in underlining the sense of historical catastrophe. It is, however, neither helpful nor accurate if it suggests that Germany broke with its institutional and cultural traditions. These traditions were refashioned and modernized, with some elements discarded but also with an important thread of continuity. This historical perspective on the origins of German regulatory culture and the institutions that support it also offers insight into regulation as a learning process. It suggests the need to see regulation from an evolutionary perspective.

Legalism and the Legal Culture

The peculiar character of German legalism and legal culture stems from the fundamental idea of law as the articulation of the state. Certain profound consequences have followed for regulatory policy. Policy is debated in juristic categories and, not least, lawyers come to assume a central role in the regulatory process. This pivotal role of law in German social, political and economic life dates back to the early nineteenth century and the reforms that followed the catastrophic defeats of the Napoleonic wars. Essentially, the concept of the *Rechtsstaat* served as the principal legitimation of the autonomy of Prussia's public bureaucracy. As servants of the state, officials (*Beamte*) were accountable to no one as long as they acted within their legally defined sphere. In short, the *Rechtsstaat* was an ideology that served the interests of a powerful administrative elite (Armstrong, 1973, p. 164). Historically, the *Rechtsstaat* has undergone two main transitions. Later in the nineteenth century German liberals sought to achieve their aim of controlling the exercise of state power by creating special administrative courts to develop and apply a body of administrative law. More importantly still, the ease with which the Weimar Republic was transformed into the Third Reich and the subsequent gross abuses of power under National Socialism led to a reconceptualization of the *Rechtsstaat* after 1945. The *Rechtsstaat* was now viewed as a political and normative concept, spelling out the fundamental principles of collective life. This concept is primarily embodied in the Federal Constitutional Court which, since its creation, has pursued an activist approach to judicial review. Regulation has, accordingly, become immersed in constitutional argument in an historically un-precedented fashion (for instance, Dyson's chapter on broadcasting). Consistent with this legal culture of judicial activism, the specialized administrative courts have also come to play a key role, most notably in industrial relations (see the chapter by Koch). In Germany issues of legal principle have become central to regulation. The consequence is that openness and accountability are built into regulation. Juridfication and open conflict have accompanied one another.

Federalism and the Federalist Culture

Like legalism, federalism has deep historical roots and has undergone significant transformation. Its central idea has, nevertheless, remained the same. The character of German federalism has derived from the idea of the close interdependence of levels of government, with an emphasis on the decentralization of administrative powers to the states and on a direct role for the states within the federal legislative process through their membership of the upper chamber of the federal legislature. This type of federal arrangement has its historical roots in the compromise through which the German Empire emerged under Prussian leadership in 1871. Essentially, the non-Prussian states sought to preserve their integrity by restricting the new national government to Berlin and retaining as much administrative autonomy as possible. With the abolition of Prussia by the Allies in 1945, a greater measure of political symmetry amongst the post-war states was created. When combined with the creation of a strong upper chamber (the Bundesrat) and an effort to decentralize power in the Basic Law of 1949, the consequence was a highly pluralistic political structure. At the same time the competitive pressures induced by such institutional pluralism were offset by a federalist culture that placed a high premium on cooperative behaviour. Here the interaction between institution and culture is clear. The mutual interdependence of levels of government created a powerful incentive to cooperate. A consequence was an elaborate infrastructure of inter-state committees topped by the conference of heads of state governments (*Ministerpräsidentenkonferenz*), and embracing a wide range of specialized policy areas. Federalism has encouraged an emphasis on bargaining within German regulation, again opening up the regulatory process to a high level of conflict. The outcome is also a conservative, slow-moving bias in regulation. Coalition building for change involves heavy costs (Scharpf, 1985). The complex and often unwieldy policy processes induced by federalism have been characterized by Scharpf et al. (1976) as 'interlocking politics' (*Politikverflechtung*). As the chapters by Dyson (on broadcasting regulation) and Moran (on financial regulation) underline, regulatory reform has been significantly impeded by this degree of dispersal of power. Federalism also provides opportunities for influence to the regulated. Essentially, state governments offer multiple points of access to regulators, creating scope to mobilize support in one or more states (for instance, for locally important businesses).

The Party System and the Party State

The party system is important in contributing to the consensual culture of German regulation. This contribution derives from the breadth of 'catch-all' coalitions which appeal to such a broad spectrum of the electorate that centre-right and centre-left governments will tend to be very similar to each other (Schmidt, 1988). In particular, the liberal Free Democratic Party (FDP) has played a pivotal role in determining which of the two main parties – the Christian Democratic Union (CDU), and its Bavarian sister party the Christian Social Union (CSU), and the Social Democratic Party (SPD) – shall be able to lead the federal government. Its continuity in government (it has been in power, far longer than either the CDU/CSU or the SPD) has given it an influence on policy far beyond its electoral and parliamentary strength. At the level of the ideology underpinning regulation the result is a highly developed consensus about the 'social market economy'. The FDP views itself as having a special responsibility to promote and protect the 'social market economy' from the two main parties. Above all, however, the parties have contributed consensus about political procedures and processes of policy. Consensus about policy substance as well as process has been facilitated by the legacy of the Third Reich and the harsh experiences of the 'other' Germany. Extremism of right and of left has, correspondingly, been slow to develop. Whilst consensus about the substance of policy has been impressive, particularly after the SPD's Bad Godesberg programme of 1959, disagreements have often been significant. With the emergence of the new social movements, and in the 1980s of the Green Party into the Bundestag and state parliaments, party conflicts have taken on a sharper tone. Significant effects have been felt in the regulation of nuclear energy and environmental regulation, as the chapters by Padgett and Weale illustrate. Overall, however, the party system has contributed a marked degree of consensus to German regulation.

Perhaps the most radical change in post-war Germany was in the structure and culture of the party system. Earlier the development of the idea of party government had been frustrated by the identification of the traditional elites with the army and the bureaucracy and a consequent unwillingness to see parties and the state as ultimately compatible. A new context was now provided for the emergence of the idea of party government by a combina-

tion of factors: the eclipse of the Weimar Republic, memories of its instability, and the loss of credibility of such traditional institutions as the army
and the public bureaucracy through association with the Third Reich. The
political parties, licensed by the Allies, presided over the political reconstruction of post-war Germany, not least constitutionalizing their role in
Article 21 of the Basic Law. Party affiliation came to play a key part in
such public institutions as the bureaucracy and broadcasting. In short,
Germany took on the attributes of a 'party state'; the parties were understood
to have a special responsibility for the health of the new republic (Dyson,
1977). Correspondingly, the political parties, aided by state financing, have
developed highly professional infrastructures. Notable also is the representation of public officials (*Beamte*) in party membership. The boundaries of
party and bureaucracy in public policy are not so sharply drawn as in
Britain. This interpenetration of party and bureaucracy is another stabilizing factor in regulatory policy.

The Public Bureaucracy and Bureaucratic Culture

Historically, the public bureaucracy has enjoyed a prestigious and central
place within the German state. Under the Prussian monarchs and the German
emperors it became a chief instrument of power, its interests aligned with
those of the ruler. Its autonomy was first asserted in the form of the concept
of the *Wohlfahrtsstaat* (welfare state), legitimating its right to intervene
widely in social and economic affairs on behalf of the public interest.
Correspondingly, the seventeenth and eighteenth centuries saw a great expansion of the regulatory role of the state. Regulation was the basis for an
orderly society. When, in the nineteenth century, the basis of the bureaucracy's
autonomy was shifted to the concept of the *Rechtsstaat*, the regulatory role
of the state was little affected. Indeed, the licensing and regulation of
guilds, trade associations, cartels and later trade unions led the bureaucracy
into a highly structured relationship with industry (Abelshauser, 1984).
Despite the enormous changes to which the German public bureaucracy
has been subject in the twentieth century, the continuity of this regulatory
tradition has been striking.

Post-1945 the main change in the bureaucracy's position has been the
erosion of its autonomy, not the prestige of its public-service values. In this
sense the legacy of the Prussian reforms of the seventeenth century and
post-1806 remained powerful. At the heart of this continuity within German
bureaucratic culture were the values of technical rationality and *Sachlichkeit*
(objectivity). Identified with the state, the senior public official (the *Beamte*)
continued to be subject to the special privileges and duties of public-
service law. As we saw above, the decisive change was in the new-found

prestige of the political parties. They penetrated the bureaucracy, as party membership became an important criterion in appointments and promotions to senior levels. The effect was to introduce much more openness and political sensitivity within the regulatory process. The bureaucratic culture became more open and responsive (Dyson, 1977).

At the level of structure, two features of German public bureaucracy are important in shaping the regulatory process. Article 65 of the Basic Law underlines and supports a pronounced 'departmentalism' within the bureaucracy. Ministers have a high degree of autonomy in running their departments, and official loyalty is adjusted to this situation. The consequence is a high level of compartmentalism in regulation. 'Sectorization' appears to be a general cross-national characteristic of public policy. However, in Germany constitutional principle and bureaucratic culture reinforce its significance. As the chapter by Humphreys on regulation of telecommunications underlines, this characteristic has reduced the prospects for radical reform. Secondly, the decentralization of administrative power to the states makes for relatively small federal ministries. These ministries in turn become heavily dependent on external sources of specialized information, whether from the states or from trade associations, chambers of commerce or firms. Regulation tends, correspondingly, to be reactive rather than assertive.

'Self-Organization' within Industry and Industrial Culture

References to a dominant ideology of the 'social market economy' all too easily deflect attention from the most distinctive and important aspect of German capitalism: namely, the degree of 'self-organization' that it contains and the attitudes towards collective action within the industrial culture. Quite simply, the institutional structure and the culture of German capitalism provide a very different context for regulation from that in the United States or Britain These differences are exhibited in four main areas: the leadership role that can be played by finance capital; the role of the chambers of industry and commerce and the chambers of crafts as the recognized, public-law 'organs' of the economy; the degree of integration and support achieved by business associations; and the emphasis on social partnership and 'codetermination' (*Mitbestimmung*) in industry.

Whilst no grand design is at work, and qualifications are needed in specific sectors, the overall effect is a capitalist system with a considerable potential for collective action. These characteristics reflect in part the historical exigencies of economic and political development. Thus, as German company law was developed in the context of nineteenth-century unification, its structure sought to secure the already entrenched position of the big banks as financers of industry. The representative structure of the supervisory board (*Aufsichtsrat*) of firms was a means of supporting the interests of the banks in industry (Dyson, 1986). That interest in turn reflected the high capital requirements of rapid industrialization and government's own encouragement of investment banking. Both the bank–industry nexus and the supervisory board have survived regime changes. The supervisory board proved in fact adaptable to the purpose of social partnership: post-1945 worker representation was introduced at this level, as a means of democratizing industries compromised by association with the Third Reich. Worker representation as an indispensible component of 'the constitution of the firm' was further established through the augmented powers of the works councils (*Betriebsräte*) (Streeck, 1984). By these means, bank and trade union influence is institutionalized within German capitalism. The effects are felt in financial regulation (Moran's chapter), in regulation of industrial relations (Koch's chapter) and in regulation of health care (Webber's chapter).

The other component of the complex institutional structure of German capitalism is provided by business representation. Here the central element of continuity is the chambers of industry and commerce and the chambers of crafts. The legislative basis of their activities was created in the nineteenth century and reflected the interests of states and localities in protecting their business interests within a unified market and state. Taking the old guild system as a point of reference, the chambers were established as a national system of public-law institutions. Their functions were spelt out in law, and membership was compulsory for firms. In this way it was intended to build the concept of *Selbstverwaltung* (self-government or autonomy) into the German economy. Regulation could be controlled by members of the chambers, within an institutional structure prescribed by the state. Such regulation was viewed as technically superior to that which might be imposed by the state. Since the nineteenth century the chambers have been recognized as the spokesmen for the collective interests of German industry and as the basis of Germany's comprehensive system of occupational training. Also, as Moran's chapter shows, the concept of *Selbstverwaltung* has been applied in other areas, like stock exchange regulation. Similarly, Webber's chapter underlines the degree of institutional inertia in the German health system. Its pattern of collectivist bargaining took shape in a long struggle over control of medical practice within the institutional framework of public health insurance created by Bismarck. Whilst trade associations are not public-law institutions, with this kind of status and integration, their development has to some extent been modelled on the organizational power of the chambers. Some have even assumed the functions of private governments regulating their members on behalf of the state (Streeck, 1983). Together, these institutional structures amount to a significant capacity for acting collectively in pursuit of long-term interests. Regulation for this purpose has been widely accepted.

What has most clearly emerged from this portrait of the institutional and cultural complexity underpinning German regulatory policies is a clear view that German regulation is embedded within distinctive 'political world pictures' and historical experiences of authority. Institutions support a set of enduring norms about the appropriate role of the state and about the appropriate ways in which to articulate and resolve issues. It seems, accordingly, appropriate to speak of certain pervasive characteristics of German regulation, for instance the federal and legal dimensions of regulation. One is alerted to the way that, in Germany, the diffusion of authority shapes the process of regulatory learning, encouraging a great deal of fine-tuning in incrementally adjusting specific rules and reconsidering regulatory instruments. At the same time, institutional and cultural analysis leaves open the question of precisely how ideas fit into the policy process and how these ideas are generated and might change.

4.   The 'Coalition-Based' Approach: The Impact of Contingencies

The somewhat integrated and holistic account of German regulation that has been presented above is not likely to be acceptable to those reared in a 'realist' tradition of political analysis. Their preference is to puncture the belief that regulation is a benign or lofty pursuit of the public interest. From this perspective regulation is bound up in certain 'hard-nosed' realities: of the complexities of regulation which is fragmented into very different sub-systems; and of the material self-interests of powerful actors. Regulation embodies a learning process, a process of adjusting coalition activities to changing realities. It is contingent on environmental change, including developments and events at the international level, on the configuration of specific policy networks, and on the rational calculations of actors.

Regulation is a contest about power and self-interest. For instance, behind regulatory façades are to be discovered the strategies of such actors as large firms. As Lindblom (1977) has stressed, firms are accorded a place of peculiar privilege within a capitalist society. For practical reasons, governments cannot systematically transgress market logic in a society in which decisions about products, prices and investment are freely taken by autonomous actors. In the political realm of bargaining about regulation the bargain struck will tend to favour business; the regulated will have an inbuilt advantage. This bargaining about regulation takes place in 'policy networks' that bring together actors who, within certain 'rules of the game', are mutually dependent. They are involved in power relationships and coalition activities, pursuing different and conflicting interests by using the various resources (such as money, information and legislative authority) available to them at any one time (Wilks and Wright, 1987). Network analysis focuses on how regulation reflects differences in the distribution of resources and power amongst a set of more or less stable actors over time. Public choice theory adds the insight that these actors will tend to behave as rational egotists. Regulation reflects their incentive and capacity to organize themselves and build effective coalitions.

This 'coalition-based' approach is appropriately seen as complementary to the 'culture-' and 'institution-centred' approaches and the 'international-centred' approach. At the macro level, the 'international-centred' approach draws attention to the broader structural context of regulatory action, the 'culture-' and 'institution-centred' approaches to the context of ideas, structure and history in which regulatory action is embedded. At the micro level, network analysis and public choice theory facilitate insight into the detailed dynamics of sectoral change. These levels of analysis are closely interdependent. External threat, for instance, prompts large firms to become newly active in pressing for regulatory change within domestic policy networks. Conversely, the strategies of powerful national firms can alter the context of international competitiveness in which domestic regulation operates. The distinctive characteristic of the 'coalition-centred' approach remains its emphasis on the material base of regulation. Regulation is to be related to its detailed economic, technical and political environment, to the changing patterns of opportunity and constraint created by this environment, and to the use that actors make of these changes, within the constraints of policy networks and as rational egotists.

Regulation and Policy Networks

In network analysis sectors are seen as generating their own distinctive patterns of political and regulatory activity. Accordingly, regulation is best studied in a 'bottom-up' manner. The network metaphor conveys the idea of a systemic pattern of interorganizational linkages and the notion of variability. Regulation is seen as bound up in the complex dynamics of sectoral networks and the interconnecting, interpenetrating and often unpredictable power relationships and coalition activities that they comprise. These dynamics cannot always be sufficiently understood by isolating specific institutions or relationships for analysis. The specific, detailed configurations of policy networks and the capacity to build reforming coalitions help to explain the success or failure of attempts at governmental reform, for instance 'deregulation' in the 1980s.

Policy networks, and the patterns of regulation that they sustain, may be influenced, but are not determined, by the pattern of relationships at the macro-political and -governmental level. They have different structures of relationships, characteristics and personnel; their agendas differ; and the policy processes by which they interact also vary. The sheer breadth and complexity of regulatory policies and processes in a single country like Germany makes generalizations about national patterns, based on institutional and cultural analysis, unhelpful. It is far more important to know which interests have privileged access to policy, and why; how they interact with each other; the degree of cohesion and stability of relationships within the network; the scope of the policy agenda of a network; and the degree of insulation of a network. Regulation will be shaped by the degree of integration or fragmentation in a policy network and by the skill with which a particular player exploits its political resources. For instance, as Dyson and Moran show, the fragmentation in their respective policy networks has shaped the agenda and pace of regulatory change in broadcasting and financial services. Similarly, in the one case the Bundespost and in the other the banks have been able to fashion change to suit their own corporate interests. A point of general application in German regulation is the influence of professionals within policy networks, to the extent that many are very professionalized. Professionals' domination of networks promotes a high level of integration.

In some policy networks, like nuclear energy (Padgett) and environment (Weale), access has proved more difficult to control during the 1980s. As popular interest in the implications of developments in these policy areas mounted, significant effects were felt both in the regulatory process and in the agenda of regulation. In such circumstances, regulatory change reflects an increasingly 'crowded' policy environment. Exposure to pressure from new actors seeking entry into a policy network produces destabilizing effects that established actors find difficult to resist. Traditionally exclusive and privileged relationships are put in question, not least as there is pressure to internalize external disturbing forces within the network. In the cases of broadcasting and telecommunications Dyson and Humphreys show how a regulatory process is destabilized as the boundaries insulating a policy network are breached by actors from other sectors as a consequence of market or technological change. Once again both the agendas and the processes of regulation were destabilized; new phases of coalition building are unleashed.

Policy network analysis is not blind to the role of ideas or to the concept of institution. The relationships between actors in policy networks are predicated upon acceptance of 'rules of the game'. In effect, there is an 'unwritten constitution' that guides the behaviour of the actors towards each other and influences the strategic deployment of their resources. Such rules embrace the legitimacy of state action, the use of legal remedy, acceptable modes of raising issues, the proper degree of formality, expectations about consultation, and the role of trust and respect for confidence (Wilks and Wright, 1987). The emphasis is clearly on the dynamics of rules; rules are not immutable. It is also on the role of 'rules of the game' as setting limits to the behaviour of actors within the policy network. 'Institutionalization' is another theme in the policy network literature. Reference here is being made to regular and valued patterns of behaviour based on stable expectations and mutual understandings, to processes that regulate bargaining relationships within the network. The emphasis is very much on their informality and their tenuous relationship to the state.

Implicit in the analysis of policy networks is a model of regulation as 'bargained' or 'negotiated' compliance (Diver, 1980; Hawkins, 1983). Compliance is problematic, to be seen in terms of the perceived costs and benefits to key actors and their capacity to comply. Significant changes in the resources available to those actors point to a 'crisis of regulation', with regulators involved in an increasingly adversarial relationship with the regulated (Teubner, 1983; Reich, 1984). Regulation is firmly embedded in its specific technical, economic and political context; institutions and culture recede into the background as 'rules of the game' that are used and mobilized by actors as appropriate. These 'rules of the game' form but part of the structural parameters of bargaining, negotiation and coalition building about regulation.

Policy network analysis is also sensitive to, and designed to draw out, the importance of the politics of the firm in the regulatory process. Particular firms may enjoy significant, perhaps monopolistic market power. They may possess a high concentration, or even monopoly of legitimate expertise, enabling them to champion their own interests. This type of analysis has been able to capture the possibility that specific firms may come to hold a pivotal position in the regulatory process, making their bilateral relationships with governmental agencies critical to the processes of regulatory change. Alternatively, sectoral interest associations, especially business associations, can come to occupy a privileged role in determining regulatory policy, in exchange for which they undertake to secure compliance from their members. Here policy network analysis shades into the literature on 'neo-corporatism' (for example, Cawson, 1985). Behind regulation may stand a complex edifice of 'private interest government' (Streeck and Schmitter, 1985). The German health system, for example, has corporatist characteristics (see Webber's chapter). A third possibility is that a regulatory agency may achieve sufficient autonomy of action and power to shape regulatory policy on its own terms. Various preconditions are needed for such a situation to arise. The agency requires independent access to information and expertise; it needs to be given sole responsibility for the sector in question; its mandate has to be drawn in broad functional terms rather than in terms of a particular client group; and the legal framework must serve to draw a clear boundary between the regulatory agency and the sector (Atkinson and Coleman, 1989).

The policy network approach also offers a framework within which to test the 'capture' theory of regulation. 'Capture' theory takes two forms, each of which emphasizes the role and impact of self-interest on regulation. In one form, the rhetoric of regulation in the public interest is seen as but a smokescreen. Regulatory agencies are habitually the captives of the regulated, especially if the regulated are businesspeople. Regulatory 'capture' occurs when a regulatory agency comes to equate the public interest with the interests of the industry that it regulates. Two factors are especially important in shaping this development. Producer lobbies are commonly better organized and better resourced than those serving the consumer interest. Additionally, the information asymmetry that creates the need for regulation makes the agency dependent on those it regulates. Bernstein (1955) developed this idea into the 'life-cycle' hypothesis of regulation. According to this hypothesis, regulatory agencies evolve from vigorous youth, through maturity, to a stage of bureaucratic sluggishness. In the process they become captured by the interests that, in their youth, they eagerly regulated in an adversarial mode. A second form of the 'capture' theory suggests that regulation can serve the self-interests of the regulators. Hirshleifer (1976) argued that regulatory agencies have their own objective needs. The career staff of such agencies are apt to identify their interests with the expansion of the regulatory system or, conversely, with avoiding a contraction of the scope of their activities. Regulation also embodies a huge amount of 'sunk costs', physical and psychological, of those who have helped create the system. Hence survival becomes a key objective need of regulatory agencies. They are unlikely to support radical deregulation.

It is clear from the above analysis that the policy network approach can support various and very contrasting pictures of regulation. This possibility is implicit in the emphasis on a disaggregated conception of regulation within the approach. Variety features as its very core.

Regulation and Group Interest

In the policy network literature the role of regulation as an instrument of specific group interests (for example, 'capture' theory) is understood in essentially political-science terms. Public choice theory presents, by contrast, such an explanation of regulation in the deductive terms of economic theory. It is founded on methodological individualism and the assumption that actors are motivated by rational self-interest. Stigler (1975) and Peltzman (1976) viewed regulation as primarily a mechanism for wealth redistribution. For Stigler, regulation was explicable in terms of a model of producer dominance. He started from the premises that those involved in regulation are rational egotists; that producers have both the incentive and the capacity to dominate regulation; that regulation originates because it is in the interests of the regulated; and that the outcome of regulation is not typically the creation of any wide public benefits but the defence of producers at the expense of other parties, notably consumers. In consequence, regulation throws up very problematic issues about costs and benefits that need detailed and critical scrutiny.

Building on Stigler, Peltzman developed a model of supply and demand for regulation. On the demand side, the contenders seek wealth redistribution through the regulatory process; the supply side consists of the votes that they are able to deliver. In short, electoral competition is built into regulation. Regulation is in effect an auction. Given the premise that those involved are rational egotists, the form that regulation takes (that is the way that wealth is transferred) is determined by the incentive that groups have to organize themselves and their capacity for organization. As the regulator is also a rational egotist, he/she will respond to the group offering the highest rewards. In such a world certain groups are more likely than others to have an incentive to bid and the resources to bid high in the regulatory auction. The advantaged will tend to be small groups with large stakes in the outcome. The disadvantaged tend to be large groups whose members are only marginally affected by the regulation. Regulation is thus biased in favour of big firms and against scattered, badly organized groups, like consumers. In Peltzman's model, changes in regulation are interpreted as the result of changes in the way that regulation distributes costs and benefits, thus altering the incentives of different groups to mobilize.

From the perspective of public choice theory, Germany's regulatory culture appears as a smokescreen behind which can be found a reality of producer dominance. The reality is in fact one of a completely commercial society in which people behave as rational egotists and regulation is in effect an auction. Lehmbruch's chapter underlines the limited impact of the model of a commercial society on inherited German political ideology, including the idea of the 'social market economy', whilst the individual case studies that follow illustrate the extent to which the politics of self-interest are built into, and shaped by, complex institutional arrangements at the national and sectoral levels. In short, the volume highlights the narrowness and shallowness of the public choice approach.

5.   Conclusion

This introduction has identified four main approaches within the literature on public policy and regulation. The 'institution-centred' and 'culture-centred' approaches yield insights into the pervasive qualitative characteristics of regulation at the national level; the 'coalition-centred' approach stresses the material bases of regulation in power relationships and self-interest; and the 'international-centred' approach draws attention away from the focus on domestic politics to broader patterns of structural change in the world economy and to the role and impact of 'hegemonic' powers. Two of these approaches radically question the state's primacy and autonomy in regulation. Within the 'coalition-centred' approach policy network analysis assigns prime importance to variations in the micro-politics of particular sectors, in effect disaggregating the state; public choice theory sees the state as no more than an arena in which regulation is put to auction. The 'international-centred' approach focuses on the external context of, and mounting constraints on, state action.

One might be forgiven for concluding that the burgeoning literature on public policy and regulation had taken on the appearance of a Tower of Babel. In fact, sensitive analysts have been forced to enter substantial qualifications about the claims of the approaches that they champion. Thus amongst proponents of the 'culture-centred' and 'institution-centred' approaches there has been recognition of the need for a more differentiated view of the state, for sectoral studies of regulation and the idea of different stories in different sectors, and to explain change as well as continuity. Conversely, 'coalition-centred' theorists have tended to the view that, whilst regulation is not simply the consequence of organizational structure, it cannot be fully understood without reference to institutions and the 'rules of the game'. No one approach has been able to adequately account for the sheer complexity and multifaceted nature of regulatory politics. This insight informs the chapters that follow.

Whilst signs of greater flexibility have been helpful, the continuing pressure to think within the confines of these four approaches has deflected attention away from critical variables in the development of regulatory policies.

1.   The relationship between domestic and international determinants of regulation is a variable in its own right. Each level of analysis has its own autonomy, but an increasing number of sectors are experiencing the problems of living with interdependence. To a greater extent than ten or twenty years ago regulation is operating simultaneously at the domestic and international levels. Regulators seek to maximize ben-

efits in one domain to enhance their position in the other. In writing about the politics of German regulation in the 1990s it will be more and more difficult to explain regulation without reference to a range of international factors, past and present. The 'international-centred' approach heightens sensitivity to exogenous factors affecting the power of one set of actors to impose its regulatory paradigm on others. Actors are disposed to use and mobilize change within the international political-cal economy in order to identify policy failure with others and thereby precipitate a shift in the locus of authority over regulation. The result will therefore be greater flexibility and more open conflicts in German regulation, particularly with the increasing EC dimension to German regulation.

2. The relationship between macro-level institutional and cultural characteristics and 'coalition-centred' behaviour at the sectoral level is a variable in its own right. Institutional and cultural factors influence how actors define their interests, how they articulate them and how they relate to other actors. In the process they assimilate and reflect characteristics of the institutional and cultural setting in which they operate. At the same time regulation will also bear the imprint of differences of market structure and the use that actors make of ideas, as reflected in the nature of policy networks. The impact of institutional arrangements, like parties, can be expected to vary across sectors, depending on detailed political and economic factors. It should not, however, be forgotten that variation expresses itself in a macro-level framework that induces certain pervasive characteristics.

A theme of this volume is that the 'international-centred' and 'coalition-centred' approaches exaggerate the erosion of the primacy and autonomy of the state. The conclusions draw attention to the continuing important impact of regulatory culture in Germany. Embraced and shaped by that regulatory culture, the dynamics of regulation take place within regulatory paradigms specific to particular sectors (Hall, 1989; Jenson, 1989). In essence, these regulatory paradigms represent frameworks of ideas and standards that specify the nature of the regulatory problems, the goals of regulation and the kind of regulatory instruments that can be used to attain these goals. These regulatory paradigms inform the very terminology of regulation, the way in which regulation is discussed and in which regulator and regulated communicate with each other. Hence it is important to identify the regulatory paradigm of each sector and the degree to which it has been challenged. This kind of analysis of regulatory paradigms needs to weave together the general cultural and institutional context with the actors most closely involved in constructing and modifying the terms of policy discourse within policy networks. Significant shifts in the locus of authority over regulation, in the resources that actors can command and in coalition activity are indicative of new regulatory paradigms. The question with which this volume is concerned is whether cumulative changes in regulatory paradigms at the sectoral level have reshaped the regulatory culture of Germany. Has the flow of ideas and influence between the two spheres been disrupted? The answer to that question will provide important evidence about the value of institutional and cultural explanations of regulation.

At heart the politics of German regulation reflect a unity in diversity, but a unity that itself is being qualified, even perhaps eroded, by the realities of interdependence at the international level. It is undoubtedly the case that the politics of regulation in Germany is increasingly to be understood in terms of pressures emanating from the international political economy and from efforts to harmonize national regulatory regimes. Yet the prestige of domestic regulatory paradigms, and EC-led harmonization on terms broadly consistent with Germany (Woolcock, Hodges and Schreiber, 1991), continue unabated to the extent that they remain associated with Germany's success within the international political economy. For this reason German regulation has a Janus-like quality. Its formal, traditional face, represented in coherent regulatory paradigms at the sectoral level that are integrated into general regulatory culture, shades into a face of pragmatic adaptation to new external pressures and redefinitions of self-interest. Whichever face one begins by studying, one ends up recognizing the importance of the other face. In this respect the rigid distinction between regulation as a framework of order and 'normative understandings' and regulation as learning breaks down. German regulation is caught up in a complex interaction, but with a new bias towards considering paradigm change at the sectoral level.

References

Abelshauser, W. (1984), 'The first post-liberal nation: stages in the development of modern corporatism in Germany', *European Historical Quarterly*, **14**, 285–318.
Almond, G. and Verba, S. (eds) (1980), *The Civic Culture Revisited*, Boston: Little, Brown.
Armstrong, J. (1973), *The European Administrative Elite*, New Jersey: Princeton University Press.
Atkinson, M. and Coleman, W. (1989), 'Strong states and weak states: sectoral policy networks in advanced capitalist economies', *British Journal of Political Science*, **19**.

Berghahn, V. (1986), *The Americanization of West German Industry*, Leamington Spa/New York: Berg.

Bernstein, M. (1955), *Regulating Business by Independent Commission*, Princeton: Princeton University Press.

von Beyme, K (1985), 'Policy Making in the Federal Republic of Germany. A Systematic Introduction' in von Beyme, K. and Schmidt, M. (eds), *Policy and Politics in the Federal Republic of Germany*, Aldershot: Gower.

Bulmer, S. (ed.) (1989), *The Changing Agenda of West German Public Policy*, Aldershot: Dartmouth.

Cawson, A. (ed.) (1985), *Organized Interests and the State: Studies in Meso-Corporatism*, London: Sage Publications.

Diver, C. (1980), 'A theory of regulatory enforcement', *Public Policy*, **28**, 257–71.

Dyson, K (1977), *Party, State and Bureaucracy in West Germany*, Beverly Hills: Sage Publications.

Dyson, K. (1980), *The State Tradition in Western Europe*, Oxford: Martin Robertson.

Dyson, K (1982), 'West Germany: The Search for a Rationalist Consensus' in Richardson, J. (ed.), *Policy Styles in Western Europe*, London: Allen and Unwin.

Dyson, K (1983), 'Cultural, Ideological and Structural Context' in Dyson, K and Wilks, S. (eds), *Industrial Crisis*, Oxford: Blackwell.

Dyson, K (1986), 'State, Banks and Industry: The West German Case' in Cox, A. (ed.), *State, Finance and Industry*, Brighton: Wheatsheaf.

Hall, P. (1986), *Governing the Economy: The Politics of State Intervention in Britain and France*, Oxford: Polity.

Hall, P. (1989), 'Policy Paradigms, Social Learning and the State: The Case of Economic Policy-Making in Britain', Harvard: Centre for European Studies, unpublished paper.

Hancher, L. and Moran, M. (eds) (1989), *Capitalism, Culture and Economic Regulation*, Oxford: Clarendon Press.

Hawkins, K (1983), *Environment and Enforcement*, Oxford: OUP.

Heclo, H. (1974), *Modern Social Politics in Britain and Sweden*, New Haven: Yale University Press.

Hirshleifer, J. (1976), 'Toward a more general theory of regulation – comment', *Journal of Law and Economics*, **19**, 241–44.

Jenson, J. (1989), 'Paradigms and political discourse: labour and social policy in the USA and France before 1914', *Canadian Journal of Sociology and Anthropology*.

Katzenstein, P. (1987), *Policy and Politics in West Germany: The Growth of a Semisovereign State*, Philadelphia: Temple University Press.

Koselleck, R. (1967), *Preussen zwischen Reform und Revolution. Allgemeines Landrecht, Verwaltung und soziale Bewegung von 1791 bis 1848*, Stuttgart: Klett-Cotta.

Lehmbruch, G. (1990), 'The Organization of Society, Administrative Strategies and Policy Networks' in Czada, R. and Windhoff-Heritier, A. (eds), *Political Choice. Institutions, Rules and the Limits of Rationality*, Frankfurt: Campus.

Lindblom, C. (1977), *Politics and Markets*, New York: Basic Books.

March, J. and Olsen, J. (1984), 'The new institutionalism: organizational factors in political life', *American Political Science Review*, **78**, 734–49.

Olson, M. (1982), *The Rise and Decline of Nations: Economic Growth and Social Rigidity,* New Haven: Yale University Press.

Peltzman, S. (1976), 'Toward a more general theory of regulation', *Journal of Law and Economics*, **19**, 221–40.

Reich, N. (1984), 'The regulatory crisis', *Government and Policy*, 140–59.

Scharpf, F. (1976), *Politikverflechtung: Theorie und Empirie des kooperativen Föderalismus in der Bundesrepublik,* Königstein: Athenäum.

Scharpf, F. (1985), 'The Joint-Decision Trap: Lessons from German Federalism and European Integration', Discussion Paper IIM/LMP 85-1, Berlin: Wissenschaftszentrum.

Schmidt, M. (1988), 'West Germany: the policy of the middle way', *Journal of Public Policy,* **7**,135–77.

Scott, R. (1987), 'The adolescence of institutional theory', *Administrative Science Quarterly*, **32**, 493–511.

Soltwedel, R. et al. (1986), *Deregulierungspotentiale in der Bundesrepublik,* Tübingen: J.C.B. Mohr.

Soltwedel, R. et al. (1987), *Zur staatlichen Marktregulierung in der Bundesrepublik,* Kiel: Institut für Weltwirtschaft.

Stigler, G. (1975), *The Citizen and the State: Essays on Regulation,* Chicago: University of Chicago Press.

Stone, A. (1982), *Regulation and its Alternatives*, Washington D.C.: Congressional Quarterly Press.

Streeck, W. (1983), 'Between pluralism and corporatism: German business associations and the state', *Journal of Public Policy*, **3**, 265–84.

Streeck, W. (1984), *Industrial Relations in West Germany*, London: Heinemann.

Streeck, W. and Schmitter, P. (eds) (1985), *Private Interest Government: Beyond Market and State*, London: Sage Publications.

Teubner, G. (1983), 'Reflexive law', *Law and Society Review*, **17**, 240–95.

Vogel, D. (1986), *National Styles of Regulation: Environmental Policy in Great Britain and the United States,* Ithaca: Cornell University Press.

Wilks, S. and Wright, M. (eds) (1987), *Comparative Government–Industry Relations*, Oxford: Clarendon Press.

Wilks, S. (1989), 'Institutions and Cultures in the Comparative Analysis of Political Economy', unpublished paper.

Woolcock, S., Hodges, M. and Schreiber, K (1991), *Britain, Germany and 1992: The Limits of Deregulation,* London; Pinter.

2 The Institutional Framework of German Regulation

Gerhard Lehmbruch

When the German Conservative–Liberal (CDU/CSU/FDP) coalition came to power in 1982, its programmatic statements reminded many observers of the 'neo-conservative' agenda of the Thatcher and Reagan governments in Britain and the United States. Chancellor Helmut Kohl and other leaders of the new majority appeared determined to effect a *Wende* ('change') of profound significance, one that was as much intellectual and moral (*geistig-moralische Wende*) as economic. The inaugural government declaration (*Regierungserklärung*) suggested that the new government had a reform agenda that aimed to strongly revitalize the market and to correct the expansion of the state that had taken place during the previous Social Democratic–Liberal (SPD/FDP) coalitions since 1969. This agenda change was also in conformity with a mood that had become quite widespread, in particular among the financial journalists of some influential dailies and weeklies.

Neo-liberal economists who took this commitment to a *Wende* seriously soon discovered that their expectations had gone far beyond what the government really was ready and able to accomplish, and that free-market policies – in particular deregulation and privatization – apparently ranked much lower on the priority scale of the federal government than they did at that same time in the United States and Britain. And in the following years, demarcation from the social democratic policies of the 1970s became increasingly irrelevant to the programmatic identity of the Conservative–Liberal majority.

With the sudden collapse of the communist rule in the GDR, however, the rhetoric of the free market received a new and unexpected impetus. This time the term *Wende* appeared in the East German vocabulary, of course in a much more profound and radical sense. But for the West German conservatives it presented an opportunity to re-employ their old electoral

29

slogan, 'freedom instead of socialism', now with reference to the economic and social heritage of the GDR. The accompanying economic discourse shifted from the advocacy of supply-side policy against Keynesian interventionism to older topics that had been current in the early post-war years (when books such as Hayek's *Road to Serfdom* were popular). Such changes in emphasis and in themes notwithstanding, it appeared that the events of 1989–90 helped the Conservative–Liberal majority to restore its original image. And the unification policy of the West German government put all its hopes in the self-regulating power of markets that, through a process of 'creative destruction' (in Schumpeter's sense), should lead to a swift recovery of the East German economy on a new basis.

In spring 1991, under the impact of escalating unemployment in the former GDR, it became obvious that this policy had failed. The result was a re-orientation in German economic and social policies that ended the emphasis on markets and on the withdrawal of government from the economy. The tax increases which virtually nullified the former tax cuts of the coalition government symbolized the transformation in a drastic manner. Did it mean that the neo–conservative (or, in economic terms, liberal) agenda was the victim of an unexpected turn of history? Or could it be that in Germany such an agenda had never had a serious chance of realization? The point can be made that the institutional framework considerably constrained its chances of realization.

One reason why the change of political strategy after the breakdown of Helmut Schmidt's government in 1982 appeared less radical than – in particular – in Britain was the simple fact that the makers of West German economic policy had never in the first place been wholeheartedly converted to Keynesian economic policy. Leading economic policy makers of the Social Democrats sympathized with a rather cautious version of 'commercial' or 'market' Keynesianism in which the role of the state would be limited to 'global steering' of macro-economic aggregates (Weir and Skocpol, 1985, p. 108). As for the 'micro relations' of the economy, the pioneer of the adoption of Keynesianism in the late 1960s, Social Democratic Federal Economics Minister Karl Schiller, always strongly emphasized the primacy of the market. It was only in the 1970s that policy concepts emphasizing stronger micro-economic intervention (*Strukturpolitik*) gained some ground within the SPD. However, they never became official government policy, be it only because of the growing influence of the FDP on economic policy. Also, the economic strategy of the Kohl government since 1982 could only to a very limited degree be understood as a copy of American or British blueprints. It followed its own logic and, as I will argue in this chapter, this logic was strongly determined by an institutional framework that differs markedly from that which, in the supposed model cases mentioned above, opened important opportunities for a policy of deregulation and privatization.

In Germany, as elsewhere, the institutional framework of economic policy has two main dimensions: the organization of the state and of its linkages with the organized economy, on the one hand, and the ideological interpretation of the relationships of state and economy, on the other. For, as March and Olsen (1989) have pointed out, the institutional definition of the framework for political action takes place through the 'institutionalization of action' as well as through the 'institutionalization of meaning'.

1. The 'Institutionalization of Meaning' In Economic Policy Doctrines and the Problem of the Welfare State

It is important to underline the point that economic policy doctrines are not, in the first place, a guideline for political choice. More often, it appears, they serve to 'make sense of the world' and as an 'interpretation of life' (March and Olsen, 1989, p. 39 ff). In the case of the West German *Wende*, the policy choices of the Conservative–Liberal majority were perhaps not so much guided as constrained by an 'institutionalization of meaning' that had its roots in the historical legacy of German economic policy doctrines. To be sure, diffusion processes played a certain role in the intellectual environment of the programme of the first *Wende*. Amongst these was the disillusion with Keynesian demand management that spread through Western Europe in reaction to the 'stagflation' of the 1970s, and the critical discussion of the expansion of the public sector and of growing budget deficits (for example, Rühle and Veen, 1978). Certainly this international discussion contributed to the climate of opinion that led to the *Wende*.

An interesting aspect of such diffusion processes was the introduction of the concepts of 'regulation' and 'deregulation'. Indeed, the language of 'regulation' was not very familiar in West Germany before the 1970s. Here, as in other European countries, it has been imported from the United States. 'Regulation', one might say, entered the vocabulary retrospectively, riding on the back of the concept – and the agenda – of 'deregulation' when the American deregulation movement reached the West European countries (Majone, 1991). That the Federal Republic was influenced by this diffusion process cannot be denied.[1] Highly reputed members of the economics profession were amongst the foremost and consistent advocates of a deregulation agenda, and it is obvious that their approach owes much to the doctrines developed by academic economists in the United States.[2] Also, some important elements of the government agenda – in particular telecommunications reform – were directly inspired by the American deregulation experience, and in this sense diffusion has certainly played a not unimportant role.

In spite of these intellectual influences it cannot be maintained that the political agenda of the West German *Wende* was essentially imitative in character. On the level of concrete economic policy concepts the backlash against interventionism in the late 1970s was largely nourished from indigenous West German sources. In that sense, although supported by the international diffusion of an anti-Keynesian mood, the change of economic policy strategy was an autochthonous West German development. The Council of Economic Experts had never been very enthusiastic about Keynesianism. From its annual report of 1976 onwards it adopted a clear and pronounced supply-side orientation (though it remained sceptical about the 'supply-side optimism' of the Reagan administration). The Bundesbank, for its part, switched to a monetarist policy from 1973. On the other hand, borrowing from American 'deregulation' as well as from British privatization programmes remained highly selective.

Some of the most salient features of American 'deregulation' policies, particularly of those emphasized under the Reagan presidency, were never emulated at all. Particularly significant is that the backlash against 'social' deregulation, be it in environmental policy, or in occupational health and safety, had practically no German equivalent. The implementation of occupational health and safety was left to the self-regulation by the *Berufsgenossenschaften* (insurance funds in which employer membership was compulsory) and was, therefore, not likely to stir similar emotional reactions of employers. Environmental regulation was continued without essential modifications after the change of government, and the more recent, market-orientated approaches pioneered by the US Environmental Protection Agency were not even given serious consideration outside a small minority of academic economists. And in fields such as control of automobile emissions the new government remarkably accentuated the regulatory emphasis (Weidner, 1989).

Essentially, the economic and social philosophy of the *Wende* had specific German roots and therefore its criticism of the welfare state was ambiguous. There was some talk, within the coalition, about the limits of social policy. In particular the Liberal party (FDP) and some elements within the CDU pleaded for a return to virtues such as individual responsibility and independence and attacked the expansion of the *Versorgungsstaat*. But the legitimacy of a policy of income redistribution was never contested in a fundamental sense. To be sure, authentic 'Heart of Jesus socialists' (as the CDU left wingers are sometimes called by their critics on the party right) are probably difficult to find. 'Leftists' in the CDU like Norbert Blüm and Geißler supported fiscal conservatism as well as the – limited–

attempts at 'deregulation' of the labour market. What distinguishes them is their outspoken sympathy for an even further extension of the redistributive welfare state. Yet even the CDU mainstream never considered a 'rolling back' of the welfare state. Hence, in spite of the efforts of Lambsdorff and other FDP spokesmen to emphasize the 'free-market' profile of the smaller coalition partner, no fundamental re-orientation of social policy was ever seriously attempted within the coalition. Although cuts in some programmes were made to rebalance the budget, strong forces within the CDU continued to press for new redistributive programmes, in particular to assist families. Finally, in the early 1990s, Blüm, the CDU Minister of Labour and Social Affairs, even led a vigorous campaign, against FDP and employer resistance and with the tacit support of the SPD, for an important enlargement of the redistributive welfare state by extending the social security principles to a new insurance to cover the rising costs of health care of the disabled elderly people (*Pflegeversicherung*). Here it became again obvious that the Christian Democrats considered this orientation as vital for maintaining the party's ideological identity.

This identity continued to depend on the reference to the German ideological tradition of a 'social market economy' defined in terms of a theory of *Ordnungspolitik*. The remarkable strength of this interpretation of economic policy is due to the paradoxical combination of an old historical legacy with the powerful myth of the 'social market economy' as a supposedly fundamental post-war political innovation. First of all, the economic policy discourse in West Germany was for long dominated by the 'Freiburg school' of German neo-liberal economics founded by Walter Eucken. A characteristic feature of this discourse was, from its very beginnings, its typological reasoning in terms of '*Wirtschaftsordnungen*', of clearly defined economic systems, as they are observable in 'morphological' historical analysis (Eucken, 1939; Eucken, 1952). The easy comprehensibility of this approach probably explains much of the strong impact it had on a broad educated public. Central typological categories, employed not only in the specialized economic literature but in school textbooks as well as in journalistic jargon, were the 'market economy' and the 'centrally administered economy', which are each supposed to obey a specific systemic logic. Such reasoning was strongly indebted to the theory of 'economic systems' as developed by the heirs of nineteenth-century historical economics, in particular Werner Sombart (Abelshauser, 1991). It was in these terms that since the 1930s – reacting to the experience of the world economic crisis – the German neo-liberals (Eucken himself, Alfred Müller-Armack, Franz Böhm and others) developed their conception of an economic 'order' based on the dynamics of a competitive market, but 'bound by the state' (*staatlich gebunden*). The fact that this doctrine could be conceived and advocated under the auspices of the official (National Socialist) 'Academy for German Law' is not as surprising as it may appear to those who identify the economics of the 'Third Reich' with the state–corporatist doctrines of the early 1930s (which soon became confined to a marginal role) or with the war economy. For, on the one hand, within the regime there were always powerful advocates of a competitive market economy based on free enterprise (Speer, 1969, p. 368 ff). Also, the ordo-liberal school could refer to an ideological tradition that was perfectly compatible with the credo of the regime. The reconciliation of a capitalist economic order with the idea of the *Sozialstaat* had already been the central concern of the *Kathedersozialisten*, those conservative economics professors who, with their disciples in the bureaucracy, guided Bismarck's social policy innovations. It can even be traced back to their intellectual mentor and precursor, Lorenz von Stein (1850), with his theory of a 'social monarchy'. Indebted as it was to this theoretical heritage, the neo-liberal theory of *Ordnungspolitik* – as it was further developed after the Second World War – regarded 'secondary' redistribution of incomes through social policy as perfectly legitimate as long as government did not interfere with the ('primary') allocative functions of the *marktwirtschaftliche Ordnung* (Müller-Armack, 1956).

Paradoxically, the strength of the idea of the 'social market economy' as a guiding interpretation of social reality seems due to the reinforcement of this historical legacy by the belief that the 'social market economy' constituted a fundamental innovation of the early post-war period under the leadership of Ludwig Erhard (1957) and the Christian Democrats. Seen in a historical perspective, the innovative element of this policy has certainly been overstated. It is of course true that the post-war version of the 'social market economy' with its strong emphasis on competition contrasted with older, 'neo-mercantilist' traditions of German economic policy, with their protectionist traits and promotion of cartels. But the attribution of the success story of post-war economic reconstruction to this new emphasis on a competitive economic order is certainly more controversial than is often assumed (see, for example, Shonfield, 1965). Also, the new myth of the 'social market economy' simplified an undoubtedly much more complex institutional reality of the political economy of West Germany (Shonfield, 1965).

Another ambiguity is created by the infiltration of the *Subsidiaritätsprinzip*, a concept with strong roots in Catholic social philosophy, into German conservative economic thinking. To be sure, it means that the state shall act only as a 'subsidiary' – but to whom? Some may interpret it as postulating the priority of market forces. However, other readings of the *Subsidiaritätsprinzip* consider the state as the subsidiary to 'society' – which may mean, for example, private associations. A 'corporatist' approach would not be incompatible with such an interpretation.

The political implications of this eclectic theoretical background were essentially twofold. First, the historical–typological approach of the Freiburg ordo-liberal school permitted an eclectic political interpretation (thus whereas Eucken was very sceptical about a policy of full employment, Müller-Armack resolutely supported it). Strict market liberals as well as the *Sozialausschüsse* (the 'social committees' of Christian trade unionists) of the CDU left wing could likewise refer to this flexible ideological tradition. It was hence highly appropriate for the purpose of integrating a political party with a socially heterogeneous clientele, such as the CDU. Second, the fundamentalist neo-conservative reaction against the redistributive welfare state encountered in the rhetoric of the Thatcher and Reagan governments remained rather alien to the 'institutionalization of meaning' established in the deeply anchored tradition of conservative German economic and social policy doctrines. Moreover, these doctrines eventually legitimized regulating the economy as long as regulation could be presented as being non-discretionary and thus 'in conformity with the market'. Müller-Armack (1976, p. 120 ff) explicitly justified regulation of the utilities, transport, credit institutions and agriculture.

It may be granted that, although dominant interpretations of the ordo-liberal tradition shielded redistributive social policy against the fundamentalist attack on the welfare state, its specific emphasis on the competitive market had become an important element of the dominant economic belief system. In consequence, 'deregulation' and 'de-bureaucratization' had become prominent issues in the government platform. But then it remains an open question why 'deregulation' and privatization did not proceed much faster than actually happened.

2. Policy Advisers, Bureaucrats, and the Institutional Segmentation of Economic and Technical Expertise

Part of the answer to this question is provided by the institutional segmentation of 'policy communities' through which interpretations of reality by the holders of economic and technical expertise are communicated into the decision-making process. Specifically, the isolation of economic policy expertise in the institutional framework of German politics was an important constraint on the adoption of a coherent agenda of 'deregulation'.

Whereas in the United States and Britain the role of conservative 'think-tanks' outside the government machinery – like, respectively, the American Enterprise Institute and the Heritage Foundation, or the Institute for Eco-

nomic Affairs, the Centre for Policy Studies and the Adam Smith Institute –
was vital for the intellectual preparation of the conservative agenda, in
West Germany the paradigm change in economic policy was to a considerable degree prepared by actors with an official status, namely the Council
of Economic Experts with its legal mandate for advising the government,
on the one hand, and, on the other, the top bureaucrats of the Federal
Economics Ministry themselves.

The most prestigious advisory body is certainly the official – but independent – *Sachverständigenrat zur Begutachtung der gesamtwirtschaftlichen
Entwicklung* (SVR, Council of Economic Experts). It was clearly established
to serve as an instrument of the economic policy of the federal government.
At the same time its relationship to the government is characterized by
'loose coupling'. On the one hand, it is *de facto* an academic body recruit-
ing itself by way of cooptation (though two of its members are appointed
on the suggestion of the employers' organizations and of the trade unions).
On the other hand, it is not permitted to formulate policy recommendations
(and therefore has to phrase its – often outspoken – prescriptive opinions in
the form of projections and causal explanations). As originally intended by
Ludwig Erhard when it was established in 1962, the Council of Economic
Experts has a considerable impact on public opinion. Its direct influence on
government policy, however, is much more uncertain.

Some economists have argued that it is precisely its institutional isolation
from the process of economic policy-making which explains the limited
impact of its supply-side orientation on the economic policy record of the
Kohl government. But this overlooks the fact that, in spite of the 'loose
coupling' between academic expertise and government exemplified by the
status of the Council of Economic Experts, its analyses had an important
role in the intellectual preparation of the agenda of the *Wende* (Singer, 1991).

However, it cannot be denied that this kind of academic expertise was
never directly translated into government policy. Rather, the decisive intellectual inputs were produced within the top of the federal government
administration. Thus the famous 'Lambsdorff paper' which, in 1982, led to
the breakup of the Social–Liberal coalition government had been prepared,
on the demand of Economics Minister Lambsdorff (FDP), by some top
bureaucrats of the ministry under the guidance of permanent secretary Otto
Schlecht, and the head of the Economic Policy Division
(*Grundsatzabteilung*) Hans Tietmeyer. This in-house expertise of the economic bureaucracy has a long tradition. Since the times of Ludwig Erhard
as Minister of Economics, the *Grundsatzabteilung* (strictly speaking division 1A) under such heads as Alfred Müller-Armack has carried considerable
weight and was always strongly committed to the market economy. Otto
Schlecht, who had already served in the *Grundsatzabteilung* under Erhard

and became its head under the Social Democratic minister Karl Schiller, played an important role in the cautious shift of the Economics Ministry toward Keynesian thinking in the late 1960s. However, since the second half of the 1970s a gradual and pragmatic re-orientation of officials like Schlecht and Tietmeyer from global demand management to a supply-side orientation and *Verstetigung* (consolidation) of fiscal policy took place.

Given this important role of top bureaucrats in policy formation, another institutional feature becomes important, namely the centrality of the *Ressortprinzip* (the 'departmental principle') in the organization of the executive. According to Article 65 of the constitution, the 'policy guidelines' are formulated by the Federal Chancellor. However, in the routine work of government this power is rather narrowly circumscribed, and Chancellor Kohl has never seriously attempted to assume leadership in economic policy. Hence the *Kanzlerprinzip* (the 'Chancellor principle') tends hence to be superseded by the *Ressortprinzip*. This 'departmental principle' is based on the stipulation of Article 65 that, 'within these guidelines, each federal minister runs his department independently and under his own responsibility'. Since the functions of the cabinet as a collective body (*Kabinettsprinzip*) remain largely confined to the ratification of bills and the arbitration of inter-departmental conflicts that cannot be solved otherwise, and since also cabinet committees have not much significant influence, the *Ressortprinzip* becomes the central principle of cabinet organization (Böckenförde, 1964, p. 168). The autonomy of ministers as heads of departments is strengthened further by the practice of coalition government where parties consider 'their' departments as domains that are normally 'off limits' to the partners in the coalition (Grande, 1987, p. 317).

One important consequence is the sectoral segmentation of institutionalized policy advice. This has two different aspects. In theory, the 'departmental principle' implies that the formation of economic policy, in particular macro-economic policy, is in the jurisdiction of the Federal Minister of Economics. The 'Lambsdorff paper' of 1982 implied indeed a claim to political leadership in this domain. However, the Minister of Economics cannot bind other ministers: for this a 'policy guideline' from the Chancellor would be required. As a consequence, as far as the formal jurisdictions of other ministers are concerned, in spite of his 'generalist' claims the Minister of Economics is confined to co-jurisdiction (*Mitzeichnung*).[3] His influence on the policy of other departments is therefore limited to 'negative coordination' (Mayntz and Scharpf, 1975, p. 145). Moreover, in 1972 the Minister for Economics lost the bureau for monetary and credit policy, and hence important instruments for the implementation of his policy, to the Minister of Finance. Accordingly, his policy-making power is in reality severely limited.

Another manifestation of the *Ressortprinzip* is that other important ministries (such as the ministries for labour, for agriculture, or for technology) develop their own in-house expertise and maintain their autonomous advisory institutions embedded into sectoral policy networks. In these networks, different scientific paradigms may guide a sector-specific 'institutionalization of meaning'. Therefore, on the level of government organization the theoretical ambiguity of the doctrine of the 'social market economy' is reflected in quite different emphases on, for example, the redistributive implications of the doctrine.

How this sectoralization of expertise can act as an important constraint on market reform strategies is well illustrated by the case of telecommunications reform (Grande, 1989, p. 188). This reform was prepared by a governmental commission which had originally been suggested by the Federal Ministry for Research and Technology but was finally established in 1985 – in accordance with the *Ressortprinzip* – by the Federal Minister of Post and Telecommunications. After long and laborious negotiations, its twelve members were drawn from different interest groups affected by telecommunications policy and from the political parties. As chairman, the Post Minister chose a renowned expert in communications policy, Eberhard Witte, a professor of business economics with close relationships to the dominant firms in the telecommunications industry (Siemens and SEL–Alcatel) and highly influential in the *Münchner Kreis*, an 'issue network' in telecommunications policy linking experts from universities, industry, and the telecommunications administration. By virtue of its claim on *Mitzeichnung*, the Ministry of Economics successfully demanded the appointment of a member of its own advisory council, himself an expert on the deregulation of telecommunications policy, to the governmental commission of the Post Ministry. But Wernhard Möschel, a professor of economic law and member of the neo-liberal *Kronberger Kreis*, found himself rather isolated within this commission. It remained under the firm grip of Witte, and Möschel's minority opinion (pleading, in particular, for the abolition of the network monopoly of the public telecommunications organization) was signed by no more than three other members (representatives of the Federation of German Industry, of the banks, and of the FDP) and had no significant impact on the 'Post Structure Law' finally voted in 1989.

The case of telecommunications policy is by no means an exception. Whereas the advisory councils (*wissenschaftliche Beiräte*) of the ministries of economics and finance are clearly market-orientated, like the Council of Economic Experts (*Sachverständigenrat*) mentioned above, important expert commissions or advisory councils in the jurisdiction of other ministries remain much more closely controlled by the sectoral 'issue networks'. In the domain of health policy, although market-orientated health economists were increasingly present in the academic discussion and were even given an opportunity to present their positions in the official journal of the Ministry of Labour and Social Affairs and in a ministry-organized symposium in March 1985, their impact on policy formation remained extremely limited. The advisory bodies in the health policy issue network continued to be dominated by the academic representatives of a 'non-market economics' approach with a strong preference for decision-making through associational bargaining (Döhler, 1990, p. 223).

The strategic consequences of the sectoral segmentation resulting from the *Ressortprinzip* were once more illustrated in the *Pflegeversicherung* issue in 1991. The political debate – which at the time of writing is still going on – culminated in a public hearing that was organized by Blüm with representatives of the interest groups for the obvious purpose of demonstrating to the employers' representatives and to the FDP that they were completely isolated within the social policy issue network, and that their counter-proposal for a form of private insurance was generally considered as unrealistic and impractical.[4]

3. Interest Associations and Sectoralized Policy Networks: The Case of Health Policy

It has already been stressed that the *ordnungspolitische* ethos of the 'social market economy' masked a considerably more complex institutional reality. One crucial element of this reality was the traditional importance of large and often strongly centralized interest associations in the governance of the German economy (see, for example, Shonfield, 1965). Already in the late nineteenth century the political weight of the industrial peak associations was such that Bismarck had recourse to their services for his foreign economic policy (Böhme, 1974, p. 596).[5] And about seven decades later, in 1950–51, Ludwig Erhard – notwithstanding his personal dislike for the peak associations of business – had to fall back on the support of the business associations to manage the crises of the supply of raw materials and of energy. Abelshauser (1981, 1983) interprets these developments as the beginnings of a 'corporative market economy' that would remain characteristic of the Federal Republic.

Given this long-established 'corporatist' role of interest associations, they were also repeatedly of crucial importance in the settlement of protracted social conflicts in modern Germany. A relatively well-known example of such 'social peace treaties' is the Stinnes-Legien agreement between organized business and labour in 1919. It was preceded in 1916 by a *modus vivendi* concluded between both parties and mediated by the military High

Command for the sake of the war effort. The importance of this associational agreement as a historical model is not diminished by the fact that it lasted only for a couple of years (Feldman, 1970, 1981). The *Zentrale Arbeitsgemeinschaft* established by the agreement of 1919 was in a way the forerunner of the *Konzertierte Aktion* ('concerted action') initiated in 1966 by Karl Schiller with the participation of organized labour and business, an experiment that in spite of its internal contradictions remains an attractive formula for many political decision-makers (Lehmbruch, 1979).

Peak associations are, however, more important in some sectors than in others. In the steel industry, they have sometimes been quite powerless against the interests of big corporations. In telecommunications policy we encounter a rather clientelist network which links the administration to some leading producers. Moreover, the Federal Republic of Germany never developed the sort of overarching trans-sectoral corporatist organization that was encountered in countries such as Austria (Lehmbruch, 1979). Rather, under conditions of a sectoral institutional segmentation of the state – as represented by the *Ressortprinzip* – German corporatism (where it ex- isted) remained itself a curiously 'sectoralized' phenomenon. Compara- tively speaking, one of the political weaknesses of the *Konzertierte Aktion* was that (different from the Austrian *Paritätische Kommission* headed by the Federal Chancellor) it remained essentially a sectoral arrangement by the Minister of Economics, and that no effective trans-sectoral coordination with fiscal policy, let alone with the monetary policy of the Bundesbank, was achieved. Scharpf (1987, pp. 165 and 253) has noted the lack of communication between the trade unions and the Bundesbank.

It is remarkable that this sectoralized character of the German variant of corporatism was a main reason not only for the 'blockade of Keynesian coordination' (Scharpf, 1987, p. 301) in the 1970s but also, in the 1980s, for the institutional blockade of a policy of deregulation. A salient example is the case of health policy. The escalation of health costs had been a subject of strong political concern already during the Social–Liberal coali- tion. But anybody who expected that the new Conservative–Liberal major- ity would turn to a policy of market-orientated reforms in the health sector was to be deceived. The Health Reform Law, which was finally voted in 1988, contained only a very limited number of 'market-conform' elements and left the corporatist character of the health system intact. It even extended the jurisdiction of a corporatist body, the *Bundesausschuß der Ärzte und Krankenkassen* (joint federal committee of doctors and health insurance funds), to the domain of pharmaceutical price regulation.

Health policy-making in Germany, as this example demonstrates, is se- verely constrained by a corporatist network of the specialized administration and the associations of doctors and the public health insurance funds. Its roots go back to Bismarck's decision to establish a system of public health insurance funds on the basis of self-administration (*Selbstverwaltung*) (Döhler, 1990, 1991; Manow-Borgwardt, 1991). With the gradual extension of this system, doctors' fees increasingly became dependent on the health insurance funds. This collective 'traumatic experience' (Döhler) led the medical community to a strong preference for collective organizational action over the freedom of contract. In 1913, after a series of doctors' strikes, and after a mediating intervention of the government, the medical associations finally succeeded in breaking the power exerted by the health insurance funds over individual doctors by the establishment of a collective bargaining system. In this system, joint committees with equal representation of both sides were made responsible for the licensing of doctors to practice in the public health system (*Kassenärzte*) and for the conclusion of contracts. The 'Berlin agreement' of 1913 thus constitutes a 'social peace treaty' that is strikingly analogous to the arrangements between organized labour and business mentioned before. Its corporatist character became still more pronounced after the establishment, in 1932, of compulsory associations (*Kassenärztliche Vereinigungen*) to represent the *Kassenärzte*. These associations have developed into powerful actors. They not only effectively defend the interests of the medical profession within the public health insurance system but also enforce the rules established in these bargaining processes on their – often very reluctant – clientele.

The essential elements of the system gradually established since the early part of the century have remained remarkably stable up to the present time. This stability can be interpreted as the result of an organizational equilibrium achieved in the triangular relationship of medical associations, health insurance funds, and the influential sectoral state bureaucracy. When, in the 1970s, the Social Democrats attempted to legally strengthen the bargaining position of the health insurance funds in order to check the escalation of health costs, this move was prevented by the CDU majority in the Bundesrat (Federal Council). Instead, the Christian Democrats gained acceptance for an institutional extension of the corporatist bargaining mechanisms through the establishment of the *Konzertierte Aktion im Gesundheitswesen* (concerted action in the health sector), modelled again on the precedents in the relationship of employers, trade unions and government. Admittedly the 'recommendations' of this semi-annual conference of all important public and private organizations of the sector, where the bureaucracy again plays a leading role, may often be ignored. But it constitutes the formal nucleus of a bargaining network in which more recently, under strong pressure from the government, the *Kassenärztliche Vereinigungen*, as the legally privileged medical associations, found themselves virtually constrained to make sizeable concessions (notably on the global sum of doctors' fees which is now 'capped'). They did so in order to preserve the essential achievements of the deal of 1913 which they continue to consider as the institutional basis of the medical community's professional autonomy. But this is obviously tantamount to an effective protection of the health policy network against market mechanisms such as those which are advocated by health economists.

4.   Vertical Cleavages in the Sectoral Policy Networks: Economic Policy between Federal and *Länder* Authorities

Interestingly, although it was the Minister of Economics who in 1982 initiated the *Wende* with the 'Lambsdorff paper', even in the jurisdiction of this department the progress of deregulation was slow, and no significant cuts were made in the subsidies for declining industries (such as bituminous coal) that were such an important part of its traditional activities. This is not simply explained by bureaucratic inertia or the successful lobbying of interest associations. Rather, in its own jurisdiction, the Ministry of Economics is constrained by the specific German variant of federalism.

It is well known that the federal government depends to a considerable degree on cooperation with the *Länder*. Not only their constitutional role in the legislative process makes federal–state accommodation essential. In particular their participation in tax legislation gives the *Länder* governments a strong voice in fiscal policy. Moreover, in most regulatory fields their participation in policy implementation is indispensable. Macro-economic policy is, of course, the chief responsibility of the Federal Minister of Economics. In consequence, however, state governments often have different priorities. For instance, in the early life of the Social–Liberal coalition Helmut Kohl, then head of the state government of Rhineland–Palatinate, said that it was not his job to make anti-cyclical policy for the socialists. *Länder* ministers of economics put much stronger emphasis on their regional structural problems and are therefore inclined to assume a more interventionist stance. In particular, after the decline of the joint federal–state activities in regional policy, the *Länder* have become increasingly active in their own right (Hesse and Benz, 1990, p. 158). In the 1980s, this activism was discernible regardless of the political orientation of state governments. The two conservative strongholds in South Germany, Baden–Württemberg and Bavaria, even got the reputation of being 'neo-mercantilists' because of their active role in industrial policy.

Quite naturally, the *Länder* also defended their vested interests against the deregulation initiatives. To take an example, in the Witte commission on telecommunications reform mentioned above, the representative of the

Länder, the conservative Bavarian Minister of the Interior Stoiber, made very clear that the large states were opposed to any reform that might cause a 'withdrawal of the Post Office from the countryside'. As a result of *Länder* opposition the 1989 law established an 'infrastructure council' with eleven representatives from the Bundestag and from the Bundesrat each to 'participate in all decisions of the Ministry of Post and Telecommunications that are of infrastructure relevance and concern essential interests of the *Länder*' (Grande, 1989, p. 228). The case of telecommunications is certainly not exceptional. Similar opposition might be expected in all domains where deregulation initiatives threaten strong regional interests. Given the quite effective leverage of which the *Länder* dispose in the complex interdependent structure of German federalism, it is only by accommodative strategies that the federal government can realize its political objectives.

5. 'Interlocking Politics' and the Party System

The institutional leverage of the *Länder* is considerably reinforced by the central position of the political parties in the interlocking federal network. This dependency is the result of *Länder* participation in the legislative process and in policy implementation, in particular via the Bundesrat. It is therefore vital for any government that wants to realize its programme to control a majority in this chamber. The reform agenda of the Social–Liberal coalition was severely constrained by this dependency because there was a Christian Democratic Bundesrat majority all the time.

Until 1990, the Conservative–Liberal coalition was not confronted with a similar situation. Between 1989 and 1991 the CDU lost control of four state parliaments (Hesse, Lower Saxony, Rhineland–Palatinate and Schleswig–Holstein) and, consequently, its Bundesrat majority. However, even when the Bundesrat majority exists, the representation of the states in the Bundesrat, through the mechanism of 'anticipated reactions' (C.J. Friedrich), results in an increased sensitivity of the federal government to electoral sanctions. Chancellor Kohl was reminded of this factor quite early in the first legislature of his coalition government. An important early issue on its 'supply-side' agenda was to strengthen employer rights in their relations with labour unions (see the chapter by Koch). As a first important step, the coalition amended section 116 of the *Arbeitsförderungsgesetz* (which regulates the functions and competences of the *Bundesanstalt für Arbeit*, the Federal Office for Unemployment and Labour Market Policy) in order to make certain strikes more difficult (see Koch).[6] Dangers arising from the resulting conflict with the trade unions were apparently underestimated by the CDU. However, after the party suffered heavy losses in subsequent state elections in North-Rhine Westphalia Chancellor Kohl swiftly moderated his strategy; deregulation of the labour market almost disappeared from the government agenda. The confrontational style of 1982 may have been useful to underline the profile of the coalition in the federal electoral arena. But it was dysfunctional in an institutional setting in which the capacity for accommodation is often a condition of successful policy formation.

6.   German Unification and the Crisis of the Market Ideology

The crisis of the free-market agenda came unexpectedly, as a consequence of the breakdown of the GDR in 1989–90. The decision for a swift monetary and economic union of both parts of Germany was an improvised response to the perception of crisis within an exceptional structure of decision-making. This situation favoured miscalculations in the transfer of monetary and economic institutions due to an ideologically motivated representation of reality. The swift transfer of these institutions resulted in a serious structural crisis of the East German economy.

In early 1990 many foreign observers and the leaders of the coalition expected that East Germany would experience a swift recovery because of its union with the powerful economy of the West, and that the united Germany would present to the world a new success story of free private enterprise. Since then, such optimism has been belied by the factual developments. The East German economy is in a process of rapid decline that is likely to result in a deep structural crisis.

In economic terms, the explanation for this dramatic decline is quite obvious: East Germany's manufacturing and agricultural sector had a much lower productivity (more pessimistic estimates put it below 25 per cent of West German productivity). According to the *Institut für Wirtschaft und Gesellschaft*, relative industrial productivity was at about 52 per cent in 1950 and stabilized at around 32 per cent in 1970 before declining further from the mid-1970s. Given these structural handicaps, with monetary and economic union almost no sector of the GDR economy was any longer competitive. Consumer goods lost even their traditional domestic market because of their inferior quality or simply because of the appeal of West German goods and the superior marketing efforts of West German distributors. Moreover, by adopting a hard currency East Germany lost most of its soft currency markets, especially in Eastern Europe and in the Soviet Union.

At the same time, the propensity of West German (or foreign) business to invest in the East remains limited. For manufacturing industries, the desolate communications infrastructure makes it clearly more profitable to produce in West Germany for the East German market than vice versa. The often enormous ecological *Altlasten* ('old burdens' that are often still unknown) involve legal risks that in many cases are difficult to assess. Insecurity about property rights remains considerable. The unification treaty stipulates the restitution of property confiscated after 1949 to the original proprietors or their successors. It is estimated that checking these claims may take several decades. Prospective investors, however, insist on clarification of the legal situation before taking any risks. What we observe looks like a deep structural crisis of an entire industrial region. Such a situation has never existed in the post-war history of West Germany. Crises were either linked to the business cycle, or they were structural crises limited to particular industries. The policy repertoire developed in West Germany after the Second World War contains no responses to this entirely new challenge.

This situation is the outcome of the exceptional structure of decision-making in the unification process. As I have argued elsewhere, the process of unification was characterized by improvisation and the lack of any strategic master-plan that might have considered aspects of implementation and eventual secondary consequences (Lehmbruch, 1990). The decision to offer East Germany a swift monetary and economic union was strongly opposed by the Bundesbank and criticized by some of the most prestigious economic advisory institutions of the government (in particular the *Sachverständigenrat* and the *Institut für Weltwirtschaft* in Kiel) and important business leaders. Their position was that a separate – but convertible – currency in the GDR was the condition for a reform of the GDR economy without serious social disruptions (a position also taken by the Keynesians of the Memorandum group). The reaction of the government to this criticism was twofold. The bureaucracy of the Federal Economics Ministry and other governmental experts argued that the strategy preferred by the bankers and economists – namely, to maintain a separate East German monetary regime – would not be viable politically. Hence the external advisers were asked to reflect about 'second-best' solutions, as Otto Schlecht, permanent secretary of the Economics Ministry, argued in the *Handelsblatt* on 23 February 1990. This still left open the question of whether the monetary union would not have to be accompanied by strong interventions aimed at creating the structural preconditions for a competitive market economy through a reorganization of the GDR economy (Singer, 1990). The majority of the government party leaders, however, persuaded themselves – and the East German public – that monetary union and the introduction of a competitive free market economy would by themselves lead to a recovery comparable to that of West Germany after the currency reform in 1948.

What happened in early 1990 was the temporary breakdown of the quasi-'corporatist' linkage structure of the West German policy network. Under the unusual circumstances of 1990, the party system cut its communication channels to other corporate actors in the West German polity and assumed the position of an unconstrained sovereign decision-maker. This had the further consequence that its peculiar belief systems which normally serve integrative rather than operative purposes came to govern its operative policy choices. The belief system that dominated not only the electoral discourse in 1990 but also the decisions of the government was the myth of the 'social market economy' in an extremely simplified version. According to this myth, under the guidance of Ludwig Erhard, the CDU adopted a new economic strategy that constituted a decisive break with the 'command economy' of the National Socialist regime and with a similar 'command economy' that had been favoured in the immediate post-war years by socialists and crypto-socialists in key posts of the Allied occupation and the German post-war administrations. Supposedly, the situation was now similar. The currency reform of 1948 and the subsequent abolition of price controls by Ludwig Erhard appeared as the key events that explained economic recovery (Abelshauser, 1983, p. 48). This may explain why monetary union was embraced in early 1990 by politicians from the opposition as well as by the government, as the panacea for the East German economic and psychological crisis, and why the promise of introducing the DM successfully captured the imagination of the East German electorate. Indeed, monetary union was first proposed by the SPD spokeswoman for financial policy in the Bundestag, Ingrid Matthaeus-Meier. On the other hand, its most determined critic was Oskar Lafontaine, the SPD Chancellor candidate who lost the first all-German elections of 2 December 1990.

The advantage of this interpretation of the 'social market economy' was that it permitted a policy without hard choices for West Germany. Monetary union, abolition of controls, and privatization of the East German economy were supposed to lead to relatively swift recovery for the former GDR territory. No economic sacrifices from an eventual redistribution from West to East would be required. Against this simple belief system, expert opinions and the pragmatic concerns of business leaders could not prevail because their cognitive framework would have implied relatively complex political strategies, developed in a long-term perspective and based upon broad political alliances. Such strategies, however, were not available within the policy repertoire of a party system that was already engaged in an intense electoral competition. The revaluation effect of the monetary union on the competitive position of the East German economy was, therefore, completely disregarded. And in the electoral campaign of autumn 1990 the coalition government asserted that– contrary to the warnings of many experts – no tax increases would be needed to rebuild the East German economy. This promise had to be broken only a few months after the election.

By autumn of 1991 the leaders of the coalition government generally acknowledged that the expectations which they entertained within this belief system were erroneous. Originally, many put the blame either on unpredictable events (notably the collapse of East European markets after the breakdown of communist rule there and the phasing out of the transfer rouble) or on incomplete information (the misleading statistical data on the East German economy). One can argue in their favour that – because of the strength of the institutionalist tradition of ordo-liberal economics – many advisers among academic economists focused 'on fixing the institutional arrangements of a liberal economic order and of a social security system' whereas – in the words of a critic representing one of the empirically orientated economic research institutes – 'a discussion of the primary economic objectives relating to unification did not take place' (Heilemann, 1991; see also Singer, 1990). In the meantime, however, the myth of the 'social market economy' has lost much of its integrative power.

In early 1991, the growth of unemployment in East Germany could no longer go unnoticed, in particular after more and more mass demonstrations against the policy of the Bonn government took place on the streets that – not much longer than a year earlier – had seen the spectacular rallies against the SED regime. An additional shock was created by the assassination of Detlef Rohwedder, chief executive of the *Treuhand,* by West German terrorists. The *Treuhand Anstalt* ('trust establishment') is a sort of public corporation originally established by the communist reform government of prime minister Hans Modrow as a sort of holding company to control and reorganize all former East German state enterprises. Its official mission was redefined to convert the former centrally controlled state monopolies into private enterprises. The first step of this task was to break up the former huge industrial monopolies (*Kombinate*), which were often characterized by an extreme degree of vertical integration, into smaller units that might be more manageable in a competitive market environment. This included in particular divesting them of those ancillary activities that could more profitably be performed by independent producers and also to reduce the labour force of companies that – as was often the case – appeared to be overmanned. Such a reorganization had, by late 1991, already been achieved to some degree. Subsequently, and as top priority, the *Treuhand* was supposed to privatize these companies and shut down those that were no longer viable. However, the *Treuhand* was often accused of neglecting the social consequences of its policies and therefore became the symbolic scapegoat for the evolving crisis. When trade unions and the Social Democrats asked for priority to be given to *sanieren* (rationalization in order to save at least part of the jobs) over *privatisieren,* even if that might mean keeping these enterprises in public ownership, the stereotypical answer of the government and coalition spokesmen was that privatization was the best form of *Sanierung*.

This dogmatic position proved increasingly unrealistic because privatization did not advance as expected. The chemical firms did not find buyers because of the ecological burdens inherited from the past (even if the *Treuhand* is ready to pay for cleaning up, there remains little incentive for prospective investors); steel and shipbuilding were no longer competitive; and the traditional sites of the automobile industry seemed likely to survive only as 'extended workbenches' of Western companies, with most of the supplies coming from West Germany. Even the traditional engineering and optical industries have lost their East European customers and have considerable difficulties in adapting to the Western markets.

In consequence, less then ten years after the arrival of a Conservative–Liberal government that promised to reduce the role of the state in the economy and that was always extremely critical of subsidized public enterprises in Italy or France, the government of the newly united Germany owns the largest public industrial complex of all capitalist countries. In the optimistic expectations of *Treuhand* spokesmen, most of its tasks will be achieved by 1993. More pessimistic projections fear that it will be forced to close most of its industrial holdings and risk a social catastrophe of dramatic dimensions, or to support them indefinitely with exorbitant subsidies.

In early 1991, growing concern about the menace of social conflicts led to a revision of policy. With respect to property rights, the priority originally given to former proprietors was modified; if they are not prepared to effect the required investments, they may lose their claim to restitution and instead may be compensated for their lost property. Repudiating its electoral promises, the government agreed tax increases that nullify most of the tax cuts effected since 1982. Most importantly, the *Treuhand* and the peak organizations of labour and employers, with the backing of the federal government, concluded a sort of social contract in order to manage the social consequences of industrial reconversion of East Germany. This corporatist pact opened the way to a new phase of the German 'corporative market economy'. The *Treuhand* agreed to attenuate the priority originally given to privatization and to envisage *Sanierung* in cases where no buyers could be found. And both the *Treuhand* and the employers' organizations acceded to the union demands for the establishment of 'employment companies' (*Beschäftigungsgesellschaften*), an instrument of active labour market policy that originally had been adopted by some West German Social Democratic state governments (especially in the Saar where the steel industry had deep structural problems), to keep at least part of the redundant workforce in employment. In these organizations, the unemployed may either undergo retraining, or they are occupied with demolishing obsolete factory premises or with removing the hazardous waste that abounds on many industrial sites. Besides, many of the unemployed have found temporary ABM (*Arbeitsbeschaffungsmaßnahme*, work creation programme) jobs. Active labour market policy has thus reappeared on the political agenda in more force than ever before. Initially, financing these activities was made possible by the tax increases mentioned above; indeed, from the early summer of 1991 it was often argued that 'money is not the problem'. The problem of government debt has at the same time lost the prominent place that it once had in the fiscal policy of the government.

This does not mean that deregulation and privatization are now dead issues. Some of the unexpected consequences of unification may even bring them back on the agenda. Rebuilding the communications' infrastructure of East Germany is a task that may overcharge not only government finances but also its planning and policy-making capacity. Hence the idea of assigning such tasks to private enterprise appeared to gain ground. Also, the administrative vacuum left in East Germany after the breakdown of the communist regime may, in the long run, prove a favourable terrain for new initiatives towards deregulation and debureaucratization. By autumn 1991 the discussion was only in its beginnings. But, to the degree that the present crisis is a crisis of the institutional framework of economic and social policy-making, it cannot be excluded that profound transformations might take place in the future.

Notes

This chapter is based on the findings of a research project on 'economic strategy change in cross-national comparison', conducted with the generous financial support of the Volkswagen Foundation. Research associates were Marian Döhler (health policy), Edgar Grande (telecommunications reform) and Otto Singer (economic policy advice). For some of the findings see Döhler (1990, 1991), Grande (1989), Lehmbruch et al. (1988), Lehmbruch (1989a, 1989b) and Singer (1991).

1 This could also be established by a content analysis of business journals and economic commentaries in the general press. Many economic commentators in the general press and the business journals often referred to these two countries as models to emulate.

2 The *Kronberger Kreis* is probably the most conspicuous group of economists and legal scholars devoted to the systematic development of an agenda for deregulation of the German economy.

3 According to the *Gemeinsame Geschäftsordnung der Bundesministerien, Allgemeiner Teil, 70, II, Mitzeichnung* (co-jurisdiction) means that the 'leading' (*federführend*) ministry has to 'clear' its initiatives (in particular, bills) with other ministries that may be affected. The term 'negative coordination' has been coined by Mayntz and Scharpf (1975, p. 145 ff.) to refer to the power of the *mitzeichende* ministry to object to initiatives by which it perceives itself as negatively affected. For a long time the Federal

Economics Ministry has been in conflicts of this type with the Ministry of Post and Telecommunications; it had, for example, prevailed on the latter not to extend its monopoly to telefax machines.

4   The most controversial problem was how to include in the scheme the generation that, because of its advanced age, would be unable to afford the contribution to a private insurance scheme. According to the counter-proposal, their benefits would have to be paid from a public, tax-financed fund. At a time when concern about the budgetary consequences of German unification was rising, it was relatively easy to present such a scheme as fiscally unsound.

5   In 1889 the diplomatic *rapprochement* with Austria was prepared by confidential negotiations – conducted on the initiative of Bismarck – between the *Zentralverband der Deutschen Industriellen* and representatives of the leading Austrian business associations (Böhme, 1974, pp. 596 ff).

6   The amendment abolished the payment of unemployment benefit to workers in plants that were not formally involved in an industrial conflict but became idle as an indirect consequence of conflicts in other regions or sectors. This measure was aimed particularly at automobile plants which could indirectly be paralysed by a strike against important subcontractors, a problem made more acute by the spread of 'just-in-time' management techniques.

References

Abelshauser, Werner (1981), 'Korea, die Ruhr and Erhards Marktwirtschaft: Die Energiekrise von 1950/51', *Rheinische Vierteljahrsblätter*, **45**, 287–316.

Abelshauser, Werner (1983), *Wirtschaftsgeschichte der Bundesrepublik Deutschland 1945–1980*, Frankfurt/Main:Suhrkamp.

Abelshauser, Werner (1991), 'Die ordnungspolitische Bedeutung der Weltwirtschaftskrise in Deutschland: Ein Beitrag zur Geschichte der Sozialen Marktwirtschaft', in Petzina, D. (ed.), *Ordnungspolitische Weichenstellungen nach dem Zweiten Weltkrieg*, Berlin: Duncker & Humblot.

Böckenförde, Ernst-Wolfgang (1964), *Die Organisationsgewalt im Bereich der Regierung: Eine Untersuchung zum Staatsrecht der Bundesrepublik Deutschland*, Berlin: Duncker & Humblot.

Böhme, Helmut (1974), *Deutschlands Weg zur Großmacht: Studien zum Verhältnis von Wirtschaft und Staat während der Reichsgründungszeit 1848–1881*, Köln: Kiepenheuer & Witsch, 3rd edn.

Döhler, Marian (1990), *Gesundheitspolitik zwischen Markt und Staat: Policy-Netzwerke und ordnungspolitischer Strategiewechsel in der Bundesrepublik, Großbritannien und den USA*, Berlin: Edition Sigma.

Döhler, Marian (1991), 'Policy networks, opportunity structures and neo-conservative reform strategies in health policy', in Marin, B. and Mayntz, R. (eds), *Policy Networks: Empirical Evidence and Theoretical Considerations*, Frankfurt/Main, New York: Campus.

Erhard, Ludwig (1957), *Wohlstand für Alle* (revised by Wolfram Langer), Düsseldorf: Econ Verlag.

Eucken, Walter (1939), *Grundlagen der Nationalökonomie*, Jena: Gustav Fischer.

Eucken, Walter (1952), *Grundsätze der Wirtschaftspolitik*, Tübingen: Mohr/Siebeck.
Feldman, Gerald D. (1970), 'German business between war and revolution: The origins of the Stinnes–Legien agreement', in Ritter, G.A., (ed.), *Entstehung und Wandel der modernen Gesellschaft: Festschrift für Hans Rosenberg zum 65. Geburtstag*, Berlin, 312–41.
Feldman, Gerald D. (1981), 'German interest group alliances in war and inflation, 1914–1923', in Berger, S.(ed.), *Organizing Interests in Western Europe: Pluralism, Corporatism, and the Transformation of Politics*, Cambridge: Cambridge University Press, 159–84.
Grande, Edgar (1987), 'Schwierigkeiten mit der "Wende". Neokonservative Ideologie und Politik in der Bundesrepublik Deutschland', *Österreichische Zeitschrift für Politikwissenschaft*, **16**, 303–23.
Grande, Edgar (1989), *Vom Monopol zum Wettbewerb? Die neokonservative Reform der Telekommunikation in Großbritannien und der Bundesrepublik Deutschland*, Wiesbaden: Deutscher Universitäts-Verlag.
Heclo, Hugh (1978), 'Issue networks and the executive establishment', in King, A. (ed.), *The New American Political System*, Washington D.C.: American Enterprise Institute, 87–124.
Hesse, Jens Joachim and Benz, Arthur (1990), *Die Modernisierung der Staatsorganisation. Institutionspolitik im internationalen Vergleich: USA, Großbritannien, Frankreich, Bundesrepublik Deutschland*, Baden-Baden: Nomos.
Heilemann, Ulrich (1991), 'The economics of German unification – a first appraisal', *Konjunkturpolitik*, **37**, 127–55.
Lehmbruch, Gerhard (1979), 'Liberal corporatism and party government', in Schmitter, P. and Lehmbruch, G. (eds), *Trends toward Corporatist Intermediation*, London: Sage Publications, 147–84.
Lehmbruch, Gerhard, Singer, Otto, Grande, Edgar, and Döhler, Marian (1988), 'Institutionelle Bedingungen ordnungspolitischen Strategiewechsels im internationalen Vergleich', in Schmidt, M.G. (ed.), *Staatstätigkeit: International und historisch vergleichende Analysen*, Opladen: Westdeutscher Verlag, 251–83.
Lehmbruch, Gerhard (1989a), 'Wirtschaftspolitischer Strategiewechsel und die institutionelle Verknüpfung von Staat und Gesellschaft', in Hartwich, H.-H. (ed.), *Macht und Ohnmacht politischer Institutionen*, Opladen: Westdeutscher Verlag, 222–35.
Lehmbruch, Gerhard (1989b), 'Marktreformstrategien bei alternierender Parteiregierung: Eine institutionell vergleichende Analyse', *Jahrbuch zur Staats- und Verwaltungstheorie*, **3**, 15–46.
Lehmbruch, Gerhard (1990), 'Die improvisierte Vereinigung: Die dritte deutsche Republik', *Leviathan: Zeitschrift für Sozialwissenschaft*, **18**, 462–86.
Majone, Giandomenico (1991), 'Cross-national sources of regulatory policy-making in Europe and the United States', *Journal of Public Policy*, spring issue.
Manow-Borgwardt, Philipp (1991), *Neokorporatistische Gesundheitspolitik? Die Festbetragsregelung des Gesundheitsreformgesetzes*, Berlin: Wissenschaftszentrum, Forschungsgruppe Gesundheitsrisiken und Präventionspolitik, 91–201.
March, James and Olsen, Johan P. (1989), *Rediscovering Institutions: The Organizational Basis of Politics*, New York: Free Press/Macmillan.

Mayntz, Renate, and Scharpf, Fritz (1975), *Policy-making in the German Federal Bureaucracy*, Amsterdam: Elsevier.

Müller-Armack, Alfred (1956), 'Soziale Marktwirtschaft', in *Handwörterbuch der Sozialwissenschaften*, **9**, 390 ff.

Müller-Armack, Alfred (1976), *Wirtschaftsordnung und Wirtschaftspolitik*, Bern and Stuttgart: Paul Haupt, 2nd edn.

Rühle, Hans and Veen, Hans-Joachim (eds) (1978), *Wachsende Staatshaushalte. Ein internationaler Vergleich der Ursachen, Folgen und Begrenzungsmöglichkeiten*, Stuttgart: Verlag Bonn Aktuell.

Scharpf, Fritz (1987), *Sozialdemokratische Krisenpolitik in Europa*, Frankfurt am Main: Campus Verlag.

Shonfield, Andrew (1965), *Modern Capitalism: The Changing Balance of Public and Private Power*, London: Oxford University Press.

Singer, Otto (1990), 'Learning by Osmosis oder Wem gehört die DDR', *Die Kommune*, **9**, 38 ff.

Singer, Otto (1991), 'Knowledge and politics in economic policy-making: Official economic advisers in the USA, Great Britain and West Germany', in Guy Peters, B. and Barker, Anthony (eds), *Advising West European Governments: Inquiries, Expertise and Public Policy*, Edinburgh: Edinburgh University Press.

Speer, Albert (1969), *Erinnerungen*, Berlin: Propyläen Verlag.

Stein, Lorenz von (1850), *Geschichte der sozialen Bewegung in Frankreich von 1789 bis auf unsere Tage*, Leipzig: Wigand.

Weidner, Helmut (1989), *Die Umweltpolitik der konservativ-liberalen Regierung im Zeitraum 1983 bis 1989: Versuch einer sozialwissenschaftlichen Bewertung*, Berlin: Wissenschaftszentrum, Forschungsschwerpunkt Technik-Arbeit-Umwelt, FS II 89–304.

Weir, Margaret, and Skocpol, Theda (1985), 'State structures and the possibilities for "Keynesian" responses to the great depression in Sweden, Britain, and the United States', in Evans, P. et al., *Bringing the State Back In*, Cambridge: Cambridge University Press, 107–163.

3 Completing the European Community's Internal Market: The Regulatory Implications for the Federal Republic of Germany

Simon Bulmer

Over the decade following the 1973 oil crisis the most striking feature of the European Community (EC) was its failure successfully to address the key issues of relative technological decline and economic stagflation. At the Milan session of the European Council in June 1985, however, the political leaders of the EC took important decisions to rectify this situation. Overruling Mrs Thatcher's opposition, they agreed to set up an Intergovernmental Conference to consider reforms to the EC treaties. At the same time they made a commitment 'to improve the operation of the Community in order to give concrete form to the objectives it has set itself, in particular as regards the completion of the internal market by 1992 and measures to promote a technological Europe' (*Bulletin of the EC*, 18 (6), 1985, p. 13). It was the combination of the two which was important, for there were two discrete problems. The existence of a single market had, after all, been provided for in the Treaty of Rome creating the European Economic Community (EEC). It had proved unattainable because member states had repeatedly refused to harmonize technical standards. Harmonization was in many cases too strong an assault upon existing national regulatory frameworks. Moreover, the practice in the Council of Ministers of only reaching agreement through consensus simply resulted in many Commission proposals being shelved. The solution set down in the internal market programme is based upon a more relaxed regulatory framework at the EC level (mutual recognition of standards rather than their harmonization), and implementation at the EC level is promised by the Single European Act's provisions for qualified majority voting in respect of most matters.

The utilization of national regulatory frameworks as non-tariff barriers to intra-EC trade in goods and services had been widespread. Though the conventional wisdom of the time was that the Federal Republic was the paragon of free trade virtues, it was in fact by no means free of protectionist practices. A classic example was to be found in the brewing industry. Beer brewed for the domestic German market had to be in accordance with the regime established under the regulatory authority of the Bavarian Duke Wilhelm IV in 1516, and reconfirmed in the Federal Republic's 1952 law on beer taxation (*Biersteuergesetz*). The EC's 1970 draft brewing directive – part of its programme to harmonize regulations relating to trade in foodstuffs – proposed to permit ingredients beyond the four specified in the German 'law of purity' (malted barley, yeast, hops and water). Thus the EC Commission proposed to overturn the practices of more than 450 years by allowing the sale in Germany of beer not brewed in accordance with the *Reinheitsgebot*.

The response of the West German brewers clearly demonstrated the potential for mobilizing resources against regulatory change. Their interest groups lobbied various federal ministries: the Economics Ministry was warned of the threat cheap imports posed to the industry, the Health Ministry of the danger of additives, and the Agriculture Ministry of the disruption to the cereals market. The interest groups formed an action committee (*Aktionskomitee Reines Bier*) to lobby public opinion, resulting amongst other things in 200,000 customers sending in beer mats registering their vote against 'chemical beer'. The Bundesrat became involved because of the regional implications – in 1970 there were well over a thousand breweries in Bavaria alone – and all the political parties courted public popularity in the Bundestag by opposing the EC draft. Suffice it to say that the EC directive suffered the fate of many others: it was shelved.[1]

And yet it proved unnecessary to propose any further legislation to achieve the goals of the 1970 draft directive. In its judgement of 12 March 1987 the European Court of Justice declared that beer produced for sale in one member state could not be kept out of another state's market except where international agencies had identified health risks (EC Commission v. Federal Republic of Germany, Case 178/84). The European Court had upheld the principle of free movement of goods as set down in Article 30 of the EEC Treaty. No enabling legislation was in fact necessary: judicial review by a supranational institution could simply declare national legislation to be a barrier to trade and thus illegal.

This brief case study indicates some important aspects of the completion of the internal market. It shows how the emphasis moved from harmonization to mutual recognition. It suggests how the Commission was able to change its institutional strategy for achieving a single market, namely by abandoning the interventionist strategy of proposing a regulatory framework for every technical standard and, instead, setting 'floor' standards — for example to ensure health or safety standards — and allowing the 'lighter touch' approach of mutual recognition to prevail. Under this latter approach the Commission has to give greater attention to its function of acting as 'guardian of the treaties' — that is, ensuring that mutual recognition is practised in the member states — and less attention to its function as 'proposer' of EC legislation

The case study also shows how the obstructionism of a single government could be bypassed once principles had been established by judicial review in Luxembourg (the seat of the European Court). Further, it indicates the distinctive feature of the EC, namely that regulatory pressures from the supranational level can assume legally binding status in member states — subject of course to national compliance. Finally, it hints at the way in which relatively innocuous pieces of German legislation, here taxation law, may conceal a superficially unrelated regulatory regime, itself supported by a powerful sectoral policy network.

The regulatory impact of completion of the internal market is by no means confined to brewing regulations. It extends across most sectors of the economy and beyond. It includes such policy areas as the various financial services, telecommunications and information technology, broadcasting, consumer protection, air transport, public procurement, indirect taxation, mutual recognition of higher education diplomas and professional qualifications, intellectual property rights, company law as well as — via the mutual recognition of technical standards — the whole of industry.

As if this were not enough, completion of the internal market is closely linked, albeit in different ways, with developments in many other policy areas. The internal market programme makes explicit reference to tightening control over state aids, thus affecting subsidies offered by governments: in the German case either by the federal or *Länder* authorities. Competition policy is being developed in order to 'ensure that anti-competitive practices do not engender new forms of local protectionism which would only lead to a re-partitioning of the market' (Commission of the EC, 1985, para. 157), whilst the Commission has acquired new powers to regulate large transnational corporate mergers. The whole area of environmental regulation is closely connected, having been given prominence in the Single European Act. Also related are immigration and policing after the dismantling of physical frontiers. Closely linked by political package deals with completion of the internal market are the reform, and doubling, of the EC's structural funds, agreed in 1988, and the Commission's proposals to ensure that completion of the internal market is not at the cost of social policy regression, namely the legislation falling under the Community Charter of Fundamental Social Rights (popularly known as the 'Social Charter'), agreed to by all member states, except the United Kingdom, at the European Council session in Strasbourg (December 1989). Finally, there are the special arrangements agreed in 1990 to facilitate German unification and the former East Germany's transition to an integral part of the EC.[2] All these dimensions have a regulatory aspect. How, then, to put some order into this vast area of subject matter and its implications for the Federal Republic?

First of all, it is necessary to assess the regulatory nature of the EC's internal market programme itself. Why was the EC deemed an appropriate framework for pursuing policies of regulatory change? Why in the late 1980s? How far is the EC a unifying force, or does it sit atop an array of highly sectorally differentiated regulatory arenas? Does the single market programme represent a wholesale transformation of the EC's regulatory goals and instruments – in other words a paradigm change – with a consequently radical impact upon member states such as Germany? This first exercise requires some application of the defining characteristics of regulation to the internal market programme. Secondly, it is necessary to sketch out the broad contours of systemic congruence between the EC's programme and the patterns of regulation within the Federal Republic generally. Finally, and on these foundations, attention will turn to the implications of the Single Market programme for German regulation. Clearly, given the extent of the EC's legislative impact on the Federal Republic, it will not be possible to give a detailed account of all the effects. Instead, this chapter will aim to provide a general framework and give a few specific examples; other chapters will refer to the EC's impact in specific policy areas.

1.   The European Community as a Regulatory Level

Central to understanding the EC as a regulatory arena is how one defines regulation. Here it is taken to comprise not only individual rules and their application but also a broad pattern of control over private interest activities.

How it is analysed is also critically important, for the subject matter of regulation and regulatory change is contested academically. Economists see regulation as ensuring that market forces do not lead to allocative or productive inefficiencies that incur adverse social costs for public welfare. For political scientists, regulation is seen as a highly politicized process in which public and (competing) private interests jockey for position in the formulation and implementation of policy. Finally, for public lawyers, there is the concern with the formal embodiment and enforcement of the regulatory apparatus.[3]

All three disciplines are relevant to analysing the EC as a regulatory arena. The Single Market programme has been regarded by some as a neo-classical economic exercise aimed at increasing the allocative and productive efficiency of the EC economy. Economic analysis is thus important. That politics is important has been demonstrated by the uncompromising line adopted by the United Kingdom government regarding the EC's 'Social Charter', the question of whether border controls should be abolished after 1992, or the extent of approximation of indirect taxation rates (with the risk to zero-rating that some goods currently enjoy under the prevailing value-added-tax regime in the UK). There is no more politicized a dispute than a gladiatorial struggle between EC governments! Finally, the substantive and procedural aspects of EC rules, their relationship with national rules, and the role of the European Court all demonstrate that the legal dimension matters. Any political analysis must be sensitive to these various dimensions of the subject matter as well as to the different methods of enquiry.

Before the Single Market Programme

Regulatory issues are not new to the EC. Right from the beginning of the European Coal and Steel Community in 1952, the Paris Treaty provided regulatory arrangements for trade liberalization in the two sectors. Further, and reflecting the role of regulation as a means of ensuring equilibrium, specific arrangements were provided for coping with either shortages or surpluses of coal or steel (by declaring a so-called 'manifest crisis'). The Common Agricultural Policy is generally regarded as the most highly regulated policy area of the EC, with its extensive provisions designed to maintain market equilibrium in the whole range of agricultural products. Clearly much more can be written about other policy areas.

Although the concern here is with the EC's Single Market programme, it is simply impossible to start telling the story from the Milan summit or signature of the Single European Act onwards. The Treaty of Rome, despite being a framework treaty and a kind of constitution for the EEC, is centrally concerned with policy issues, unlike national constitutions. It already provided for the removal of tariffs and quantitative restrictions on intra-Community trade. Furthermore it set down the principle of prohibiting such practices that would distort or prevent competition between the member states. What is striking, therefore, is that this latter principle was not generally implemented. That is to say, while there was some limited progress on harmonizing technical standards through legislation, the potentialities for

European Court rulings were not exploited. In essence, the momentum for regulatory change was lacking. Why was this so?

A number of possible explanations can be adduced. First, over the initial decade of the EEC the preoccupation was with removing tariff barriers and quantitative restrictions. The persistence, and indeed increased incidence, of non-tariff barriers to trade indicated the member governments' reluctance to proceed further at that time with the programme originally agreed in the Treaty of Rome. Second, the political climate of support for integration had declined in the context of de Gaulle's incumbency of the French presidency and particularly following on from his insistence on the Luxembourg Accords of 1966. The failure to proceed to the introduction of majority voting in the manner set out in the Treaty of Rome signalled an unravelling of the package deal which the EEC and Euratom treaties had formed. The willingness to transfer authority to the supranational authorities waned and the Commission, the 'loser' from the Luxembourg Accords, was badly placed for launching a counter-offensive – whether through legislation or reference to the European Court. Third, the EC economies enjoyed a reasonable level of growth on the basis of the progress which had already been made. Finally, divergent patterns of industrial policy were pursued by the member governments, in some cases with overtly nationalist goals such as creating national champions. The time was not ripe in the late 1960s and 1970s for the EC to consider supply-side prescriptions.

By the mid-1980s it was. Why?

- The old economic policy recipes were increasingly held to have aggravated the stagflation problem of the period following the oil crisis.
- The Japanese and American economies were perceived to be more dynamic, especially in the high technology sectors; the newly industrializing economies were making great advances as well.
- Despite its continued dynamism, the American pre-eminence in the management of the international economy had declined significantly. In short, the United States' role as 'governor' of the international economy had diminished (Cerny, 1989). This gradual development over the last two decades was characterized by the collapse of the Bretton Woods international monetary system and the decline of other international agencies set up in the post-war period. More recently, it has been reflected in the difficulties in reaching agreement in the Uruguay Round of the General Agreement on Tariffs and Trade (GATT). These developments have resulted in a need for greater sharing of the responsibilities of international economic management. Hence the growth of regional trading blocs as the focus of economic policy initia-

tives: the phenomenon of 'global regionalism'. The EC has been to the fore in this trend.

- The European Community as the world's largest foreign trading bloc could not isolate itself from the supply-side developments under way in the United States. Similarly it could not isolate itself from the harnessing, by the Americans and Japanese, of new technologies to internationally traded services such as securities.
- The ideological commitment to 'deregulation' (and privatization) had made advances in some of the EC member states. The viability of governmental intervention as a solution to economic malaise was in doubt and symbolically demonstrated by the 'U-turn' in the Mitterrand experiment in 1983.
- Commencing in 1984, the EC found a period of respite from the twin crises of the Common Agricultural Policy (CAP) and of the budget.
- Last but not least, a winning coalition emerged within the EC itself.

This winning coalition brought together 'players' with divergent objectives. Two supranational institutions, the Commission and the European Parliament, began to lay emphasis on the incomplete internal market. The Commission began in 1981 to draw attention to this, and a list of proposed remedies was drawn up. In 1983 the Albert–Ball report to the Parliament drew attention to the so-called costs of non-Europe (Albert and Ball, 1983). Both institutions sought more generally to raise their own profile. The Commission was most able to achieve this objective through its direct input to the main strategic policy-making agency of the EC, namely the European Council. The EC's programme for completion of the internal market was an important component of the package that was to emerge (Commission of the EC, 1985).

The Commission's hand was strengthened by two landmark decisions of the European Court: in 1974 relating to the so-called Dassonville case and in 1979 on the 'Cassis de Dijon' case (Rewe–Zentralfinanz v. Bundesmonopolverwaltung für Brandwein, Case 120/78). The latter is particularly pertinent since it involved German regulatory arrangements. A German company found itself unable to import the French blackcurrant liqueur cassis into the Federal Republic because its alcohol content (15–20 per cent) fell below the minimum permissible level of 25 per cent set under German law. Despite the defence's argument that 'the need to state a minimum alcohol level in liquor was necessary in order to protect public health because low-strength liquors had a rather more insidious effect on consumers and might lead to alcoholism', the European Court ruled that this was a distortion to trade (Davidson, 1989, p. 115). This landmark decision thus had a similar outcome to the later case on the law of purity; in both instances German regulations were deemed incompatible with the Treaty of Rome. The central point was that the Court had ruled against measures having equivalent effect to quantitative restrictions. By extension it had ruled in favour of the broad principle of mutual recognition, so the Commission's subsequent internal market programme was consistent with the outcome of judicial review. Legislation and legal enforcement could proceed simultaneously in the same direction.

There were of course more partners in the winning coalition than the supranational institutions. Some governments, such as Mrs Thatcher's, favoured more liberal regulatory regimes; the more interventionist states pressed for an enhancement of the EC's role in technological cooperation. Some pressed for stronger EC powers on environmental legislation, others for greater social and regional equity within the EC. Some sought stronger powers for the European Parliament, others wanted a commitment to closer cooperation in monetary policy. Others still wanted closer foreign policy cooperation. The EC's success lay in its finding a package deal – the Single European Act – which satisfied all concerned.

The Regulatory Nature of the Single Market Programme

What are the regulatory characteristics of the Single Market programme? An answer to this question depends on the level of analysis. At the *level of the member states* the programme inevitably imposes constraints upon the extent to which national authorities can continue to enforce the regulation of a wide range of policy areas. The obverse of this is the requirement that member states recognize the principle of mutual recognition. So, whilst national authorities may continue to regulate or set technical standards, they may not be enforced as barriers to trade. The result is a pattern of 'competing jurisdictions' (Curzon Price, 1989, p. 32), with the market determining which member state's rules are the most desirable. In both these respects the Single Market programme must be regarded as deregulatory in nature.

At the EC level, by contrast, the Single Market programme creates increased regulatory authority. Firstly, it involves a significant amount of EC legislation. This clearly reinforces the importance of the EC institutions as the framers of regulatory arrangements. Secondly, it requires the Commission to increase its vigilance as the agency responsible for supervising the application of EC legislation. Thirdly, it underlines the European Court's importance as the agency adjudicating over the enforcement of EC law. Then there are the regulatory arrangements themselves. The basic thinking has been that the EC should legislate to set EC-wide minimum standards. In new technology applications European standards should be set so that

national standards would be superseded. Much of the latter activity has
been delegated to European standards agencies, notably CEN (the European Committee for Standardization), CENELEC (the European Committee for Electrotechnical Standardization) and ETSI (the European Telecommunications Standards Institute). So, fourthly, in the area of technical
standards it is these bodies which are the regulators. In other areas, such as
mergers and acquisitions, it is the Commission itself which acts as regulator.
But the overall pattern is the same, namely an increase in regulatory authority
at the EC level.

The net effect is a combination of deregulation at the national level and
reregulation at the EC level. The Single Market programme appears to give
these developments a coherent logic but, in reality, the situation is rather
less clear cut. As Woolcock et al. point out:

> ... in sectors in which the old national regulatory regimes have become coun-
> ter-productive, national regulators have begun to look to EC-wide measures to
> re-establish regulatory control. In the case of the natural monopolies, such as
> telecommunications, energy and transport, there is a need to anchor national
> regulations in a European framework to defend them against any undermining
> by global competition.... (Woolcock et al., 1991, pp. 5–6).

It must therefore be noted that, whilst the Single Market programme's
economic objective is to facilitate member states' access to each other's
market, it may also be designed to restrict the access of non-members. A
particularly striking example of this relates to the EC's public procurement
legislation. Under the utilities draft directive it was proposed that EC
purchasers should be able to exclude bids where the EC content would fall
below 50 per cent. In fact, this position has been used as a bargaining chip
in GATT negotiations on the Government Purchasing Agreement because
of similar content clauses in the legislation of competitors, including the
United States (see Woolcock et al. pp. 38–9).

As this assessment indicates, there are three levels at which the regulatory nature of the Single Market programme must be assessed: the national,
EC and international levels. In general terms, the programme envisages
deregulation at the national level translating into reregulation at the EC
level. At the same time, EC-level reregulation is regarded by some member
states as a necessary step to retain some control in the face of *international*
deregulation. EC reregulation can be seen as a response to the observation
that '[G]overnment regulations are essentially nation-state-level phenomena,
but markets – and the factors which shape, constrain and "distort" markets
– are increasingly transnational in scope' (Cerny, 1991, p. 174).

A number of additional points need to be made about the enhancement of the EC-level's regulatory powers with particular reference to the policy process. In this context it is worth noting the distinction that Swann has drawn between *de jure* and *de facto* regulation (Swann, 1989, p. 7). The EC's powers have been enhanced in both senses.

First, the Single European Act provides for majority voting on most matters relating to completion of the internal market whereas, under pre-Single European Act treaty provisions, unanimity was required for the harmonization of laws, regulations or administrative actions. Hence an individual national government cannot necessarily obstruct EC legislation as before. This effectively represents a transfer of regulatory power to the supranational level (where the national governments are of course represented in the Council of Ministers). A further change relates to the new cooperation procedure which brings the European Parliament into a fully fledged legislative role for the first time, albeit in a restricted number of policy areas. These include matters relating to the internal market. Thus the policy-making arena has undergone fundamental change. It is no longer adequate, whether for producer or consumer groups, to mount intensive pressure at the national level and then, if necessary, rely on the government to impede agreement in the Council of Ministers. Influencing the regulatory regime now requires a much more sophisticated mix of lobbying: forming transnational alliances, contacting Members of the European Parliament and attempting to bargain with the Commission.

Second, not only does the Single European Act provide for new policy-making procedures but majority voting is also being practised to a much greater degree than before. There is a much greater correlation between the *de jure* provision for majority voting in the Single European Act and *de facto* practice than is the case regarding the provisions in the original EEC Treaty. Similarly, to the extent that the European Court's powers to uphold treaty provisions are employed, by contrast with the period prior to the Cassis case, so Community regulatory competence is enhanced *de facto*.

These general remarks should not be taken to suggest that there is a tidy uniformity about the EC's policy process. On the contrary, it is very untidy with differing dynamics between individual policy areas and policy issues. In this sense the EC is not a regulatory arena but a level of government which the member states deem appropriate for the pursuit of certain policy goals. It is a 'location in space' for regulation/deregulation (Hancher and Moran, 1989a, p. 132). Its suitability in this respect is determined by the need for the member states to compete in a trilateral international economy. In other words the EC is a unifying force in that it is the level of government which predominates in the regulation of the single market. However, the patterns of regulation differ according to the policy issue.[4]

In light of these findings, then, does the Single Market programme represent a wholesale transformation of the EC's regulatory goals and instruments? Does it create a 'paradigm change' for German regulation; or are there strong elements of continuity? These questions require a differentiated answer. There is a strong case for arguing that, *at the EC level*, there is a wholesale transformation of regulatory goals and instruments. Despite the differences in the pattern of regulation according to policy issue, the mere presentation of the package of measures as part of an integrated single market programme, together with the symbolic deadline of the end of 1992, has transformed the process of achieving the EEC Treaty's original objective of a common market. In addition, the regulatory goals have been transformed. No longer is the creation of a common market a self-contained programme of European economic integration, as it was originally conceived in the second half of the 1950s. Rather it is part of a self-defence objective in a trilateral international economy. Meeting the competitive challenges from Japan and the Pacific Rim, on the one hand, and the United States and the emergent North American Free Trade Area, on the other, lies behind the new regulatory objectives of the EC. A clear indication of the importance of the pressures of global regionalism is evident in the October 1991 agreement on the part of the EC and the EFTA (European Free Trade Association) countries to create a European Economic Area.

The new emphasis upon mutual recognition and equivalence, rather than upon harmonization, represents a transformation in the EC's regulatory instruments. This is enhanced by changes to the procedures of EC regulation, in particular the increased use of qualified majority voting. Taken together, the changes in the EC's regulatory goals and instruments can indeed be regarded as a 'paradigm change'. But does this represent a 'paradigm change' for Germany?

The answer to this question is much less clear-cut. It would require an aggregation of *all* the effects of the Single Market programme on German regulatory practice: something that cannot be attempted in this chapter. However, it is possible to make two broad observations which amount to an argument that there is no Single Market-induced paradigm change in German regulatory practice.

Taking the Single Market's programme of liberalizing practice in technical standards first of all, it must be remembered that mutual recognition does not eliminate national regulation. The work of the main German agency responsible for technical standards, the *Deutsches Institut für Normen* (DIN), will be placed within European constraints but it will not be eliminated. Numerically, German DIN standards – of which there are some 20 000 – will prevail over European standards – of which there are about 1 250 – for some time yet (Woolcock et al. p. 47; Oehler, 1990). Two further factors are likely to reinforce this situation. First, the Commission's commitment to the principle of subsidiarity is likely to prevent any attempt to accelerate the centralization of standard-setting. Secondly, to the extent that the single market witnesses a 'competition among rules', the German economy's status as the largest market in the EC, and reinforced by unification, is likely to ensure that DIN standards play a prominent role.

Over the longer term, European agencies such as CEN and CENELEC will come to predominate as standards are set for new technologies. However, even in this respect it must be noted that DIN is a participating member organization. Woolcock et al. note that 'In March 1989, Germany's DIN/DKE held 75 out of 212 CEN/CENELEC secretariats for technical committees, i.e. 35.4 per cent' (1991, p. 48).[5] This was the biggest representation of a national standards body and suggests that German influence will continue to be felt in the setting of harmonized standards, albeit indirectly.

A further point to note is similar to this but relates to other aspects of the Single Market programme. Again for the EC to create a paradigm change in German regulation assumes that the character of legislation agreed in the Council of Ministers is fundamentally different in nature from that already obtaining at the national level. Whilst this might happen in isolated instances, it is hardly likely to be the general picture (see below for further discussion). Germany may be seen as occupying the middle ground of regulation: between the less regulated Anglo–American pattern represented by much practice in the UK, and the more closely regulated practice of France or Italy.

The second fundamental observation – and reflected in the chapters which follow – is that the EC is not the only source of pressure for regulatory change. The three other sources are technological change, international pressures, and national pressures. Thus the new technology of direct satellite broadcasting, regulatory change in the key international financial centres, and domestic pressures for the maintenance of existing labour market practice are arguably more important to explaining developments in these policy areas than the influence of the EC. As one source of regulatory change among several, the EC cannot alone create a disjuncture in German goals and practice. To a significant degree the EC is merely mediating other forces for regulatory change.

2.   Systemic Congruence?: German Governance Structures and the Single Market Programme

Assessing the systemic congruence between German regulatory structures and the direction of the EC's Single Market programme is a further necessary component to evaluating the likely impact of the latter. What are the key characteristics of German regulatory practice? In broad terms they correspond to several of the elements of unity and diversity that characterize the German policy process in general (Bulmer, 1989).

Unity is provided first of all by the pervasive role of the law as a regulatory instrument. This corresponds to the characterization by Hancher and Ruete of German administration as a 'formalized regulatory or legal culture' that contrasts with the United Kingdom's 'flexible bargaining culture' (quoted in Katzenstein, 1987, p. 31). Regulation is largely – but not exclusively – achieved by means of the rule of law (the *Rechtsstaat*). As N. Johnson puts it (1978, p. 178):

> The law is unambiguously in politics both as a structuring instrument defining institutions and the rights and duties of citizens, and equally in the guise of a statement of political and social values to which the society as a whole is committed and to the promotion of which those active in politics are held to be especially bound.

Public administrative law – a major regulatory instrument – is central to Germany's law-based culture.

In the context of public policy, and particularly economic policy, the legal dimension is encapsulated in the notion of *'Ordnungspolitik'*: the legal embodiment of the framework rules for economic activity. But *Ordnungspolitik* is not just a matter of legal prescription. In those policy areas where German legislators have wished to assign discretionary powers, they have done so by means of creating parapublic agencies such as the Bundesbank, the Federal Cartel Office, the Federal Environment Office, the Federal Employment Office and so on. As Katzenstein puts it: '[T]hese institutions express a general German principle of organization: independent governance of social sectors under the general supervision of the state' (1989, p. 333). This 'independent governance' extends beyond parapublic institutions, narrowly defined, to include co-determination arrangements at the corporate level, works councils and other forms of private interest government. The last of these is characterized by the regulatory agency for standards, DIN itself, which receives about one-fifth of its funds from the public purse, whilst remaining a private organization.

The presence of parapublic agencies has been one source of what can either be seen as policy immobilism or, more positively, policy stability (Bulmer and Humphreys, 1989). In either case there is an inbuilt defence against any excessive centralizing zeal on the part of the European Commission. The clearest case of this relates to the debate on Economic and Monetary Union; in crude terms the federal government is able to advance its case for an independent European central bank by pointing out that the Bundesbank would have some constitutional–legal difficulty in relinquishing its authority to any other form of EC central bank. Where private interest government exists, the institutionalized representation of the affected interests again represents a potentially formidable coalition against change. Is it really feasible to demolish the cosy but consensual edifice that private interest government represents?

This reference to consensualism brings us to the three 'Cs': consensus, corporatism and cooperative federalism, essential characteristics of German regulatory practice. All regulatory regimes must rely on some basic level of consensus if compliance problems are to be avoided. But in Germany this consensus is extensive, institutionalized and quite distinct from the pattern which has prevailed under British Conservative governments over the period from 1979. This is because, in Germany, the consensus has to be constructed along two axes. First, the commitment to social harmony is reflected in the wish to incorporate the views of the affected interest groups in both policy-making and regulatory procedures. This strong corporatist tradition is present to some degree at the 'macro' level, but is especially prominent at the sectoral or 'meso' level, as well as at the corporate or plant, 'micro' level.[6] In the specific context of the Single Market, for instance, a series of meetings was held involving government and leading interest associations. Indicative of this was an initial meeting of peak interest groups, held in Bonn on 15 March 1988, and addressed by both Chancellor Kohl and Commission President Delors. The first (tripartite) national 'Europa-Konferenz' was held in December 1988. These meetings reflected the powerful pull of a consensual approach to addressing the challenges of the Single Market.

Second, there is the need for a (vertical) consensus between the two tiers of federal government. This is necessary because of the extent to which legislative competence is shared between the federal and *Länder* authorities in Germany's system of 'cooperative federalism'. Moreover, the *Länder* authorities are responsible for the implementation of much of federal (and EC) policy, so their views are taken seriously in Bonn. In several cases this necessitates cooperation between governments of different party political complexions and is thus a factor strengthening the consensus for policy and regulatory practice. Thus aspects of the mutual recognition of diplomas, regulation of the professions, vocational training, environmental protection, transport policy, health and safety matters, fiscal harmonization and public procurement are amongst those components of the Single Market programme that, in terms of domestic responsibility, affect important or exclusive powers of the *Länder*. Similarly, some aspects of technical standards regulation fall within the competence of the *Länder*: Woolcock et al. (1991, p. 53) quote the case of the EC's building products directive.

The coherence of the German political system is thus manifested in the role of the law, parapublic agencies, private interest government, corporatist arrangements and cooperative federalism as the institutional expression of the pattern of regulation. National regulatory regimes in Germany thus have a highly integrated, organic nature. The institutions of regulation, like those of the German policy process more generally (Bulmer and Humphreys, 1989), are not susceptible to radical change. Change is not excluded, however, for if all the key actors in a policy sector reach a consensus for change – such as happened in respect of regulation of the securities sector (see Chapter 6) – an unstoppable coalition for reform can emerge from what appeared to be a severe case of institutional atrophy. None the less, the overwhelming impression is one of regulatory practice being relatively entrenched in an array of institutional arrangements. That this is the case was born out by the Kohl government's efforts to promote deregulation. These met with as little success as efforts earlier in the decade to promote privatization. Thus the establishment in 1987 of a committee of experts, known as the Deregulation Commission, to examine the scope for the loosening of regulatory control produced a number of proposals. But '... consultations with interest groups created a storm of protest during 1989 ... the Kohl government was not prepared to attempt to change the agreed regulation without seeking a political consensus' (Woolcock et al., 1991, p. 102).

The diversity present within German practice is precisely that the institutional profile of regulation varies on a case-by-case basis. Different parapublic agencies monitor different issues; different patterns of private interest government exist; different balances exist in the division of competence between federal and *Länder* authorities; different ministries may hold responsibility at the federal level creating problems of policy fragmentation in Bonn. All these factors necessitate a differentiated, case-study approach to the politics of regulatory change.

How congruent are these German arrangements with the EC's approach to regulatory change? Just as Germany has only in relatively recent times addressed issues of regulatory reform – unlike the United Kingdom – so, too, is this the case with the EC authoritites. Unlike the UK, Germany has not pursued regulatory change as part of a neo-liberal ideological programme. This is also true of the EC as a whole. German familiarity with the importance of the law as a regulatory instrument also finds parallels in EC practice, as demonstrated by the European Court judgements which paved the way for the Single Market programme and by the importance of EC legal norms more generally. The programme has not yet given rise to an extensive array of EC-level parapublic institutions but private interest government has played an important role, as shown in the delegation of standard-setting to bodies such as CEN, CENELEC and ETSI. Moreover, the Commission has – like the federal government – been keen to maintain a distance from neo-liberal deregulation by its initiation of the Community Charter of Fundamental Social Rights: an attempt to ensure that the Single Market programme is based on the support not only of 'capital' but also of 'labour'. The Social Charter has commanded wide support from the political forces in Germany. Finally, the Commission has sensitized itself to the dispersion of power within member states by its repeated reference to the principle of subsidiarity (Wilke and Wallace, 1990). Since the Commission adopted this position in part as a response to German circumstances – the concern of the *Länder* about the loss of authority occasioned by the Single European Act – it should help avoid future conflict with Germany's cooperative federalism.

Thus, in general terms, there exists a fair degree of congruence between the approaches to regulation in both the EC and Germany. In the next section several brief case studies serve to explore this in more detail.

3.   The Regulatory Implications for Germany

As was indicated at the start of the chapter, the Single Market and related EC policy initiatives will have an extensive impact upon Germany in terms of the breadth of subject matter affected. This section can only aim to give some examples; it cannot be comprehensive.

Road Haulage

Road haulage has been one of the most regulated sectors in the German service sector. The roots of the 'exceptionalism' of German transport policy date back to the last century and the close relationship that was established between the state and the railways (Diekmann, 1989). Despite the EEC Treaty's commitment to introduce a common transport policy, Germany's heavily regulated road haulage sector was scarcely affected because the member states failed to translate their commitment into action. However, the EC's transport policy was given momentum by a 1986 ruling of the European Court (case 13/83) which upheld the European Parliament's allegations that the Council had failed to 'introduce measures to secure freedom to provide transport services, as required by Articles 75, 59, 60 and 61'. As a result of this judgement, and of the impetus given by the Single Market programme, the Council sought to liberalize cross-border road haulage as one of several transport policy initiatives.

This development placed the German regulatory arrangements for road haulage in conflict with the objectives of EC policy. German

'Ordnungspolitik' derived essentially from the freight transport law (*Güterkraftverkehrsgesetz*, GüKG). This excluded foreign companies from commercial freight transport in Germany but also restricted market access for German companies. Under the so-called 'controlled competitive order' which resulted,[7] market entry was restricted in three ways: the need to pass a quality threshold in order to qualify as an operator; a quota system operated by means of licensing; and a closely controlled tariff structure. The quota and tariff arrangements both illustrate typical features of German regulatory control. Global quotas were set by the Federal Ministry of Transport for road haulage and then divided up by federal state, taking into account transport needs and transport safety. The setting of transportation rates took on the familiar features of private interest government, with the representatives of the hauliers making decisions in working parties (*Tarifkommissionen*), in which customers (that is, those companies with goods to be conveyed) had only an advisory role.

This controlled competitive order served to pose several fundamental questions and to create a number of distortions (Zobel, 1988; Soltwedel et al., 1986, pp. 192–274). First, it raised the question of whether the state possessed sufficient information to determine the most efficient road haulage arrangements. Second, it risked knock-on effects in other modes of transport (also heavily regulated!). Third, the quota arrangements led to a poor use of capacity. And the system created various distortions. The allocation of permits for specific vehicles – rather than for an operator – resulted in a predominance of general purpose transport vehicles rather than the more specialized ones which customers might prefer. Finally, it prompted the growth of 'in-house haulage' (*Werkfernverkehr*). This arrangement was permitted under paragraph 48 (1) GüKG, provided that the company concerned carried its own goods, did so as a secondary activity, and used its own vehicles and employees. The growth of in-house haulage was the customers' response to the constraints imposed by the regulatory order.

The German road haulage sector was concerned about its competitive position, especially with its Dutch counterpart. Its response to the EC's liberalization of the sector, the first steps of which were ironically agreed during Germany's 1988 presidency of the Council of Ministers, was a plea for a 'level playing-field'.[8] This would include a harmonization of vehicle excise duty, fuel duty and safety codes at German levels. In a related move the German government proposed in February 1989 that all heavy lorries using German autobahns should pay an annual tax, initially for three years, commencing in 1990 (*Neue Zürcher Zeitung*, 26–7 February, 1989, p. 17). When finally adopted in October 1989 the tax was set at between DM1 000 and DM9 000, depending on factors such as number of axles (*Neue Zürcher Zeitung*, 25 October 1989). Significantly the government proposed to reduce the excise duty levied on German lorries by up to DM3 500. In July 1990 the European Court agreed to an interim injunction on the grounds that the proposals would discriminate against non-German hauliers. The proposed tax had to be abandoned.

Despite German opposition bilateral quotas – governing the haulage of goods between member states – were increased by 40 per cent under the 1988 agreement and are to be phased out by 1993. Even with this EC-led move to a less regulated, more competitive road haulage regime, there is no guarantee that this will bring all the anticipated results. For instance, as Cooper and Browne (1989) suggest, German hauliers are relatively prosperous as a result of their former, protected arrangements. This may enable them to buy into the French market, for example, in order to maintain their position by a strategy of acquisition. The full regulatory impact may only become clear at the end of the century. In addition, the German government pressed ahead with its reduction in the excise duty for German hauliers: reputedly worth DM1.5 billion per annum! Thus the EC may have achieved some deregulation of the German road haulage sector but the sector's successful lobbying seems to have transformed the issue into one of subsidies and state aids.

On top of this, the German government has had to contend with the transport policy implications of unification. In brief these comprise the incorporation of a poor network of roads that was not designed for the East–West flows of a united Germany (except where the infrastructure predates Germany's division!); and the former East Germany's far greater bias in favour of rail as the preferred mode for carrying freight. In the five new *Länder* a road haulage sector has to be created from almost nothing.

State Aids

The monitoring of state aid to industries or regions is provided for under Articles 92–94 (EEC); it is not an innovation of the Single Market programme. However, completion of the internal market has given the issue of state aid greater salience: it would defeat the goal of achieving a more competitive European Community if the least efficient industries were simply to be compensated by means of governmental hand-outs in the form of subsidies. The intensification of the Commission's scrutiny of state aids has been witnessed in several cases, for example regarding British governmental aid to Rover in connection with that company's acquisition by British Aerospace, or aid to Renault from the French government.

Over the years Germany has enjoyed the reputation of pursuing a 'social market' model of industrial policy. Under this formula intervention in industry is only permitted if it is limited in quantity and of a short-term duration. Intervention of this nature, for instance through subsidies, is regulated under the framework of the 1967 Law on Stability and Growth (*Gesetz zur Förderung der Stabilität und des Wachstums der Wirtschaft*). A restrictive attitude towards intervention is the official policy position. The reality looks rather different, particularly when one takes into account that policy is being conducted at both the federal and *Länder* levels. German aversion to the term '*Industriepolitik*' – due to the Nazi and East-German anti-models – should not be allowed to deceive.

The exact regulatory arrangements differ from sector to sector but typically reflect a consensus between the industry concerned and the relevant trade union (Germany's industry-based union structure makes it an effective part of any consensus, unlike a craft-based system). Regional interests, articulated through *Länder* politics, are frequently an additional component.

In the context of the Single Market programme the Commission conducted a survey of the pattern of state aid (Commission of the EC, 1988). This report revealed the Federal Republic to be in second place behind Italy in terms of the total amount of financial aid and tax concessions averaged over the period 1981–86. However, when measured as a percentage of Gross Domestic Product the Federal Republic was located in the middle range, below the EC average, albeit with a rising tendency. The main areas of subsidy by the German authorities were revealed as transport (especially the railways), coal and regional aid (especially the Zonal Border Area and the special arrangements for West Berlin).

The situation regarding the last of these three has been transformed as a result of German unification. The EC Commission pushed for a swift end to the favourable taxation regime for West Berlin, given its new attractiveness as an investment location in the united Germany. However, if this reduced state aid, the Federal Republic's assumption of responsibility for the industry of the former East Germany has involved vast amounts of financial support pending privatization. German state aid has thus increased. The rapidly agreed formula for accession of the five new *Länder* to the EC anticipates an end to special arrangements by 1993. It remains to be seen whether the German authorities' commitments (and hopes) will be fulfilled by this date, given the persistence of unemployment in the East. There thus remains a potential major conflict between the EC and German authorities responsible for regulating state aid.

Energy

There are various aspects of creating a single European energy market. One which links in with the issue of state aid concerns the coal industry. Under an agreement dating back to 1980 – known as the *Jahrhundertvertrag* –

German consumers effectively pay a premium of 8.5 per cent on electricity bills (the so-called *Kohlepfennig*) for the privilege of having German rather than foreign coal burned in their power stations. Without this premium the Ruhr and Saar coalfields would be subject to numerous pit closures. The subsidies, which are calculated at DM10 billion per annum, have increasingly come to be seen as an obstruction to the creation of a single energy market (Nowak, 1990). Under the arrangement (West) German generators have burned some 41 million tons of domestic coal – over half of domestic production.

The European Commission's concern has grown as its attempts to create a single market have gathered pace. It has also been bolstered by the French electricity sector which sees the single energy market as an opportunity to sell its surplus nuclear energy on the German market. Non-EC coal producers have also been lobbying against German coal subsidies in the context of trade negotiations in order to gain a market for their cheaper coal. In May 1991 the European Commission informed the German government that it sought the abolition of the *Kohlepfennig* by the end of 1993, claiming that it was in breach of Article 85 (1) EEC, which governs EC competition policy. For its part the coal industry has indicated that an end to its subsidy will threaten its viability.

The issue has been compounded by unification. Attempts to have privatized generators in the five new *Länder* utilize large quantities of the locally mined lignite, which is a 'dirty' fuel, seemed likely to compound the pre-existing regulatory constraints on market liberalization. On the other hand, the need for significant investment in the infrastructure and environmental components of electricity generation in the five new *Länder* might just necessitate a fundamental rethink of the *Jahrhundertvertrag*. Financial aid for the (West) German coal industry may come lower down the list of priorities than re-structuring energy production in the five new *Länder*.

Other Sectors in Brief

In the financial services sector the Single Market programme is likely to lead to a loosening of regulatory control: for instance in the insurance sector (Woolcock et al, 1991, pp. 73–93). The extent to which this presents opportunities to lower-cost suppliers of insurance services is not yet clear. The sector has resisted the EC's more radical reform proposals. Moreover, the three multi-purpose German banks have entered the sector by means of diversification or acquisition. So, whilst the German insurance market may undergo regulatory change, reports of the sector's demise are premature.

In the context of the Single Market the Commission has sought to advance legislation assisting the development of corporate-level cooperation in the EC. The proposed Fifth Directive relating to EC public limited companies forms part of this effort. The Commission proposals have been particularly influenced by German corporate practice and, in consequence, envisaged a two-tier board structure. This arrangement – with a supervisory board for policy issues and another for more routine management matters – was to apply to all public limited companies with more than 500 employees. Moreover, the proposal envisaged adoption of worker participation on the boards. The Fifth Directive was originally proposed in 1972 but met considerable opposition and underwent several reformulations which essentially had the effect of making the proposal more flexible. However, these changes have still not enabled agreement on the proposal.

As a parallel exercise the proposal for a European Company Statute was put forward by the Commission in 1970. This proposal aimed to provide a company law structure which could be adopted where a company wished to operate in more than one member state. This also envisaged a two-tier company structure and worker participation in corporate decision-making, for instance through a European works council and participation in the appointment of members of the supervisory board. Unlike the Fifth Directive, however, the European Company Statute is designed to be a recommended prescription. It will be up to the companies concerned to decide whether to adopt it as opposed to relying on a combination of national laws from the jurisdictions concerned. In its most recent form the proposal would allow companies to choose between three models of worker participation, broadly equating to the German, Franco–Belgian and British practices. But, like the Fifth Directive, this proposal has also been caught up in apparently interminable negotiations between the national governments and had not been agreed by mid-1991. From the German perspective there is concern that either the absence of agreement, or agreement on a less regulated form of company law than that which prevails in Germany, could result in EC competitors being subject to less costly labour market regulation and upset existing practice.

Other sectors, such as the regulation of telecommunications and the environment, are examined in subsequent chapters. The picture that emerges is one of German regulatory practice being subjected to reform but with the extent of that reform varying from one policy area to the next. Even where the congruence of EC regulatory proposals and pre-existing German practice is low, this does not translate into a disjuncture in practice. As the road haulage case demonstrated, the impact may be deflected by changing another set of rules, in this case those governing the excise duty for lorries. If a clear pattern emerges, it is that German regulatory practice is based on an entrenched consensus with those who are regulated. This creates a strong resistance to radical change. Where there is a significant change in regulatory arrangements, the preference for consensus tends to result in the objectives of the previous arrangements being re-created through other means. There is some evidence to suggest that the abrupt nature of German unification has created as much pressure for regulatory change as the Single Market programme.

4.   Conclusion

Over the period 1986–93 the Single Market programme should reduce the extent to which German authorities are able to regulate important aspects of the economy. Some of the legislation remains to be agreed; some that has been agreed is not yet in effect. Thus a definitive assessment is not yet possible.

It has been argued here that the Single Market does not represent a 'paradigm change' for German regulation. Mutual recognition will leave some authority at the national level in the core area of technical standards. Moreover, there are strong elements of systemic congruence between the method of regulation being pursued by the EC and that which has been followed in Germany. The extent of congruence is greater than that between the EC and UK practice.

Above all, it is important to bear in mind the time-scale which is needed in order to judge the impact of regulatory change. In the United States it was in 1978 that the Airline Deregulation Act was introduced, providing for the progressive and ultimately complete deregulation of fares and market entry. By the early 1990s the fall in fares had been arrested and the US airline industry had become dominated by some six 'mega-carriers'. Market entry has become more difficult as a result of problems of access to favourable take-off/landing slot times; of the 'mega-carriers' acquiring (or building) the most modern airport terminal infrastructure; and of on-line reservation systems that present travel agents (and thus potential passengers) with a restricted choice of airline. The flying public may now have a better choice of service. But it often involves plane-changes or intermediate stops at such airport 'hubs' as Raleigh/Durham or Minneapolis/St Paul – locations which appear to owe more to the airline's convenience than the passenger's.

If it has taken a decade or more for these new distortions to become evident in the US air transport sector, then regulatory change is still young in the European Community. The new regulatory changes of the single market are only just achieving take-off. A lengthy journey lies ahead, and diversion to an alternative destination may prove necessary. The ultimate extent of turbulence over Germany is not yet known!

Notes

1 This episode is charted in Bulmer, 1986, Chapter 7.
2 This chapter will not consider the whole issue of Economic and Monetary Union (EMU), which originally gained some impulses from the internal market programme, but then much stronger ones from the wish to step up integration in the context of German unification. Clearly, once the proposals on EMU are agreed, there will be important impacts upon Germany's regulatory arrangements for fiscal and monetary policy. Similarly, once the proposals on Political Union are agreed – and these reforms were also stimulated by German unification – there will be further regulatory impacts upon the Federal Republic. At the time of writing neither of these initiatives had reached fruition so that consideration of their impact would be unnecessarily speculative.
3 The different approaches can be seen, for example, in Button and Swann (1989), and Hancher and Moran (1989b).
4 See for instance the different dynamics relating to mergers and acquisitions, public procurement, technical standards, telecommunications and financial services, as demonstrated in Woolcock et al. (1991).
5 DKE, the *Deutsche Kommission für Elektrotechnik*, is responsible for electrotechnical standards and is the German member organization in CENELEC.
6 On this differentiation of corporatism, and on the importance of meso-corporatism generally, see Cawson (1985).
7 Significantly this 'kontrollierte Wettbewerbsordnung' necessitated a derogation from German competition policy, enshrined in paragraph 99 (1) of the 1957 *Gesetz gegen Wettbewerbsbeschränkungen*. The derogation was justified on the grounds of the danger of ruinous competition; inadequate infrastructure; and the need to protect German Railways *(Deutsche Bundesbahn)* (Zobel, 1988, p. 58).
8 For a revealing statement of the German hauliers' position, see Neumann (1988). Neumann's comments were made in his capacity as *Hauptgeschäftsführer der Zentralarbeitsgemeinschaft des Strassenverkehrsgewerbes*.

References

Albert, M. and Ball, R. (1983), *Towards European Recovery in the 1980s*, Working Documents 1983–4, Luxembourg: European Parliament.

Bulmer, S. (1986), *The Domestic Structure of European Policy-Making in West Germany*, New York: Garland Inc.

Bulmer, S. (1989), 'Unity, diversity and stability: the "efficient secrets" behind West German public policy', in Bulmer, S. (ed.), *The Changing Agenda of West German Public Policy*, Aldershot: Dartmouth Publishing, 13–39.

Bulmer, S. and Humphreys, P. (1989), 'Kohl, corporatism and congruence: the West German model under challenge', in Bulmer, S. (ed.) *The Changing Agenda of West German Public Policy*, Aldershot: Dartmouth Publishing, 177–97.

Button, K. and Swann, D. (eds) (1989), *The Age of Regulatory Reform*, Oxford: Clarendon Press.

Cawson, A. (1985), *Organized Interests and the State: Studies in Meso-Corporatism*, London: Sage Publications.

Cerny, P. (1989), 'The "Little Big Bang" in Paris: financial market deregulation in a *dirigiste* system', *European Journal of Political Research*, 17, (2), 169–92.

Cerny, P. (1991), 'The limits of deregulation: transnational interpenetration and policy change', *European Journal of Political Research*, 19 (2/3), 173–96.

Commission of the EC (1985), *Completing the Internal Market*, Luxembourg: OOPEC.

Commission of the EC (1988), *First Survey on State Aids in the European Community*, Luxembourg: OOPEC.

Cooper, J. and Browne, M. (1989), 'Freight transport – a great journey of change', *Eurobusiness,* 1 (5), 12–17.

Curzon Price, V. (1989), 'Three models of European integration' in Dahrendorf, R. et al., *Whose Europe? Competing Visions for 1992*, London: The Institute of Economic Affairs, 23–38.

Davidson, S. (1989), 'Free Movement of Goods, Workers, Services and Capital' in Lodge, J. (ed.), *The European Community and the Challenge of the Future*, London: Pinter Publishers, 111–28.

Diekmann, A. (1989), 'Intervention als Konstante deutscher Verkehrspolitik', *Zeitschrift für Verkehrswissenschaft*, 60 (2/3), 85–101.

Hancher, L. and Moran, M. (1989a), 'Introduction: regulation and deregulation', *European Journal of Political Research*, 17, (2), 129–36.

Hancher, L. and Moran, M. (eds) (1989b), *Capitalism, Culture, and Economic Regulation*, Oxford: Clarendon Press.

Johnson, N. (1978), 'Law as the articulation of the state in Western Germany: a German tradition seen from a British perspective', *West European Politics*, 1, (2), 177–92.

Katzenstein, P. (1987), *Policy and Politics in West Germany: the Growth of a Semisovereign State*, Philadelphia: Temple University Press.

Katzenstein, P. (1989), 'Stability and Change in the Emerging Third Republic', in Katzenstein, P. (ed.), *Industry and Politics in West Germany: Toward the Third Republic*, Ithaca, NY: Cornell University Press, 307–53.

Neumann, W. (1988), 'Binnenmarkt auf Europas Strassen', in Weidenfeld, W. (ed.), *Binnenmarkt '92: Perspektiven aus deutscher Sicht*, Gütersloh: Verlag Bertelsmann Stiftung, 129–31.

Nowak, I. (1990), 'Elektrizitätswirtschaft: lange Leitung nach Europa', in Vorkötter, U. (ed.), *Aufbruch nach Europa:* »*1992« Herausforderung für die deutsche Wirtschaft*, Stuttgart: Verlag C.E. Poeschl, 131–5.

Oehler, K.D. (1990), 'Normen und technische Standards: Abenteuer im Vorschriften-Dschungel', in Vorkötter, U. (ed.), *Aufbruch nach Europa:* »*1992« Herausforderung für die deutsche Wirtschaft*, Stuttgart: Verlag C.E. Poeschl, 34–8.

Soltwedel, R. et al. (1986), *Deregulierungspotentiale in der Bundesrepublik*, Tübingen: J.C.B. Mohr.

Swann, D. (1989), 'The Age of Regulatory Reform: an Overview', in Button, K. and Swann, D. (eds), *The Age of Regulatory Reform*, Oxford: Clarendon Press, 1–23.

Wilke, M. and Wallace, H. (1990), *Subsidiarity: Approaches to Power-sharing in the European Community*, London: RIIA discussion papers no. 27.
Woolcock, S. et al. (1991), *Britain, Germany and 1992: the Limits of Deregulation*, London: Pinter Publishers/RIIA.
Zobel, A. (1988), *Der Werkfernverkehr auf der Strasse im Binnengüterverkehr der Bundesrepublik Deutschland. Zur Problematik staatlicher Regulierung im Verkehrsbereich*, Berlin: Dunckcr & Humblot.

4 Regulatory Culture and Regulatory Change in German Broadcasting

Kenneth Dyson

On 23 February 1984, at the *Ministerpräsidentenkonferenz* in Bonn, the heads of the state (*Land*) governments opened the way for the allocation of a television channel on the ECS satellite for the new private commercial broadcaster SAT 1. This event, coupled with the opening of the pilot cable projects in Ludwigshafen (January) and Munich (April), represented the dawn of a new era in German broadcasting. The strict division of powers in media policy between public-service broadcasting and a private-sector press was brought to an end, and a new age of a 'dual' broadcasting system born. Until 1984, the public-service broadcasters and the private-sector press had operated in completely separate spheres. Public-service broadcasters had kept out of local broadcasting, thereby not challenging the local media and advertising monopolies of the press: whilst the press had confined itself to the printed media in order to protect this local monopoly. In fact this traditional division of powers had been challenged since the 1950s by the large publishers in the Federal Association of German Newspaper Publishers (BDZV), especially by their *Pressevereinigung für neue Publikationsmittel*. The events of 1984 could be seen as a victory for their long-term lobbying, especially for their argument that the introduction of local broadcasting must be accompanied by regulation that would safeguard the commercial interests of the local press by giving them a privileged role in new media development. Also witnessed in 1984 was the start of an avalanche of new media legislation at the state level to provide new regulatory frameworks for commercial broadcasting and the intensification of a protracted debate (till 1987) about a new state treaty to regulate new media.

This chapter seeks to analyse the character of the broadcasting revolution in Germany and especially the nature and scale of regulatory change. At first glance broadcasting appears to be an obvious case of paradigm change in regulation and of a process of rapid regulatory learning by Social Democratic (SPD) states. In Germany the drama of regulatory change has been played out in a particularly public and competitive manner. The goals and instruments of regulation have been debated and contested in a radically new way, with new actors (like the Bundespost and the big publishers) entering the regulatory arena and new coalitions being formed (for instance, the reformist coalition of the Bundespost and certain CDU states). In the process the paradigm of broadcasting regulation altered from a clearly and firmly defined public-service model to a competitive 'dual' broadcasting model. Successive judgements of the Federal Constitutional Court spelt out the nature and implications of this paradigm change. Yet, paradoxically, this change took place within the context and bounds of a 'broadcasting constitution' that has adapted but still retained its essential character. In short, broadcasting regulation provides an outstanding case study of the politics of regulation in both its senses – as an enduring, yet adaptive framework of order, within an overarching regulatory culture; and as a learning process in which regulatory problems, goals and instruments are being redefined. Seen from one perspective, that of coalition activity and interest politics, the story of broadcasting regulation is one of surprises, a saga of threat and counter-threat, bluff and counter-bluff: the impression is of discontinuity. From a longer-term perspective of cultural and institutional development, the impression is of an underlying continuity: whilst from an international perspective regulatory change in Germany appears as late and tentative. In short, much depends on the vantage point from which one chooses to investigate the regulation of German broadcasting.

1.   The Nature of the Broadcasting Revolution

In Germany, as elsewhere, deep-seated changes in the international political economy of broadcasting from the 1970s onwards seemed to promise a radical paradigm change in broadcasting regulation. The new technological and economic forces at work suggested that the assumption on which the monopoly of public-service broadcasting had been based was becoming rapidly outmoded (Dyson and Humphreys, 1988; Dyson and Humphreys, 1990). This assumption was understood to be the scarcity of broadcasting frequencies: the scarcity and subsequent high value of this resource required stringent public regulation. With new cable technologies (copper-coaxial and fibre-optic) and new satellite communications (including direct broadcasting satellite, DBS) the opportunity was created for an explosive growth in the number of channels, for programming to suit special interests ('narrowband' broadcasting) and for a huge new demand for programme production (Knoche and Seufert, 1987; Peasey, 1989; and Schrape and Kessler, 1988). In the process, new economic opportunities were being created, alongside increased choice for the viewer. The opening of these opportunities, and the realization of their potential, required in turn a liberalization of broadcasting regulation. Profound effects could be expected, not just in the number of channels and viewing habits, but also in the politics of broadcasting regulation. Broadcasting regulation would no longer be an autonomous realm of a very few privileged actors. Through technological and economic change it would converge with such sectors as telecommunications and publishing from which actors would seek to diversify into broadcasting. It would also become increasingly internationalized, both because satellite television was inexorably a cross-frontier operation (especially in a crowded Western Europe) and because new channels opened new commercial opportunities to produce and market programmes internationally. The lead of the American broadcasting industry in new technologies, cost-effective programme production and resources suggested that the presence of the United States in international broadcasting markets would increase sharply. Together, these forces intimated a paradigm change in broadcasting regulation, from the public-service model to the commercial model. No longer would broadcasting regulation be dominated by the idea of broadcasters as trustees of the public interest, with a special responsibility for providing information and education programmes of cultural significance. Broadcasting was now an industry in which the purpose of regulation was to maximize competition in the interest of the consumers. In turn, the centre of economic gravity in broadcasting would shift from ownership of channels (no longer so scarce and valuable as before) to the capacity to produce programmes and to sell programme rights and advertising time (the increasingly scarce resource). Economic opportunities focused less on the traditional broadcasting organization and more on control of the studio system as the central managerial point in programme production.

The implications of the process of internationalization for a country like West Germany were brought home by the European Community's television directive of October 1989 (Council of the European Communities, 1989), as well as by its sister, the Council of Europe's Broadcasting Convention (adopted in May 1989). This new EC directive gave clear primacy to a market model of broadcasting in which the priority was the requirement to guarantee freedom of reception to cross-frontier television and a generous attitude to advertising on commercial channels. In essence, the EC viewed broadcasting as a service in which, consistent with the Single Market programme, freedom of movement was necessary. Politically, the directive was a considerable victory for the advertising industry's lobbying to open up large and relatively unexploited markets, notably West Germany.

This 'international-centred' account of a broadcasting revolution seems to be substantially supported by evidence drawn from the changes in German broadcasting and in its regulatory framework. By the end of 1990, thanks to the rapid expansion of cable and the availability of new terrestrial frequencies, only 30 per cent of West German households were unable to receive commercial television (Darschin and Frank, 1991). By September 1989 22.8 per cent of total German households were connected to cable (5.85 million), 51.2 per cent were capable of being connected (13.8 million). West Germany had become the only one of the four major West European states in which cable played a significant role in broadcasting. It possessed the largest cable network in Europe. The two main private commercial channels had even greater penetration by means of terrestrial frequencies: in October 1989 RTL plus reached 7.46 million households terrestrially, SAT 1 6.22 million (Woldt, 1989). In 1990 RTL plus looked like becoming the first satellite television programme in Europe to achieve an annual profit, with SAT 1 close behind. This commercial success reflected the enormous changes in the West German advertising market (Pretzsch, 1991). In 1982 television advertising had accounted for 17.3 per cent of total German advertising; in 1990 the proportion had risen to 24.8 per cent. Press advertising had fallen in the same period from 75.3 per cent to 65.7 per cent. Advertising turnover of RTL plus rose 134.7 per cent in 1990. By contrast, the two largest public-service broadcasters, *Westdeutscher Rundfunk* and *Norddeutscher Rundfunk,* saw advertising turnover fall by 40 per cent and 25.6 per cent respectively. In 1990, for the first time, private television operators took over 50 per cent of the market share of television advertising.

Programming had also undergone significant change. Traditionally, the West German viewer had been able to receive the First Programme of ARD, the Third Programme of the respective regional public-service broadcaster, *Zweites Deutsches-Fernsehen* (ZDF) and, depending on geography and topography, the Third Programmes of other regional broadcasters and cross-frontier foreign programmes. By September 1989 an average of 15.3 programmes was available in cabled households with, for instance, 26 in Munich. Of 19 cable programmes available in Frankfurt, ten were public-service and nine commercial. Four commercial channels had established themselves with a national presence: RTL plus, SAT 1, Tele 5 and Pro 7. RTL plus and SAT 1 had, under pressure from the state regulatory authorities, begun to establish regional television programmes, though they had little economic incentive to do so. Local radio too had blossomed since

1984, albeit in the face of severe economic problems. Here the main success story had been the new state-wide commercial radio stations.

The expansion of television programmes had been accompanied by an increase of daily television viewing from an average of 237 minutes (1986) to 257 (1990) (Darschin and Frank, 1991). Cabled households increased viewing by 21 per cent in 1990 alone. The increased reception of commercial television channels was also accompanied by a growth of their audience figures. Daily viewing of RTL plus was up from 3 minutes (1987) to 31 minutes (1990) and of SAT 1 from 3 minutes (1987) to 24 minutes (1990). By contrast, ARD viewing had fallen from 107 minutes (1986) to 78 (1990) and ZDF from 94 to 72. Viewing figures for public-service news and current affairs programmes had dropped significantly, especially in cabled households. In cabled households the proportion of viewing time for the public-service channels was 62 per cent in 1990, with RTL plus achieving 16.1 per cent and SAT 1 14.9 per cent.

The significant increase in the number of commercial channels and privately-produced programmes went along with an increasing engagement of large media companies in broadcasting, notably by Bertelsmann, Holtzbrinck, Kirch and Springer (Röper, 1989b). In particular, a complex web of cross-ownership emerged between commercial broadcasting and the press (Röper, 1989a). By June 1989 294 newspaper publishers were involved in broadcasting, notably in local commercial radio where often, notably in Bavaria and Baden–Württemberg, they were able to secure a double monopoly of local press and of local radio. In commercial television and the big state-wide commercial radio channels, however, the media giants played the key role. Three have been particularly active in broadcasting. Bertelsmann, the largest media company in the world, had struck two international alliances: with CLT of Luxembourg to launch RTL plus, and with Canal Plus of France to launch a pay-television channel Première. Both ventures benefited from the strength of Bertelsmann's broadcasting holding company Ufa as the most important German company in the field of (non-film) television transmission rights (for example, the German football league, Wimbledon). The Springer Group, diversifying from its large role in newspapers and publishing, held the leading position in shareholdings in the new state-wide commercial radio channels, not least in the SPD states of Hamburg, Hesse and North-Rhine Westphalia. It was also locked in a long-standing struggle with Leo Kirch, notably about control of SAT 1 but also about the strategy underlying Kirch's 10 per cent shareholding in Springer. With its base in films, the Kirch group developed international collaboration in programme production on a greater scale than any other German company, including a collaboration with Berlusconi, Maxwell and Seydoux and another with the American firm Tribune Broadcasting. The largest shareholder in SAT 1 was PKS; 49 per cent of PKS's shares are held by Leo Kirch, another 49 per cent by the Deutsche Genossenschaftsbank (DG Bank), Kirch's 'house bank'. This strong position of Kirch in SAT 1 in turn unleashed a conflict with Springer. More clear-cut was the Kirch Group's success with the Pro 7 entertainment film channel which benefits from the sizeable film holdings of the Group. A notable feature of the relations between these big three, as well as with Burda and Holtzbrinck, has been the instability of the complex webs of cooperation and competition that have evolved as local and state-wide commercial radio channels have been awarded. The consortia that they have formed have proved fragile, with manoeuvring and counter-manoeuvring very much the order of the day. Cooperation in one region or market was threatened by competition in other regions or markets.

The evidence that has been presented would seem to suggest that West German broadcasting has been caught up in a general pattern of change within the international political economy – that the broadcasting revolution has been an international phenomenon that is to be accounted for in international terms. And yet by 1990 there were some clear signs that claims of a broadcasting revolution were overstated, or at least premature. The inroad of the new commercial television channels into the viewing figures for public-service television slowed down considerably in 1990. An average of 68.7 per cent daily television viewing was directed at the public-service channels, compared to 11.7 per cent for RTL plus and 9.1 per cent to SAT 1. This dominant position of the public-service broadcasters, even in cabled households (62.1 per cent), reflected the popularity of its entertainment programming. On the other hand, there was no evidence that the public-service broadcasters had reduced their commitment to information, educational and cultural programming. Public-service news and current affairs programming had by 1990 begun to maintain its audience position. Also, West Germany remained an oasis of relative calm in the increasingly internationalized broadcasting markets. German media companies were most attracted by opportunities within the German-speaking world, initially Austria and Switzerland, and later the former GDR. Only with German unification did overseas media giants, like Rupert Murdoch and Robert Maxwell, seek an involvement, and then in press and publishing rather than broadcasting.

German unification was important in a more deep-seated sense. It did more than represent the relevance and importance of an 'international-centred' account of broadcasting regulation. As a consequence the German media sector found itself at a turning point in its development, not dissimilar from that created by private broadcasting earlier in the 1980s. The German media giants responded by heavy investments in the new markets for newspapers and journals. Media concentration achieved a new scale, with enormous new investments in press and publishing in the former GDR by Bertelsmann, Burda and Springer. New rivalries for market leadership, especially between Burda and Springer, diverted attention away from commercial broadcasting. In the process some of the market pressures on the public-service broadcasters were eased. More importantly still, as Lehmbruch emphasizes, the new conditions of uncertainty introduced by German unification raised new questions about the relevance and viability of the neo-liberal policy model. Not least in broadcasting the new tasks of social integration, cultural unification and democratization endowed public-service broadcasting with a new importance.

2. Cultural and Institutional Legacies

The limitations of an 'international-centred' account become even more apparent when one considers the development of German broadcasting regulation. At this level it becomes clear that broadcasting regulation is anchored in a solid cultural and institutional context that has adapted but retained certain essential and readily identifiable features. Regulatory development has not been able to break free from the domestic historical context. Within this context two characteristics have continued to have a notable impact on broadcasting policy – the cooperative pressures of the federal culture and a highly legalistic policy culture. These two characteristics have in turn been reflected in the central role of two institutions within the process of developing broadcasting regulation – the *Ministerpräsidentenkonferenz* and the Federal Constitutional Court. Their role, particularly in broadcasting, is to be understood against the background of the post-war efforts to learn lessons from the collapse of the Weimar Republic and to prevent any future slide into the kind of regime represented by the Third Reich.

Memories of the capture and use of film and radio by the Third Reich had a profound formative influence on regulatory policy for broadcasting. Influenced by the BBC, regulation enshrined the model of public-service broadcasting and cast it in terms of inherited German ideas and experience (Bausch, 1980; Humphreys, 1989). The public-service model involved a broadcasting system independent both of the state and of any particular social group or interest. This regulatory goal achieved a distinctively German expression in the concepts of *Binnenpluralismus* and *Binnenkontrolle*, 'internal pluralism' and 'internal control' within broadcasting. The main tool of regulation was the provision for pluralism *within* the regulatory process: the governing bodies of the broadcasting corporations were to comprise representatives of a wide range of 'socially relevant' groups (like the churches, trade unions, chambers of commerce, and so on). This principle of representation as a tool of regulation had deep roots in German political tradition, in the concept of *Proporz* drawn from the medieval period. It meant that each broadcasting corporation was regulated by a broadcasting council (*Rundfunkrat*) whose purpose was to safeguard the public interest through 'socially-balanced' representation. Among other functions, the broadcasting council was responsible for ensuring that each channel reflected a balance and diversity of opinions (*Meinungsvielfalt*). The regulatory goal of *Meinungsvielfalt* was to be realized by means of the tools of *Binnenpluralismus* and *Binnenkontrolle* within self-governing 'institutions of public law' (*Anstalten des öffentlichen Rechts*) independent of the state.

Another effect of the background of the Weimar Republic and the Third Reich was to increase the political importance and visibility of broadcasting to the state (*Land*) governments and to the political parties. The importance of broadcasting within the federal system derived from the fact that it was one of only four areas in which the states had exclusive jurisdiction over policy. Consequently, the public-service broadcasting system with its nine regional broadcasters was constructed by individual state legislation (for example, creating *Bayerischer Rundfunk* or *Westdeutscher Rundfunk*) or by interstate treaty (used to create *Norddeutscher Rundfunk* by Hamburg, Lower Saxony and Schleswig–Holstein and, by all states, to create the second television channel, *Zweites Deutsches Fernsehen*). This complex diversity was in turn held together by a powerful compound of economic and technical factors with an ideology of 'cooperative' federalism. The result was ZDF, the periodic agreements amongst the states to fix the licence fee, and the ARD (*Arbeitsgemeinschaft der öffentlich-rechtlichen Rundfunkanstalten*) through which the regional broadcasters cooperate to produce the First Programme. They acted as symbols of mutual dependence and cooperation within a federal system in which the states were zealous guardians of their sovereignty over cultural affairs (*Kulturhoheit*).

Broadcasting regulation was also bound up in the post-war realities of the *Parteienstaat* (party state). From the ashes of the Third Reich the political parties emerged with a new legitimacy and power. The traditional anti-party elites, based on the bureaucracy and the military, had lost credibility through association with the Third Reich. By contrast, a licence from the Allies to operate as a political party conferred respectability; membership of a licenced party suggested prima-facie evidence that one could be trusted. Against this background of doubt about democratic credentials and reliability, the political parties took on from the outset an important patronage function. As they had powerful incentives to take a close interest in broadcasting, not just because of its power but also because of Germany's past, the interest of the political parties in German broadcasting proved both sustained and intrusive. This background of mistrust combined with the electoral rivalries of competitive party politics to create pressures towards majoritarian party patronage and to fuel a debate about the abuse of power in broadcasting. This debate contributed in turn to an erosion of respect for the public-service system within parts of the political party system, particularly during the period of Social Democratic-led governments in Bonn (1969–82). German broadcasting was enmeshed in party politics to an unusual extent because of the heritage and implications of the *Parteienstaat*.

The greatest impact of the Third Reich was undoubtedly felt in the strengthening of Germany's legalistic policy culture, enshrined in the concept of the *Rechtsstaat* ('state governed by law') and given material expression in the detail and rationalism of the Basic Law of 1949 and in the new Federal Constitutional Court. In a series of key judgements the Federal Constitutional Court has spelt out and adapted the basic goals and tools of broadcasting regulation and constrained policy-makers to respect inherited principles and practices. The so-called *Fernsehurteil* (television judgement) of 28 February 1961 represents the classic defence of the traditional regulatory paradigm (*Bundesverfassungsgericht*, 1961). The Court ruled against Chancellor Konrad Adenauer's design to introduce a second television channel that would be both Bonn-regulated and commercial for two reasons. Firstly, broadcasting policy fell under the exclusive jurisdiction of the states and was not a matter for federal regulation. Secondly, the Court drew a distinction between broadcasting and the press. The German press was characterized by a multitude of publications which are independent and mutually competitive according to their basic social values and political leanings. By contrast, in broadcasting the number of those providing services was relatively small, both for technical reasons of scarce frequencies and because of the extremely high financial investment involved. In short, the public-service monopoly was upheld.

Subsequent technological, economic and political changes produced, as we have seen, a new situation so that, beginning in 1981, the Federal Constitutional Court produced a series of key judgements dealing with the introduction of commercial television. These judgements can be seen as representing three stages of development. The first major step in adjusting the ideology of regulation to change was the so-called *'FRAG-Urteil'* of June 1981 (*Bundesverfassungsgericht*, 1981). This judgement gave notice to the states that there was no constitutional impediment to the introduction of commercial television now that the obstacle of a scarcity of frequencies had been overcome. At the same time it reaffirmed the normative constitutional requirement, derived from Article 5 of the Basic Law, to 'regulate for pluralism' in the interest of broadcasting freedom. For commercial broadcasting the Court outlined a new model of regulation based on

Aussenpluralismus ('external pluralism') by means of an *Aussenkontrolle* ('external control') of broadcasting. As for public-service broadcasting, the basic goal of regulation was a balance and diversity of opinion. However, a new set of regulatory tools was required. Instead of the *Binnenkontrolle* characteristic of public-service broadcasting it was essential to create new regulatory authorities at the state level to licence and oversee the establishment of a greatly increased number of channels and programmes. This judgement gave the signal for the states to begin the legislative process of establishing new state media authorities and determining their powers. Whilst the political beneficiaries appeared to be the CDU states and CSU Bavaria, it was notable that the Court insisted on a continuity at the level of regulatory principles and goals.

In its two consecutive judgements of 1986 and 1987 dealing with the new media legislation of the CDU states of Lower Saxony and Baden–Württemberg the Federal Constitutional Court developed and modified its views on the appropriate regulatory paradigm for broadcasting. Of the two judgements, the Lower Saxony judgement of 4 November 1986 was the most significant (*Bundesverfassungsgericht,* 1986; Stock, 1987). It introduced the concept of a 'dual broadcasting order'. On the one hand, regulation must ensure that public-service broadcasting was able to provide 'a basic service for all', concentrating on investigative, cultural and educational programming and offering minority programmes. In order to fulfil this function, public-service broadcasting had to be given 'necessary' financial, organizational and technical guarantees. On the other hand, regulation of commercial broadcasting must recognize that its rationale was to offer entertainment programming in order to maximize ratings and thereby attract necessary advertising income. Hence the same high requirements about balance and variety of programming expected of public-service broadcasters were not to be imposed on commercial broadcasters.

The ruling indicated a clear order of priority in regulation: adequate guarantees for public-service broadcasting were a condition of lower regulatory standards for commercial broadcasters. However, the Court seemed to suggest that negative effects on the quality of broadcasting were unavoidable. It confined itself to underlining in general terms the importance of regulating for 'balance' and 'diversity of opinion' in the commercial sector. Regulation must include the opportunity for a regulatory body to act if general programming developed in an unbalanced way by requiring that each individual programme be 'balanced in itself'. It has also to counter the 'danger of a concentration' with the development of a 'multimedia power over opinion' (that is, a combination of influence through both broadcasting and the press). Whilst the Lower Saxony broadcasting law was judged to be 'in its essentials' in conformity with the Basic Law, one feature in

particular was singled out as unacceptable. Franchising by the State Chancellery (the office of the *Ministerpräsident*) offended against the principle
of broadcasting's independence from the state. Finally, mindful of the
continuing failure to agree a state treaty to regulate the new media, the
Court stressed the requirement of *bundesfreundliches Verhalten* (behaviour
that was conscious of federal responsibilities). 'Mutual accommodation'
and 'cooperation' was indispensable for cross-frontier broadcasting. This
injunction, plus the affirmation of the substantive principles to guide regulation, was important in facilitating a characteristically German consensual
outcome in the form of the state treaty of 1987.

This process of constitutional adjudication to adapt regulatory principles
to new technical and economic circumstances reached a new stage of
maturity in the North-Rhine Westphalia judgement of 1991
(*Bundesverfassungsgericht,* 1991; Berg, 1991; Stock, 1991). In this case
the Court was dealing with complaints brought by the CDU and FDP
against two SPD laws: the *Westdeutscher Rundfunk* law and the North-Rhine
Westphalia state broadcasting law. These laws were declared in their basic
essentials compatible with the Basic Law. Taking the guarantee of broadcasting freedom of Article 5 as its starting point, the Court stressed the
indispensable role of public-service broadcasting and the paramount need
to ensure that its functions were not impaired by the 'dual broadcasting
order' or the dysfunctional effects of importing a press model of minimalist
regulation into broadcasting. Hence regulation could seek to achieve a
'dual order' or a public-service system; it was not able to opt for a purely
commercial model. In a 'dual order' there could not be a consistent regulatory model (*Modellkonsistenz*). The real regulatory problem was how to
organize internal relationships within the 'dual order'. Here the Court
broke new ground by arguing that it was not possible to correct imbalance
in commercial programming by simply relying on the continuing compensating role of public-service broadcasting. Given the financial and
programming problems of the commercial sector the constitutional
requirement of regulatory guarantees for public-service broadcasting was
re-emphasized, along with the indispensability of the licence fee as the
prime source of finance. Reflecting this priority to the constitutional role of
public-service broadcasting approval was given to the legislative provision
for *Westdeutscher Rundfunk* (WDR) to collaborate with commercial partners
in developing broadcasting services, as long as the programme mission was
compatible with its public-service rationale. In particular, the relatively
stringent requirements of the North-Rhine Westphalia Broadcasting Law
on commercial broadcasting were confirmed: especially the 'two-pillar'
model (*Zwei-Säulenmodell*), which divided management from programming decisions; the provision for editorial participation to secure an inter-

nal *Meinungsvielfalt* in commercial broadcasting; and the requirement for representation of the 'socially-relevant' groups (notably representing cultural interests) in the state regulatory agency for commercial broadcasting as well as in WDR. Representation of the 'socially-relevant' groups was an appropriate instrument of regulatory control in both sectors of the 'dual broadcasting' system.

These landmark rulings of the Federal Constitutional Court provided both the constitutive principles and the constraints within which state media legislation was drafted (and typically redrafted) and within which the *Ministerpräsidentenkonferenz* sought to hammer out basic nationwide agreement on cross-frontier broadcasting. Federalism represented a second level of institutional action that shaped and contained the progress of broadcasting regulation. In a general sense the German federal system comprised a complex set of mutual dependencies and interdependencies. This observation was particularly true in relation to broadcasting, with a heritage of collaboration in public-service broadcasting (ARD, ZDF and the regulation of the licence fee) and a need for cooperation in order to develop commercial broadcasting by ensuring a genuinely national market for the new channels. The route to a state treaty proved long and stormy, but there could be little doubt that the destination would be a state treaty. The process lasted from the abortive Bremerhaven compromise of October 1984 till April 1987. In the interim agreement was reached on the allocation of two channels on the ECS communications satellite: one to 3SAT, a public-service compilation programme produced by ZDF in collaboration with Austrian and Swiss broadcasters; and the other to a commercial consortium (SAT 1 was selected). Also, in 1986, the Federal Constitutional Court's Lower Saxony ruling spelt out the parameters of, and need for, cooperative action, consistent with the underlying spirit of German federalism. Together, federalism and the law provided a powerful cultural and institutional framework within which broadcasting regulation developed. Regulation could not in the process escape from historical legacies which, if they did not totally imprison policy development, conditioned and shaped it.

3.   Policy Coalitions and Regulatory Change

Despite their strengths, neither the 'international-centred' nor the 'culture-' and 'institution-centred' approaches – separately or together – offer a fully adequate account of broadcasting regulation. Regulation is also embedded in power relations which in turn reflect the way in which policy actors, including those outside the state itself, develop and use ideas and resources within cultural and institutional contexts. Explanation of the way in which broadcasting regulation developed in Germany must attend to the complex changes underway in the policy sector within which regulation was embedded. From the 1970s two main changes affected the broadcasting policy sector – an expansion of the number of actors involved, and a new labyrinthian process of threat and counter-threat as 'reformist' coalitions battled with 'conservationist' coalitions (Dyson, 1989). In the process the old idea of a relatively closed and privileged policy community, resting on a shared ideology of public-service broadcasting, gave way to a much more pluralistic and competitive picture in which self-interest seemed closer to the surface of regulatory politics.

From this perspective the central catalyst for change appears to be the change of power in Bonn in 1982: from the SPD/FDP government of Helmut Schmidt to the CDU/CSU/FDP government of Helmut Kohl. Under SPD ministers the Bundespost had pursued cautious policies towards the new communications technologies, focusing on their role in industrial modernization. The *Kommission für den Ausbau des technischen Kommunikationssystems* (KtK, 1974–76) had been kept firmly under the wing of the Bundespost and had recommended only 'pilot projects' for cable television. By 1982 no 'cable project' had yet begun, and the cabinet had rejected a proposal for the cabling of major cities, motivated by particular concern about the prospect of commercial broadcasting. SPD priority was to the long-term development of an Integrated Services Digital Network (ISDN), using broadband fibre optic cable, and to preservation of the public-service monopoly in broadcasting.

The determination of the CDU to make broadcasting into a centrepiece of its *Wende* policy in 1982 owed a great deal to the appointment of Christian Schwarz-Schilling as Bundespost minister and the sheer political tenacity with which he used his control over telecommunications policy as an instrument to achieve a revolution in broadcasting. In opposition Schwarz-Schilling had developed close links to the commercial interests pressing for deregulation of media policy. There were also powerful party political arguments for prioritizing this area of policy: political friends were to be won in the CDU states pressing for an opening of broadcasting to commercial operators; whilst an influential body of opinion within the CDU/CSU held the public-service broadcasters responsible for conveying a negative view that had led to successive federal electoral defeats for their parties. The scale of Bundespost action was formidable and designed to break the resistance of the SPD states to a liberalization of broadcasting. In 1982 Schwarz-Schilling announced a massive programme to provide the Federal Republic with an infrastructure of copper-coaxial cable with the main aim of an 'opening of the broadcasting market'. By the end of 1989 over DM9 billion had been invested, with over DM1 billion in 1989 alone, at an average cost of DM613 per household (Woldt, 1989). As we have seen, West Germany became the major European market for cable television – in effect a huge public subsidy for the establishment of commercial broadcasting.

The cable programme was implemented despite a huge barrage of public criticism – from the large electronics companies which complained about wasted investment in outdated technology; from the Federal Audit Court (*Bundesrechnungshof*) which in a report of 1984 attacked the lack of commercial logic behind the programme; and from the SPD which attacked the misuse of the telecommunications monopoly for the purpose of subsidising a broadcasting revolution and which promoted the alternative of a concentration of investment in the ISDN (Mettler-Meibom, 1986; Zerdick, 1982). In order to promote marketing and respond to the criticisms of the Federal Audit Court, in 1986 the federal government took the initiative in establishing the Regional Cable Service Companies (RKS), with minority participation by the Bundespost's subsidiary *Telepost Kabelservice* (TKS) (*Programm zur Verbesserung der Rahmenbedingungen des privaten Rundfunkmarkts,* 1986). The result was a new range of different price deals for cable customers that was successful in substantially improving the connection rate to 44.3 per cent in September 1989. In practice, however, the political priority of a broadcasting revolution took precedence over the cable programme. The Bundespost made active use of satellite transponder capacity to assist the new commercial broadcasters, not least in the huge public subsidy in the TV-Sat 2 DBS satellite and the DFS1 Kopernikus. In July 1985 Schwarz-Schilling announced that regulations for satellite reception were to be liberalized. This move not only opened a larger potential audience to the commercial operators but also made life much more difficult for SPD politicians. More significantly still, reacting to the concerns about slow penetration of cable and large operating losses from the new broadcasters, from 1985/86 the Bundespost began to make available new terrestrial frequencies to speed their penetration and attract more advertising. In this way a total of 65 towns and cities, with a total population of 16 million, was opened to the new broadcasters. Priority was given to CDU/CSU states which were quick to benefit SAT 1. Together, this battery of measures helped to establish the two main commercial channels, RTL plus and SAT 1, in a secure financial position by 1991.

The other two main partners in the 'reform coalition' were the commercial interests that stood to benefit (led by the large publishers and by the advertising industry) and the CDU/CSU states. By 1981 the BDZV was suggesting a flight of capital abroad and evasion of domestic regulatory control by negotiating with CLT of Luxembourg about a joint European Television Company to operate a commercial television channel. This prospect became a reality when Bertelsmann, excluded from SAT 1, went into partnership with CLT to produce RTL plus, initially from Luxembourg. A complex amalgam of political and economic motives underpinned the behaviour of the CDU/CSU states, in particular the creation of what they saw as a more sympathetic broadcasting environment, the establishment of a new national image and the attraction of new economic and cultural activity away from the traditional broadcasting centres, like 'SPD' Hamburg and Cologne. Viewed from the economic perspective of investment, jobs and tax revenue, and of cultural prestige, broadcasting regulation became subsumed in industrial location policy (*Standortpolitik*). In alliance with a politically and financially supportive Bundespost, the states of Rhineland–Palatinate, Lower Saxony and Bavaria set the pace of regulatory reform (the reason why the SPD appealed the Lower Saxony Broadcasting Law of 1984 to the Federal Constitutional Court).

There were at the same time some clear differences of emphasis amongst the CDU states, typically reflecting characteristics of their industrial structures. In Baden–Württemberg, for instance, where the electronics industry was notably powerful, priority was given to non-broadcasting telematic services as early as the report of the *Expertenkommission Neue Medien* (1981). By contrast, Rhineland–Palatinate sought to build on its broadcasting potential as already the location for ZDF. The behaviour and ambitions of CSU Bavaria also excited concern within the CDU, especially its efforts to promote the public-service channel Bayern 3 as a national satellite programme and the threat of a monthly charge per cabled household in Bavaria to be paid by non-Bavarian programmers. Despite such differences, however, the case for commercial broadcasting held together a relatively solid CDU/CSU reform coalition. Bavaria benefited not least from the successes of the Munich-based Leo Kirch and the location of Tele 5 there.

Regulatory change in broadcasting was caught up in the complex political dynamics unleashed by the initiatives and *fait accompli* of the Bundespost and by the search for political and economic advantage and, in the case of the SPD states, damage limitation. The CDU/CSU states were especially keen to take advantage of the '*FRAG-Urteil*' of 1981 to establish the regulatory principles of 'external pluralism' and 'external control', along with new state regulatory authorities to implement them, and to encourage the local and regional press into a role in the new broadcasting, both radio and television. Also, the Ludwigshafen pilot project was used as a means to licence SAT 1 as the first federal commercial channel. Like Schwarz-Schilling, the CDU states were creating *fait accompli* for the SPD. Additionally, the CDU states could use the threat of refusing to renew the licence agreement on which the finances of the public-service broadcasters ultimately depended. This multidimensional political pressure for regulatory change culminated in the two mini-state treaties on satellite broadcasting drawn up by the CDU/CSU states in 1986, a northern treaty and a southern treaty.

The SPD states found themselves on the defensive, seeking to conserve the benefits of public-service broadcasting; whilst the public-service broadcasters were somewhat politically inhibited by a desire not to associate themselves too closely with the SPD and thereby impair their reputation for neutrality and impartiality. One significant bargaining resource was available to the SPD: the sanction of refusing the new commercial broadcasters access to key state markets, like North-Rhine Westphalia. Initially, SPD opposition to commercial broadcasting was one of principle. However, by a narrow majority, the SPD party conference at Essen in May 1984 adopted a new Media Action Programme that was distinctly more pragmatic in approach (SPD, 1984). This new period of 'constructive opposition', championed by the SPD's general secretary Peter Glotz, meant acceptance of commercial broadcasting but left open the question of the terms of its acceptance. Hesse, where the SPD was in coalition with the Greens, remained in strong opposition, adopting a law for the retransmission of satellite programmes as late as 1987 (Hessen, 1987); North-Rhine Westphalia was prepared to compromise but on terms that privileged the regional public-service broadcaster WDR and that ensured editorial and programming independence (the so-called *Zwei-Säulen Modell*) (Prodöhl, 1987); whilst Hamburg had a pressing incentive to compromise in order to maintain its key position in German press and broadcasting. For Hamburg the threat of a loss of media investment, jobs (some 30 000 were employed in the media) and tax revenue, at a time of general industrial decline, was a potent factor in its breaking ranks to accede to the northern state treaty of the CDU.

The legitimation of commercial broadcasting by the Federal Constitutional Court's ruling of 1986, including the new legal pressure for agreement of a state treaty, came at a time of political weakness for the SPD. Its room for bargaining was limited. With the state treaty of 1987 the SPD accommodated itself to the reality of a 'dual broadcasting order', as outlined in the 1986 ruling (Hartstein et al., 1989). It accepted that the balance of satellite channel capacity was to lie in favour of the commercial broadcasters. The new DBS satellite, TV-Sat 1, would carry two public-service channels, 3SAT and EINS PLUS, and RTL plus and SAT 1, with a new third channel on TV-Sat 2 also going to a commercial operator. Two other retreats were made by the SPD. Restrictions on advertising on commercial channels (but not on public-service channels) were lifted, and *Hessischer Rundfunk* was required to withdraw advertising from its regional service. With the accession of the four main commercial channels (SAT 1, RTL plus, Pro 7 and Teleclub) to the Luxembourg ASTRA direct broadcasting satellite in December 1989, the limitations of the state treaty as a regulatory instrument were in any case underlined.

Despite these reverses events in 1990–1 brought new confidence to the public-service broadcasters. The 1991 ruling of the Federal Constitutional Court legitimated some of the key arguments of the SPD about regulatory policy. Also, German unification brought about a wholly new and threatening political situation in which politicians in general were more disposed to see a positive role for public-service broadcasting in stabilizing and integrating the five new *Bundesländer*. The central problems were the need to reduce the role and high costs of the *Deutscher Fernsehfunk* (DFF), the former television service of the GDR, and to achieve a transitional solution till the five new states were in a position to enact their own broadcasting laws and create new broadcasting companies. The unification treaty provided for a new council, representing the new states, to advise and control the new special broadcasting commissioner (*Rundfunksonderbeauftragter*) in designing transitional arrangements. Also, it stated that, as part of these arrangements, the DFF could continue to operate until 31 December 1991. In practice, the federal government found itself operating in a vacuum, with the states failing to establish the new council and with a sharp conflict between the SPD and CDU states about the appointment of the broadcasting commissioner. Chancellor Kohl used this situation to coordinate with the four CDU new states to agree new television plans for eastern Germany. In November 1990 Rudolf Mühlfenzl, the broadcasting commissioner, announced the allocation of the east German frequencies in such a way that DFF in its existing form ceased to exist. This procedure provoked sharp criticism from the SPD as an arrogant intrusion of federal power into broadcasting. The real beneficiaries were, nevertheless, the ARD and the ZDF: ARD took over the frequency of the DFF's first programme; ZDF gained a frequency unused by DFF; whilst DFF's second programme was to be transformed into a new channel that would offer a new regional service for the new *Bundesländer* and was expected to form the basis for their new television structure. Once again the federal government had found a means to become active in broadcasting, but this time in the cause of public-service broadcasting.

4. A Case Study of the *Landesmedienanstalten*

An important result of this protracted process of debate, legislation and ministerial initiative was the creation of a new system of state media authorities (*Landesmedienanstalten*), cooperating at the federal level in their own directors' conference (*Direktorenkonferenz der Landesmedienanstalten*) (for example, *Gemeinsame Richtlinien*, 1988). By the 1990s they had come to represent a new interest in the regulatory process, important both for policy development – they enjoyed very substantial discretion – and for the critical process of implementation of the state media laws and of the principles underlying the rulings of the Federal Constitutional Court. The state media authorities had the task of licensing and controlling commercial broadcasting according to the model of 'external pluralism'. Accordingly, particular attention had to be paid to the requirements for 'balance' and 'diversity' of programmes, as spelt out in the 1986 ruling of the Court, and for realization of the broadcasting freedom under Article 5 of the Basic Law, as stressed in the 1991 ruling. Regulation in the public interest was, however, only part of their brief. According to the state treaty of 1987, they could also – for the period 1988 to 1991 – subsidize the initial investment and running costs of the technical infrastructure to support the establishment of commercial broadcasting. Regulation became inseparable from, and complicated by, this promotive function of the *Landesmedienanstalten*. Active regulation in the public interest was not a noticeable characteristic.

In order to ensure their independence from the state in discharging these functions, the state treaty guaranteed the *Landesmedienstalten* the equivalent of 2 per cent of the broadcasting licence fee for their financing. By 1990 their total budget amounted to some DM109 million, and their total employees to over 200 (Wöste, 1990). By 1990 three *Landesmedienanstalten* in particular had achieved a formidable scale of operation: the *Landesanstalt für Rundfunk* in North-Rhine Westphalia, with a budget of DM27.5 million and 40 employees; the *Bayerische Landeszentrale für neue Medien* with DM21 million and 47 employees; and the *Landesanstalt für Kommunikation* in Baden–Württemberg with DM17.9 million and 18 employees. State governments took in fact a close interest in these budgets. Some state media laws specified the use of the licence fee income: for instance, Lower Saxony required that 90 per cent of this income be dedicated to improvement of the technical infrastructure (by implication only 10 per cent was left for the regulatory function). The media laws of Bavaria and Hamburg introduced extra charges for cabled households to contribute to the financing of the new regulatory system. The Bavarian law allocated 10 per cent of this revenue to the regulatory authority, the rest to cable companies and Bavarian programme providers. In Berlin, Hamburg, Lower Saxony and Schleswig–Holstein a special programme provider charge was introduced. In this respect perhaps the most innovative state was North-Rhine Westphalia. In a law of 1990 it introduced a so-called 'self-commitment' of the *Landesanstalt für Rundfunk* to co-fund the state's new *Filmstiftung*, established by the state government and WDR to develop the state's film industry. By 1993 45 per cent of its licence income was to pass to WDR for investment in the *Filmstiftung*. These stipulations manifested the ethos of mercantilism that surrounded the operation of the *Landesmedienanstalten*..

The expenditure patterns of the *Landesmedienanstalten* reveal that just less than half was devoted to licensing and control activities. In the period 1988–90 over DM95 million was spent on development of technical infrastructure, just over one-third of the total. The largest spending was by states that had deliberately restricted spending on regulatory activities. Baden–Württemberg allocated DM33 million (though, because of a protracted dispute with the Bundespost, much less was actually spent) and Lower Saxony DM29.9 million. The chief beneficiaries in Lower Saxony were RTL plus and SAT 1 whose terrestrial telecommunications charges were largely subsidized. In Schleswig–Holstein the same broadcasters had their telecommunications charges reduced by half in the same way, whilst in Bavaria the total transmission charges of local radio broadcasters were met. Once again, a substantial indirect public subsidy was being made available to commercial broadcasters.

In this context it is hardly surprising that the interests of the regulators and the regulated became inextricably entangled. The processes of regulation by the *Landesmedienanstalten* bear the indelible imprint of their origins in the attempt of CDU governments to use every available means to establish and promote commercial broadcasting. Prior to the 1986 ruling of the Federal Constitutional Court the State Chancelleries of Lower Saxony and Rhineland–Palatinate had played a strong role in ensuring the early licensing of SAT 1 by their regulatory authorities. From the outset the relations between the CDU government of Rhineland–Palatinate, the state's *Anstalt für Kabelkommunikation* (AKK), and the cable and satellite lobby were close to the point of intimacy. The first chief executive of the AKK, created as early as 1980 to oversee the Ludwigshafen pilot cable project, was a former managing director of the BDZV (to which he returned in 1985); he was also a co-director of an early commercial programme producer, PKS, which was selected for the Ludwigshafen project and was a partner in SAT 1 which the AKK selected in 1984 to operate on the ECS 1 satellite. A senior official from the State Chancellery in Rhineland–Palatinate left to become managing director of SAT 1 and deputy chairman (later chairman) of the *Bundesverband Kabel und Satellit* (BKS), the main lobby for commercial broadcasters. This situation reflected a combination of the intense political commitment of the state government with the competitive pressures for policy success in a federal system. It also revealed the scope of the reach of the *Parteienstaat*.

The enmeshment of regulation in promotive political ambitions had a profound effect on the nature of licensing and control processes. Regulation did have an impact, notably in the development of regional television programming by RTL plus and SAT 1, a licence condition that was not commercially attractive to these operators. Also, the *Landesanstalt für Rundfunk* in North-Rhine Westphalia became a symbol of a more committed SPD approach to preventing commercial media concentration and privileging public-service broadcasting. The overall impression remained, however, that *Landesmedienanstalten* tended to give priority to economic over cultural criteria, assuming a measure of responsibility for the economic success of commercial broadcasting as well as for its regulation (Hellstern and Reese, 1989; Lange, 1989). Foremost amongst these criteria were the economic interests of the state (*Standortpolitik*) and the commercial viability of the applicants or operators. Problems of the newly licensed commercial radio operators in, for instance, Berlin and Hamburg underlined the centrality of the latter criterion. An example of the influence of these economic criteria was provided by the *Hamburgische Anstalt für neue Medien* which awarded its first and commercially most attractive commercial radio licence to Radio Hamburg, a consortium of the major Hamburg-based publishing companies (notably Gruner und Jahr of the Bertelsmann group and Springer). The attraction of this consortium was its potential to mobilize Hamburg media interests against new commercial radio competition from Lower Saxony and Schleswig–Holstein. In this respect the pioneer was Rhineland–Palatinate's AKK which, in awarding to Radio 4 the first commercial radio licence in the Federal Republic, privileged the main newspaper publishers of the state. Through their dominance of the regional studios of Radio 4 these publishers were able to establish local media monopolies. A high point of local media concentration was reached in Baden–Württemberg, with the dominance of local radio by the local press. The case of Radio 4 in Rhineland–Palatinate also shows how the regulatory authority could be drawn into a detailed involvement, organizing cooperation amongst commercial interests when the private sector on its own proved incapable of delivering an effective consortium (Klingler and Walendy, 1986). In fact, as was revealed by the experience of Radio 4 and by the deep financial and organizational problems of Radio in Berlin and Radio 107 in Hamburg, the *Landesmedienanstalten* were unable to control the complex market forces and economic relations at work. Their capacity to regulate in such areas as advertising practice and to adequately research rival consortia in the licensing process was further undermined by sometimes stringent legal restrictions on staff expenditure (for instance, only seven staff in Lower Saxony in 1990). Faced by a lack of adequate staffing and the speed and complexity of change the *Landesmedienanstalten* tended to resort to an ideology of trust in the market and to judge pluralism by reference to the simple criterion of the number of partners in a consortium. In essence, they adopted a relatively passive regulatory role, consistent with the realities of the market power to which they were subjected and the political ambitions in which they operated. At the same time, as we have seen, they could exert a regulatory muscle when the economic and cultural interests of the state were clearly affected.

5.   Conclusions

This account of broadcasting regulation in Germany has underlined the deep-seated changes that have accompanied the transition to a 'dual broadcasting order'. Regulatory change has been above all directed at the themes of testing, introducing and legitimating commercial broadcasting and at the issue of the proper relationship between public-service broadcasting and commercial broadcasting. The major conflicts and changes that ensued cannot be properly understood outside the context of international developments – the availability of new transmission technologies, the internationalization of markets, and the consequent increasing pressures from economic and political interests. The formation of a new domestic coalition for regulatory reform was part of a wider pattern of international development. Yet this account has also emphasized how regulatory change in Germany has been conditioned by powerful cultural and institutional legacies, expressed most resonantly in successive rulings of the Federal Constitutional Court and in the impact of the character of the federal system. Broadcasting regulation has remained framed within a constitutional legacy that, shaped by the experience of the Third Reich, continues to place prime emphasis on the necessary conditions for broadcasting freedom, amongst which still figures a pre-eminent role for public-service broadcasting.

In the German case the characteristic problems of markets and regulation have been compounded by the federal dimension. Regulatory activity has been caught up in the problems of managing paradox: on the one hand, a regulatory system that concentrates authority at the state level facing, on the other, a broadcasting structure in which commercial power is gravitating to the federal and international levels. In this context the question arises of just how much respect and credibility is attached to state regulatory authorities by the large media conglomerates. The very effort of the *Landesmedienanstalten* to organize their own federal cooperation served if anything to benefit these conglomerates. By developing the principle of 'equal broadcasting conditions' the *Direktorenkonferenz der Landesmedienanstalten* created a new pressure on individual states to licence

RTL plus and SAT 1. Yet, at the same time, the sheer complexity of domestic new media regulation caused serious problems of consortia-building and maintenance amongst the media conglomerates. As different consortia emerged in different broadcasting jurisdictions, so the conglomerates found themselves in a mozaic of relationships of cooperation and conflict that posed for them too serious managerial problems. In these various ways institutional structures made their impact felt.

Alongside an affirmation of the new impact of the international environment and the continuing impact of culture and institutions, this chapter conveys a powerful message about the independent role that policy actors have been able to play in the processes of change in broadcasting regulation. This role has involved more than just using and shaping the impact of international forces and cultural and institutional legacies to promote particular self-interests. In the case of broadcasting it has included the creation of new regulatory institutions, the *Landesmedienanstalten*. In other words, institutions and the cultural forms that they express are not to be seen as simply a historical legacy; they are themselves the product of specific contemporary contingencies and the efforts of actors to reshape the environment in which they operate. What is clear is that the institutional environment of broadcasting regulation has itself undergone deep-seated change for which explanation has to be sought in the complex interface of international developments with the refashioning of domestic policy coalitions and the subsequent emergence of gaps in institutional provision for regulation.

In the early 1980s the prospect was of a paradigm change in broadcasting regulation, the replacement of one model of regulation (public-service, *Binnenpluralismus*) by another (commercial, *Aussenpluralismus*). Paradigm change in this sense did not occur, in large part because of the Federal Constitutional Court's insistence on continuity within change. New regulatory instruments were developed to parallel the new goal of licensing and controlling commercial broadcasting. However, in the process old regulatory goals were not displaced; the pre-eminence of the values of balance and diversity of opinion were reinforced by successive constitutional rulings. In effect the Federal Constitutional Court was seeking to define the terms and limits of a regulatory learning process that was, as we have seen, led by a powerful combination of technological, economic and political forces. The new 'dual broadcasting order' was an attempt to add to, but not supplant, the existing regulatory paradigm. In this important respect it is possible to speak of an enduring but adaptive framework of order in German broadcasting regulation.

Seen from a longer-term perspective, one can divine an underlying continuity. Supportive evidence can be drawn from the extent to which, in the new 'dual broadcasting order', the public-service broadcasters have retained their classic programming philosophy and, reinspired by the constitutional rulings of 1986 and 1991, have undergone a resurgence of self-confidence (Krüger, 1989). By 1991 they were showing signs of having stabilized their share of viewing at around two-thirds. Also, as we have seen, German unification underlined the enormous importance of the role of public-service broadcasting within the 'dual broadcasting order'. Safeguards for the quality of information and educational programming took on a new significance against a much more uncertain political background.

From another perspective, however, regulation has involved a complex learning process in which regulatory problems, goals and instruments have been redefined in a story of surprise, of threat and counter-threat, bluff and counter bluff. Commercial broadcasting has successfully established itself, providing a great deal more (imported) entertainment programming than before (Stock, 1990). In effect, it has strengthened the entertainment function of broadcasting. Regulation in this sector has proved to be weak, with regulation in the interest of *Aussenpluralismus* heavily adapted to the commercial realities of an entertainment medium. In fact, as we have seen, the relationship between the state and the commercial sector in broadcasting has been defined less by regulation than by huge public subsidies – from the Bundespost, via its cable programme, and from the *Landesmedienanstalten*, via support for the development of the technical infrastructure.

The character of German attitudes towards broadcasting regulation can perhaps be best gleaned by responses to two developments: German unification, as we saw above, and the EC's television directive. The degree of distance to a market model of broadcasting was apparent in the breadth of criticism of the proposed EC directive and the eventual reluctance and reservation with which the federal government agreed to vote for it in October 1989. On several occasions the Bundesrat attacked the EC's proposals for failing to recognize that broadcasting was a 'cultural phenomenon' and could not simply be equated with an ordinary service sector; whilst Bavaria took the issue of the federal government's competence to negotiate an EC agreement on broadcasting to the Federal Constitutional Court. German lawyers were in general agreement that the regulatory paradigm underlying the EC directive was incompatible with the Federal Constitutional Court's concept of a 'dual broadcasting order' and of the role of public-service broadcasting in providing a 'basic provision' of broadcasting service. They, and German politicians, could at least take some comfort from the wide political discretion left to national authorities to interpret the meaning of many of the directive's provisions. Despite its liberalizing thrust, the EC's broadcasting directive looked set to highlight national differences rather than encourage similarities.

References

Bausch, H. (1980), *Rundfunkpolitik nach 1945,* München: Deutscher Taschenbuchverlag.

Berg, K. (1986), 'Weichenstellung. Das Niedersachsen-Urteil als Leitlinie der künftigen Rundfunkordnung', *Media Perspektiven,* 11, 689–91.

Berg, K. (1991), 'Grundversorgung und Programmzeitschriften des öffentlichrechtlichen Rundfunks nach dem 6. Rundfunkurteil des Bundesverfassungsgerichts', *Media Perspektiven,* 4, 217–19.

Bundesverfassungsgericht (1961), 12, 205 ff (the first broadcasting judgement).

Bundesverfassungsgericht (1981), 57, 295 ff (the third Karlsruhe broadcasting judgement or 'FRAG-Urteil').

Bundesverfassungsgericht (1986), 73, 118 ff (the fourth broadcasting judgement or Lower Saxony judgement).

Bundesverfassungsgericht (1987), 74, 297 ff (the fifth broadcasting judgement or Baden–Württemberg judgement).

Bundesverfassungsgericht (1991), 1, 85 ff (the sixth broadcasting judgement or North-Rhine Westphalia judgement).

Council of the European Communities (1989), *Council Directive on the Coordination of Certain Provisions Laid Down by Law, Regulation or Administrative Action in Member States concerning the Pursuit of Television Broadcasting Activities,* 5858/89, Brussels.

Darschin, W. and Frank, B. (1991), 'Tendenzen im Zuschauerverhalten: Fernsehgewohnheiten und Fernsehreichweiten im Jahr 1990', *Media Perspektiven,* 3, 178–93.

Dyson, K. (1989), 'Whither West German Broadcasting? The Transformation of a Policy Sector', in Bulmer, S. (ed.), *The Changing Agenda of West German Public Policy,* Aldershot: Dartmouth.

Dyson, K. and Humphreys, P. (1988), *Broadcasting and New Media Policies in Western Europe,* London and New York: Routledge.

Dyson, K. and Humphreys, P. (eds) (1990), *The Political Economy of Communications: International and European Dimensions,* London and New York: Routledge.

Expertenkommission Neue Medien (EKM): Baden–Württemberg – Abschlussbericht (1981), Stuttgart: Kohlhammer Verlag.

Gemeinsame Richtlinien der Landesmedienanstalten zur Durchführung der Werberegelungen des Rundfunkstaatsvertrages: Entwurf der Direktorenkonferenz der Landesmedienanstalten (DLM) vom 10, November 1998.

Hartstein, R., Ring, W-D. and Kreile, J. (1989), 'Kommentar zum Staatsvertrag der Länder zur Neordnung des Rundfunkwesens (Runfunkstaatsvertrag) von 3.4.1987', in Ring, W-D, *Medienrecht 1, Rundfunk, Neue Medien, Presse, Text, Rechtsprechung, Kommentierung,* München, 379–405.

Hellstern, G-M. and Reese, J. (1989), 'Ziele, Organisation und Leistung der Landesanstalten für Rundfunk' in *Rundfunkaufsicht, Bd.3: Rundfunkaufsicht in vergleichender Analyse. Bd.16/III Begleitforschung des Landes Nordrhein-Westfalen zum Kabelprojekt Dortmund,* Düsseldorf, 3–56.

Hessen: Gesetz über die Weiterverbreitung von Satellitenprogrammen vom 30 Januar 1987, reproduced in *Media Perspektiven Dokumentation* (1987), **2**, 116–20.

Hoffmann-Riem, W. (1986), 'Law, Politics and the New Media: Trends in Broadcasting Regulation', in Dyson, K. and Humphreys, P. (eds), *The Politics of the Communications Revolution in Western Europe*, London: Frank Cass.

Humphreys, P. (1989), *Media and Media Policy in West Germany*, Leamington Spa: Berg.

Klingler, W. and Walendy, E. (1986), 'Radio 4: kommerzielle Hörfunkkonkurrenz in Rheinland-Pfalz', *Media Perspektiven*, **7**, 444–55.

Knoche, M. and Seufert, W. (1987), 'Entwicklung und Finanzierung des Fernsehprogrammangebots bis zum Jahr 2005', *Media Perspektiven*, **4**, 209–28.

Krüger, U. (1989), 'Konvergenz im dualen Fernsehsystem? Programmanalyse 1989', *Media Perspektiven*, **12**, 776–806.

KtK (1976), *Telekommunikationsbericht mit acht Anlagebänden*, Bonn: Bundespostministerium.

Lange, B-P. (1989), 'Landesmedienanstalten und "Aussenpluralismus" auf dem Prüfstand', *Media Perspektiven*, **5**, 268–76.

Mettler-Meibom, B. (1986), *Breitbandtechnologie*, Opladen: Westdeutscher Verlag.

Peasey, J. (1989), 'Der Markt für Fernsehprogramme in Westeuropa 1988 bis 2000', *Media Perspektiven*, **8**, 481–9.

Pretzsch, D. (1991), 'Werbefernsehboom hält an: die Entwicklung in den klassischen Medien 1990', *Media Perspektiven*, **3**, 147–60.

Prodöhl, H. (1987), 'Organisationsprobleme des lokalen Rundfunks: Das "Zwei-Säulen Modell" im nordrhein-westfälischen Landesrundfunkgesetz', *Media Perspektiven*, **4**, 229–38.

Programm zur Verbesserung der Rahmenbedingungen des privaten Rundfunkmarkts (1986), Bonn: Bundespresse- und Informationsamt.

Röper, H. (1989a), 'Stand der Verflechtung von privatem Rundfunk und Presse 1989', *Media Perspektiven*, **9**, 533–51.

Röper, H. (1989b), 'Formationen deutscher Medienmultis 1989', *Media Perspektiven*, **12**, 733–47.

Rundfunkgesetz für das Land Nordrhein-Westfalen vom 19 Januar 1987, reproduced in *Media Perspektiven Dokumentation* (1987), **2**, 120–38.

Schrape, K. and Kessler, M. (1988), 'Film Fernsehen-Video. Programmbedarf bis zum Jahr 2000', *Media Perspektiven*, **9**, 541–54.

SPD (1984), *Medienpolitik: eingeschränkte Öffnung für private Veranstalter: Beschlüsse des Essener Parteitages der SPD zur Medienpolitik*, Bonn: SPD.

Staatsvertrag zur Neuordnung des Rundfunkwesens (Rundfunkstaatsvertrag) vom 12 März 1987, reproduced in *Media Perspektiven Dokumentation* (1987), **2**, 81–8.

Stock, M. (1987), 'Ein fragwürdiges Konzept dualer Rundfunksysteme', *Rundfunk und Fernsehen*, **35**, 5–24.

Stock, M. (1990), 'Konvergenz im dualen Rundfunksystem?', *Media Perspektiven*, **12**, 748–57.

Stock, M. (1991), 'Das Nordrhein-Westfalen-Urteil des Bundesverfassungsgerichts', *Media Perspektiven*, **3**, 133–46.

Wöste, M. (1990), 'Nur knapp die Hälfte für Lizenzierung und Kontrolle: Die Einnahmen und Ausgaben der Landesmedienanstalten 1985 bis 1990', *Media Perspektiven*, **5**, 281–304.
Woldt, R., (1989), 'Mythos Kabel', *Media Perspektiven*, **10**, 589–605.
Zerdick, A. (1982), 'Ökonomische Interessen bei der Durchsetzung neuer Kommunikationstechniken', *Rundfunk und Fernsehen*, **30**, 478–90.
Zwischenbericht der Enquete-Kommission 'Neue Informations- und Kommunikationstechniken'; (28 March 1983), Drucksache 9/2442, Bonn: Bundestag.

5 The Politics of Regulatory Reform in German Telecommunications

Peter Humphreys

Reform of the telecommunications sector, like that of the financial markets (see chapter by Moran), has to be seen primarily as part of the Federal Republic's structural adjustment to transformations in an intensely competitive, and increasingly global, international political economy. Like the financial sector telecommunications reform demanded a capacity for an authoritative, strategic, and fairly dramatic break with entrenched traditional regulatory practices and structures. As with the financial sector the problem for the Federal Republic was that this kind of radical change of course appeared to be to a certain extent 'incongruent' with the country's policy-making 'style' (Bulmer and Humphreys, 1989).

German attempts to adopt policies of radical structural adjustment have encountered a number of significant problems inherent in a 'fragmented' political system characterized by decentralized government and weak central institutions (Scharpf, 1976; Friebe, 1984; Humphreys, 1989; Grande and Schneider, 1991). As a key to understanding this problem, the Federal Republic's political system might usefully be understood in terms of Arend Lijphart's (1984) influential and useful model of 'majoritarian' and 'consensual' democracies. Accordingly, the political system of the FRG can be described as having a complex mix of majoritarian and consensual traits. Despite the moderately adversarial polarity of political conflict, between large *Volksparteien* of the centre-left (SPD) and the centre-right (CDU/CSU), the political system has a number of pronounced consensual features: notably, a proportional election system (and a tradition of *Proporz* in the administration, representation on governmental commissions, and so on); federalism; strong bicameralism; a written constitution, which is strictly adhered to; a very strong form of judicial review in the Constitutional Court system; and it has always had coalition governments, albeit not typically grand coalitions. To this catalogue, which points to the fragmented as well as consensual nature of the political system, should be added the corporatist institutionalization of the major organized interests of labour and capital in the decision-making system (Lehmbruch and Schmitter, 1979 and 1982). Although important 'unifying' benefits may result from 'social partnership' (social peace, enhanced policy implementation and compliance, and so on), the scope for autonomous state action is further restricted to the extent that powerful socio-economic interests are 'incorporated' into political decision-making and regulatory structures.

The presence of such a large number of consensus mechanisms means that, perforce, majoritarian inputs – which might be a source of authoritative and strategic decisions – are seriously constrained. To be successful, reform proposals, however 'rational', have to be capable of acceptance by a broad coalition of domestic forces. To put it in slightly different terms, although the expert-fixated policy-making culture may attach great importance to rationality (Dyson, 1982), it is not enough that a policy is rational: it has also to cater to the requirements of a wide range of interests and so, in practice, rational policy-making is often muted by the demands of a complex process of partisan mutual adjustment.

Together, this highly fragmented political system, characterized by so many consensus features, combined with the constant requirement of negotiation and agreement between the different parts and parties of government, explains the incremental style of policy-making which has been a major hallmark of the West German system (Katzenstein, 1987). The federal government has first to agree a policy amongst its constituent parts (the coalition partners). The federal authorities in Bonn also have to negotiate and cooperate with the incorporated organized interests and the *Länder* which, in the country's federal system, are co-responsible for policy formulation and largely responsible for policy implementation/compliance. This simple structural fact is highly conducive to a pattern of bargaining and trade-offs which characterizes the West German policy style. As a result the system bears strong features of a mix of competition and cooperation, but in the last analysis in the absense of a commitment to maintain a broad consensus there is a danger that the system simply will not function. As a result, radical reform proposals are a comparative rarity: more usually, reform will be moderate and capable of achieving a new consensus.

In this connection, it has been commonplace to suggest that – unlike Britain after 1979 – the two great German alternances of government (the *Machtwechsel*) of 1969 and 1982–3 have resulted in allegedly very little substantive change ('*Wende*'). In a recent text on public policy in West

Germany, Klaus von Beyme has suggested that, in the Federal Republic, '... alternation leads to small policy changes' (von Beyme, 1985, p. 21). Similarly, one of the main themes of Katzenstein's (1987) work on West German public policy was the absence of large-scale policy change in the face of governmental changes. Von Beyme, Katzenstein, and indeed many others, are inclined to lay the burden of the explanation of this absence of significant *Wenden* on the incrementalism of policy-making, which is to be explained in turn by reference to West Germany's fragmented political structures.

However, to return to the crux of the problem of structural adjustment: incrementalism is arguably a very appropriate mode of reaction to routine events, yet dramatic technological, industrial and international market changes are anything but routine in their nature. Rapid and far-reaching technological, industrial and international market changes place a pressure on policy-makers to reject incrementalism in favour of a more 'heroic' style of policy-making. Before we turn to an empirical examination of how this problem has been solved in the telecommunications sector, it is first necessary to sketch out the imperatives for such a reform arising from these technological, industrial and international market developments; and, secondly, to examine the nature of the domestic resistance to change, namely the array of forces and factors which supported the *status quo* – in other words, the traditional consensus which had to be overcome, or at least transformed.

1. The Imperatives for Deregulation of Telecommunications

The first imperative for deregulation is technological in nature. A Kondratievian cluster of technological innovations has placed communication networks at the heart of the computerization revolution. The field of transmission has been revolutionized by the advent of optic-fibre cable, satellite technology and semi-conductors; similarly, that of switching by the transition from electro-mechanical to fully electronic, digital switching technology; and that of terminals by the microprocessor. In turn, technological 'convergence' with the computer sector has vastly expanded the scope of the telecommunications sector, which now embraces a proliferation of new transmission methods and value-added services. Telecommunications will provide no less than 'the central nervous system of the evolving world economy of the twenty-first century' (Snow, 1988, p. 153).

Information providers and suppliers of value-added services have joined forces with corporate business users, at both international and domestic levels, to call for a deregulation and liberalization of the monopolies of post and telecommunications authorities (PTTs). The corporate sector, including powerful multinational companies, has lobbied more and more vocally for a more favourable structure of telecommunications tariffs and much greater freedom to connect new privately-owned and -operated value-added communication systems. Moreover, technological convergence has meant that new industrial producers, mainly from the computer sector, have sought to enter the telecommunications markets, challenging the existing cartel of manufacturers with privileged access to the PTTs. The most commonly cited example of this new market entrant is the powerful US multinational IBM. As will be seen, both IBM Deutschland and the native German computer producer Nixdorf (since taken over by Siemens) joined a growing domestic lobby for market liberalization. Finally, in view of this technological convergence, and also given the climate of very rapid technological change, liberalization was rapidly being acknowledged by telecommunications experts, within PTTs and also national Research and Technology or Industry Ministries, as essential for states to remain competitive. Influential international organizations, like the OECD, were also preaching the message that the idea of a state telecommunications monopoly was apparently fast becoming anachronistic (OECD, 1983; OECD, 1987).

The need to remain competitive is rendered all the more acute in view of the second imperative, namely the massive expansion – and internationalization (globalization) – of the world's telecommunications market. In 1985 the world telecommunications market already amounted to no less than US$65 billion. One year later this figure had leapt to $83 billion (Snow, 1988, p. 153). In 1988 Bundespost experts estimated that by 1990 world-wide turnover was expected to reach $280 billion, equalling revenues from the automobile industry. They were led to conclude that '... information and communications technologies will have a major influence on the growth and productivity of [national] economies. Therefore, all industrialized countries must attempt to create the optimum conditions for growth. To achieve this objective and to stimulate these dynamic industries, existing structures must be modified' (Deutsche Bundespost, 1988, p. 3).

The direction of this 'modification' (as this chapter will argue the choice of the word 'modification' is revealing) was conditioned by a third imperative: namely, a global wave of deregulation and liberalization unleashed by the United States. In the early 1980s the deregulation and divestiture of AT & T in the United States, the liberation of IBM from its former anti-trust constraints and the removal of COMSAT's satellite monopoly effected a thorough-going liberalization of the US telecommunications markets. At the same time, the US began to bring enormous pressure to bear on European countries for reciprocal access to the latters' heavily protected markets. Very strong pressure was aimed at the notoriously protectionist Germans,

the US Congress even threatening market-closure to West German electronics imports in the absence of German liberalization.

Britain swiftly followed the US lead during the first half of the 1980s:
the dismemberment of the Post Office and privatization of British Telecom
in the United Kingdom, followed by a massive liberalization of the market
for value-added networks, was a further stimulus to her European competitors to adapt their regulatory structures to maintain competitiveness in
telecommunications services. Britain began to benefit from the perception
of foreign multinationals that it had the most liberal telecommunications
regime in Europe and accordingly offered the most attractive locational
conditions for their European headquarters (Morgan and Webber, 1986, p.
59). A wave of competitive deregulation promised to sweep across Western
Europe as first the Netherlands followed the British lead, then other countries
began to examine their national regulatory structures in the light of
Standortpolitik (location policy – policies to attract investment).

Meanwhile, in the latter half of the 1980s, the European Community
(EC), seeking to create a large internal market by the end of 1992, responded
by developing a programme of extensive liberalization of terminal equipment
sales and value-added services, opening up the highly protectionist public
procurement policies of its member states, and calling for the separation of
the regulatory and business sides of the PTTs' operations. Again West
Germany found itself in the eye of the storm, the object of considerable
external pressure: in the first instance, the European Commission pressured
the Bundespost, on more than one occasion, to open up its terminals equipment monopoly. The '1992' programme meant that German regulatory
practices and structures would have to change even more significantly
(*Financial Times*, 1987, p. IV).

2. The *Status Quo Ante* in the Federal Republic

What were, then, the essential characteristics of the West German regulatory 'style' in the telecommunications sector? Firstly, far from being purely
commercially orientated, the sector has traditionally been very strictly
regulated along 'public-service' principles, such as that of uniform charges
for services (*Tarifeinheit*) and universality of service provision
(*Flächenversorgung*). These principles have been deeply embedded in the
consciousness of politicians of all parties, imbued as they have commonly
been with the spirit of social contract, the post-war *Sozialstaat*. Accordingly, quite apart from the consensual configuration of the macro-political
system already mentioned, instruments of consensus and consultation have
played a most important role in the specific regulatory regime of the sector.

This has placed an additional important limitation on the capacity of governments to dictate policy (Woolcock et al., 1991, p. 6).

Perforce, policy has emerged as the result of detailed, often prolonged, and institutionalized – to a quite formal degree – processes of consultation with business, unions, consumers, and *Länder* authorities, these being apart from central government the main policy actors in the sector. In short, regulation has been 'corporatistic'. As Woolcock et al. (1991, p. 6) have emphasized, regulation has accordingly been geared much more towards long-term *Ordnungspolitik* than to close 'hands-on', discretionary interventions by the government of the day. In the telecommunications sector, typically, *Ordnungspolitik* has involved policy formulation by 'corporatist' commissions (such as the Witte Commission – see later); and policy implementation has been overseen by a special corporatistically composed supervisory body – the *Verwaltungsrat* – within the Bundespost.

According to Article 1 paragraph 1 of the Post Administration Law (*Postverwaltungsgesetz*) the Bundespost is directed by the Minister for Post and Telecommunications (Bundespost Minister), but this article contained the important clause 'with the cooperation of' the *Verwaltungsrat*. The *Verwaltungsrat* (Administrative Council) had to approve the Bundespost's budget and also had a considerable say in the matters of infrastructural and technical innovation and the fixing of tariffs. According to Webber (1987, p. 4), the '... council's composition reflect[ed] the generally high level of institutionalization of corporate interest-representation in the FRG'. Half of its 24 members came from the two sides of industry, five more were federal politicians and, significantly, another five had to be *Land* politicians. Moreover, the influence of Siemens, West Germany's giant telecommunications national champion firm, has been effectively quasi-institutionalized in the form of a special member of this body, one of two further members nominated by the Bundespost Minister from the realms of the telecom industry and the banks. The Bundestag's influence, on the other hand, was very limited indeed: generally confined to questioning the Bundespost Minister. According to Webber (1987, p. 4), '... there [was] wide scope for policy to be changed without changing laws'. In one sense then the Bundespost enjoyed a large degree of institutional autonomy. It could effectively bypass parliament, although it remained subject to the superior control of the Bundespost Minister himself. Against this, though, established organized corporate and provincial interests exerted considerable influence through their representation within the Bundespost's supervisory body, the *Verwaltungsrat*.

Secondly, the role of markets and governments of the day alike have been limited by West Germany's public law tradition, which is reflected in a large body of administrative law (the aforementioned *Post-*

verwaltungsgesetz); and even by constitutional law which has determined the limits to government marketization of the sector. The Bundespost was actually part of the state administration; under the direction of the Bundespost Ministry, it did not even have the semi-autonomy of a public corporation. Moreover, state ownership of the Bundespost was enshrined in the West German constitution (Basic Law, Article 73). This status could only be changed by constitutional amendment, which required a two-thirds majority in both houses of parliament. Under the West German constitution and law, the Bundespost had the task of 'serving the common good', and consideration of the interests of all users was part of its public responsibility. To this end, the Bundespost possessed a legal monopoly of the provision of all telecommunications networks and services (OECD, 1987, p. 238; Morgan and Webber, 1986, p. 68).

Thirdly, often behind the veil of 'public service', regulatory policy in the telecommunications sector has been geared towards the pursuit of industrial policy goals. In fact, during the 1980s West Germany was increasingly criticized for being a 'fortress on the Rhine', so protected were its telecommunications industry and markets (Webber, 1987). The telecommunications sector was dominated by a huge state telecommunications authority, the Bundespost (the Federal Post Office). Through its telecommunications monopoly, the Bundespost dominated the supply side of the West German telecommunications markets. According to Grande (1987, p. 4), '... the Bundespost purchased 100 per cent of the national supply of switching equipment, telegraphy equipment and telephone mainstations; as well as 80 per cent of transmission facilities'. In fact, '... the only relevant market in which it [was] not the dominant purchaser [was] that for PABXs, where its share of demand [was] around one-fifth' (Webber, 1987, p, 6). The Bundespost's policy for public procurement was notoriously protectionist *vis-à-vis* a privileged coterie of German (or German-based) suppliers. For example, four West German companies – Siemens, SEL (the German subsiduary of ITT), DTW (Deutsche Telephonwerke) and T & N (Telenorma, part-owned by Bosch) – entirely controlled the market for switching equipment (Siemens dominating with a market share of 46 per cent). The markets for equipment were also similarly concentrated on a larger number of German or German-based firms (Grande, 1987, p. 4). The Bundespost maintained highly incestuous relations with these 'client' firms whose position in both domestic and international markets was directly related to the Bundespost's preferential treatment (subsidies, research grants and massive state contracts). These relations were both formal and institutional through the Central Association of the Electronics Industry (*Zentralverband der Elekrotechnischen Industrie*, ZVEI) and informal and bilateral between the Bundespost and the individual firms themselves (Morgan and Webber,

1986, p. 69). Under these circumstances, competition within the West German domestic markets was weak. Market forces were further inhibited by consultation and agreements among the national producers and the Bundespost about market shares, public procurement, and telecommunication standards and specifications. Of particular interest were the close informal links that existed between the national telecommunications producers and the Bundespost and its Central Office for Telecommunications Technology (the *Fernmeldetechnisches Zentralamt*, FTZ), as the result of which foreign producers were effectively debarred from market entry to a considerable extent (Grande, 1987, p. 4; and Monopolkommission, 1981).

The Bundespost's power derived not only from its administrative status and its considerable institutional autonomy, but also from the fact that it was the largest economic concern in the FRG (indeed in Western Europe). In 1987 it had over half a million employees and a staggering annual turnover of DM50 billion. In the period 1975–80 alone the Bundespost invested between DM6 billion and DM10 billion per annum, rising to DM12 billion in 1981, and no less than DM18 billion in 1987 (Humphreys, 1990, p. 196). This massive investment capacity gave the Bundespost considerable political power, which was further strengthened by its aforementioned dominance of the demand side of the telecommunications sector. Moreover, the business policy of the Bundespost had a great significance for the development of the wider economic policies of the FRG. According to Webber (1987, p. 7), '... its investments, some 90 per cent of which [were] in telecommunications, regularly amount[ed] to between one-fifth and a quarter, or more, of those carried out in the whole of German manufacturing industry' (by the state). The Bundespost also enjoyed an unusual degree of fiscal independence. According to Article 3 of the Post Administration Law (*Postverwaltungsgesetz* or PostVwG), the Bundespost was responsible for its own budget (with the one constraint that the Finance Minister had to agree with it).

Most significantly, the Bundespost's institutional autonomy was further strengthened by a particular feature of the West German political system: namely, the principle of ministerial autonomy (the *Ressortprinzip*), which is established by Article 65 of the West German constitution. According to this Article, ministers have a large measure of autonomy to run their departments without outside interference (always, of course, within the Federal Chancellor's general policy guidelines). The result has been described as the 'sectorization of policy-making' (Bulmer and Paterson, 1987, 1988). Indeed, as will be seen, this latter feature is very important in explaining both 'why' and 'how' the considerable obstacles to reform, flowing from the fragmented political system and the entrenched nature of the coalition for the *status quo*, were overcome. To no small extent the telecommunications reform which was to emerge from the complex policy process bears many significant hallmarks of having been tailored to the new market and technological requirements by the Bundespost technocrats themselves, and implemented by the Bundespost Minister not least with the future interests of the Bundespost in a more competitive environment in mind.

3. The Obstacles to Regulatory Change

Clearly, in the past at least, the Bundespost itself had had a compelling institutional self-interest in maintaining its monopoly status. This was reinforced by the opposition to any change from the German Post and Telecommunications Workers' Union (the *Deutsche Postgewerkschaft*, DPG). The latter was both highly organized and incorporated into the policy community, not least through its institutionalized representation in the Bundespost's *Verwaltungsrat* (see above). Several authorities on the subject have drawn attention to the special industrial strength of the DPG, which organizes no less than three-quarters of the Bundespost's workers (the West German average is 35 per cent unionization) (Grande, 1987, p. 8; Herrmann, 1985, pp. 285–300; and Webber 1987, p. 7). The privileged insider group of leading telecommunications manufacturing companies also had an obvious motive for supporting the maintenance of the Bundespost's monopoly and firm opposition to any privatization or liberalization of the West German telecommunications markets. In addition, there existed a larger number of small and medium-sized West German equipment suppliers believing that their very survival depended upon the maintenance of the Bundespost monopoly.

Among the political parties too, there was considerable support for the *status quo*. Firstly, the Social Democratic Party (SPD) was intensely committed to a regulated economy. The SPD had an interventionist policy orientation and, even after its abandonment of its 'class-party' (*Klassenpartei*) image in the 1950s, had maintained its identification with the organized labour movement. Certainly, the SPD subscribed to the notion of the social market economy, built up during the Federal Republic's formative years of CDU/CSU political hegemony. Yet at the same time the SPD remained firmly committed to the principle of organizing and regulating markets. Moreover, the SPD remained concerned to represent employee interests and to give important support to the public sector and to public-service principles. Secondly, the CDU/CSU had always promoted what might be called 'social capitalism' characterized by a primacy to free enterprise and business but, very significantly, modified by a concern for social peace and welfare and not least a concern for the electoral support they gained from low-income earners.

By no means was the strength of this group-political support for the *status quo* the only factor for strict state regulation. It is also necessary to consider the very politico-economic culture of the country. In this respect, one of the major background factors impeding deregulation and liberalization was the traditional role of the state in regulating the West German economy. Jeremy Leaman (1989) has argued persuasively that it is important not to be taken in by the mythology surrounding the 'social market economy': the West German state has always played a far stronger role in managing the economy than is often realized. Similarly, Manfred Schmidt (1988, p. 147) has pointed to the '... high degree of political control to which West Germany's economy and society are exposed'. This can be explained, in turn, in terms of the country's 'policy of the middle way', namely its unique path between 'Social Democratic welfare capitalism' and 'market capitalism'. Schmidt rightly points to the (often ignored) state interventionist component of post-1949 policy which can '... at least partly be attributed to the tradition of state-led industrialization, the tradition of a conservative-reformist welfare state, and the relative weakness of a *laissez-faire* ideology' in Germany (Schmidt, 1988, p. 144).

4.   Domestic Pressures for Reform

Domestic criticism of the way the telecommunications sector had been organized throughout the post-war period had been mounting ever since the late 1970s. One major charge laid against the Bundespost monopoly was that it had been run by the Bundespost bureaucrats largely for their own purposes of institutional aggrandizement and other organizational-political goals. Moreover, the constitutionally prescribed political control supplied by the Bundespostminister was also open to the poignant criticism that the ministry itself had fallen victim to a bureaucratic kind of 'agency capture': successive ministers were felt to have become pawns of the Bundespost's technocrats.

More importantly still, the group politics of the telecommunications sector was changing dramatically. During the 1980s there developed a powerful domestic coalition for reform. In the language of policy analysis, a new and dynamic 'policy network' emerged to challenge the established and entrenched 'policy network' (Wilks and Wright, 1987, pp. 275–313; Wright, 1991). In the first place, West German business users of telecommunications services began to demand more competition in the supply of services in the belief that this would lead to lower prices and rental charges.

Both the influential German Chamber of Industry and Commerce (*Deutscher Industrie- und Handelstag,* DIHT) and the powerful Federation of German Industry (*Bundesverband der Deutschen Industrie,* BDI) increasingly voiced the rising frustration with the Bundespost monopoly of companies in both the service and manufacturing sectors. The demands of telecommunication user firms were also expressed through the specialized Association of Bundespost Users (*Verband der Postbenutzer,* VPB), a very bitter adversary of the Bundespost and a champion of radical policies of privatization and liberalization. In the second place, computer manufacturers – most notably, Nixdorf and IBM – which had previously been largely excluded from the Bundespost's privileged coterie of suppliers became proponents of privatization and liberalization (Morgan and Webber, 1986, p. 72).

A third factor was the stimulus to reform which now came from the German *Monopolkommission* (Anti-Trust Commission), one of the many autonomous para-public bodies which play an important role in institutionalizing relations between the state and the market in the Federal Republic's fragmented political system (Katzenstein, 1987). Authoritative interventions by such bodies are very important for introducing direction and order into the otherwise convoluted policy process (Bulmer and Humphreys, 1989, p. 187). In 1980, the eminent *Monopolkommission* produced a trenchant criticism of the procurement policy of the Bundespost and the domination of the Bundespost in the telecommunications equipment markets. In particular, the *Monopolkommission* questioned the Bundespost's 'double role' as a player and referee in the West German telecommunications markets. The *Monopolkommission* demanded no less than an extensive liberalization of the terminals market. Beyond this it recommended the introduction of a limited degree of competition for telecommunications services offered by the Bundespost (Monopolkommission, 1981, pp. 91–110).

According to Schneider and Werle (1989, p. 40), this report of the *Monopolkommission* came at a highly unpropitious time for the Bundespost. Its competence was already being publicly questioned because of mistaken investment decisions concerning the adoption in the 1970s of an obsolete electronic switching system, the EWS-A system supplied by Siemens. In this case, over-reliance on the national champion had seemed to demonstrate the Bundespost's bureaucratic and monopolistic inertia. The report of the *Monopolkommission* seemed to confirm growing fears that the Bundespost's dominant role in the industry was leading to complacency and inefficiency. The report gave powerful expert support to the fast growing policy network pushing for deregulation and liberalization (Humphreys, 1988, p. 3).

A fourth important factor was political/ideological in nature. In 1982 the Social–Liberal (SPD/FDP) coalition, which had ruled in Bonn since 1969, was replaced by a new Christian–Liberal (CDU/CSU/FDP) coalition with a putatively radical neo-liberal programme. In tune with the global *Zeitgeist* of the 1980s, the new government appeared to espouse a dramatic reduction of state intervention and a renewal of the free-market economy. This promised *Wende* seemed to herald a significant departure from the previous government's more state-interventionist approach to the problem of structural adjustment. The CDU/CSU/FDP slogan for the 1983 election had been 'more market, less state' (*Mehr Markt, weniger Staat*).

In this the role of the pivotal Liberal party, the FDP, was crucial. The latter party, which had itself been responsible for the *Machtwechsel* (by changing coalition partners), had veered observably to the 'free-market' right during the 1980s. It was now once again a full-blooded continental style neo-liberal Liberal party (rather than a more socially orientated force akin to the British Liberals) pledged to the restoration of free-market principles and private entrepreneurial initiative to the West German economy. The FDP now went so far as to call for the complete removal of the Bundespost's network monopoly and exclusion of the Bundespost from the terminals market. Some Liberals even proposed privatization of the Bundespost itself.

Importantly, the FDP Economics Minister Count Otto Lambsdorff was an enthusiastic proponent of the new economic liberalism (the ministry being, in Dyson's words, the 'guardian of the social market economy'). Given the political will, the Economics Ministry could bring a certain measure of veto-power to bear on the development of telecommunications policy. The Economics Minister had to approve all telecommunications charges and thus had an important say over the introduction of new services. In fact, the latter issue had caused growing tension between the Bundespost and the Economics Ministry ever since the mid 1970s when the Liberals took the Ministry over from the SPD.

Finally, the Bundespost's authority and legitimacy had come under attack at the hands of the new Bundespostminister, Christian Schwarz-Schilling (CDU). Admirably qualified for the post, Schwarz-Schilling had occupied himself in the twin fields of media and telecommunications for years leading up to the *Machtwechsel*, having been the chairman of the CDU media committee since 1975. However unfairly, Schwarz-Schilling's motivations came in for serious questioning when he launched an expensive national cable programme in 1983. The wisdom of the sheer scale of investment in this programme – no less than DM1 billion per annum – was widely criticized, even from within the ranks of the CDU. Moreover, the suggestion that the Bundespost should begin to allow the involvement of private cable companies in this exercise became the object of some damaging political sniping in view of the fact that the new Bundespost Minister himself had had an interest in one such company, although in fact he had actually sold his share before taking his ministerial oath (Bruce, 1987; *Der Spiegel*, Nr. 45, 1982, pp. 124–6).

5. The Witte Report

Despite the government's promise of 'more market and less state' (*Mehr Markt, weniger Staat*), the CDU/CSU/FDP coalition government was in fact deeply divided internally over telecommunications policy. The so-called social committees of the CDU's left wing subscribed to the corporatist, consensus-orientated model of political economy and favoured state intervention and employee protection. This current received some support too from the CDU Minister of Research and Technology, Heinz Riesenhüber (although he accepted the need for some liberalization in the cause of technological innovation). In addition, there were a significant number of CDU/CSU members of the Bundestag who were less than enthusiastic about liberalization and deregulation for the simple reason that, as Morgan and Webber (1986, p. 71) have put it, the CDU/CSU '… were parties of the countryside'. These parliamentarians feared that radical reform of the telecommunications sector might lead to higher charges and inferior service provision in the more rural constituencies, the conservative heartlands. Moreover, by no means all of the CDU/CSU members of the Bundestag were won over by the neo-liberals (or seriously expected neo-liberal rhetoric to be carried through into practical policies). The CDU/CSU were not instinctively neo-liberal parties. As Christian Democratic parties, they contained strong elements that continued to adhere to a certain ingrained respect for regulation – in particular, the Christian 'moral conservatives' (*Wertkonservativen*). Finally, the CSU was keen to promote Bavarian interests in the *status quo*. Bavaria, dominated by the CSU, hosted a large concentration of the established telecommunications and electronics industry. Munich was the home-base of Siemens in particular and benefited much from Bundespost investment.

The characteristic first step in the West German policy process is to establish a commission of inquiry – in other words, to have recourse to the experts. The establishment of a government commission comprising representatives from trade and industry, science and politics to explore the restructuring of telecommunications was first mooted in the government's 'Concept for Promoting the Development of Microelectronics, Information and Communications Technologies' of 14 March 1984. One year later, on 13 March 1985, the so-called Witte Commission was formally set up in order to examine 'present and future tasks in telecommunications'. The corporatistic Commission consisted of 12 members: five representatives of trade and industry, the industrial associations and the trade unions (one each for the latter), three representatives of the sciences, and four representatives of the political parties (one each for CDU, CSU, FDP and SPD – no Green). The Commission became known as the 'Witte Commission' after its chairman, Professor Eberhard Witte, who had been nominated by the federal government. Particular consideration was to be given to both 'national and international aspects'; 'scope, limits and structure of government tasks in telecommunications'; 'organizational, economic and legal prerequisites for the efficient fulfilment of government tasks by the Deutsche Bundespost'; and a 'framework to be defined by the government for the fulfilment of private enterprise tasks'. In other words, the Commission was mandated to examine the entire future balance of state regulation and free market in the telecommunications sector. The Witte Commission presented its report to the federal government over two years later, on 16 September 1987.

The majority of its members voted in favour of moderate, rather than revolutionary, change. This included the separation of the (loss-making) postal and the (highly profitable) telecommunications branches of the Bundespost, and also of its 'sovereign' (regulatory) tasks and the 'entrepreneurial' tasks. It was suggested that, at least for the time being, the Bundespost should retain its monopoly over the telecommunications network. Within the Commission there had been no majority for a proposal that licences be issued to allow for network competition, but there was a very clear majority in favour of providing leased lines on 'fair and competitive conditions'. Moreover, the report suggested that prices would have to become more realistic and competitive and orientated to costs rather than the externalities of public-service obligations. In the event of the Bundespost's failure to curb the excesses of its monopoly situation, the Commission recommended that the government reserve the option of intervention to introduce competition in network supply. Moreover, the report suggested that the Bundespost's monopoly should be reviewed every three years. As for equipment supply and services, it was argued that the Bundespost should merely retain a monopoly of telephone equipment and services; in all other services, there should be more competition. On the other hand, the Bundespost should be allowed to compete with private systems in the supply of new 'unregulated' services beyond those basic services called 'monopoly' and 'regulated' services which it was obliged to provide (Witte, 1987).

The majorities in favour of all 47 of its detailed recommendations were deceptive. In reality, there was no consensus. Albert Stegmüller, the trade union representative on the Commission, voted against it and instead produced a categoric statement of dissent (*abweichende Stellungnahme*) in which he complained about the 'one-sided composition' of the Commission and laid out his main lines of opposition to the proposed reform. He argued in effect that telecommunications was a classic case of natural monopoly and should be run along public-service lines rather than give primacy to market mechanisms. Peter Glotz, the SPD representative, also attached a dissenting note (*abweichende Vorstellung*), although in his case he noted that the report contained much to be agreed with and even greeted. However, one of his main reservations was that by weakening the Bundespost the proposed reform might prove to be a competitive handicap for German industry, and that it tended to favour big business over small and medium-sized firms and the Bundespost's larger customers over smaller ones (Witte, 1987, pp. 140–9).

On the other hand, no fewer than four representatives registered a 'special vote' (*Sondervotum*), welcoming the 'overwhelming part' of the reform proposal but also stating that in their view it did not go far enough. They complained that as presently constituted the reform would foreclose to the market up to 90 per cent of the telecommunications sector measured in terms of the Bundespost's returns. They defended the virtues of free competition and advocated a more dramatic demonopolization and marketization, including the introduction of competing networks or, if this should prove to be politically unrealizable, at least the legal right to private use of a range of new transmission systems. They also recommended opening all services including voice telephony to competition. These four were the representative of the FDP, the president of the BDI, the representative of the banking sector (a leading executive of the Commerzbank) and lastly an academic jurist from Tübingen university. Notably, the representative of the Peak Association of the Electronics Industry (*Zentralverband der Elekrotechnischen Industrie* – ZVEI) did not number among them (Witte, 1987, pp. 134–9).

After the presentation of the report the initiative passed directly to the Bundespost Minister reflecting the already-mentioned very high degree of ministerial autonomy (the *Ressortprinzip*) in the West German governmental system and policy process. In the German legislative process government bills are first produced in the form of an 'experts draft' (*Referentenentwurf*) by experts in the relevant ministry before being discussed and voted in cabinet (Southern and Paterson, 1991, p. 112). Schwarz-Schilling had until the beginning of 1988 to present an outline for new legislation to the cabinet. He then had until early 1989 to bring about a corresponding reorganization of West Germany's post and telecommunications services which fulfilled the requirements of modern realities and yet was also politically saleable. Schwarz-Schilling himself immediately gave some indication of the main directions of the restructuring that he would seek to pursue with the help of the Witte report's recommendations. It quickly became clear that Schwarz-Schilling was determined to ignore the more radical minority recommendations of the representatives of the FDP and the BDI among others. He made it quite clear that the Bundespost would essentially retain its monopoly of the telecommunications network and voice telephony, though the scope for liberalization in other areas was to be seriously explored (Schwarz-Schilling, 1987).

This seemed to suggest that, while keen to introduce an important measure of long-overdue reform, Schwarz-Schilling also remained sensitive both to the need to defend the Bundespost's most fundamental interests and to the emotive public welfare considerations of the issue. If he needed any, Schwarz-Schilling could also point to a number of persuasive 'alibis' for the need for striking a cautious balance. The most obvious was the disruptive power of the German Post and Telecommunications Workers' Union (DPG) which had been quick to condemn most of the Witte report's recommendations and had meanwhile mobilized a large-scale action campaign against the Witte proposals. The SPD opposition and his own party's CSU coalition partner alike were also opposed to any large degree of change. Finally, the powerful Finance Minister Gerhard Stoltenberg (CDU), who had been an advocate in principle of reform, had very pragmatic reasons to be cautious about its extent. The exchequer had been accustomed to draw upon a strong and profitable Bundespost as a healthy source of government revenue and Stoltenberg was aware that this would be lost if the Bundespost were privatized or weakened by too much competition.

On 1 March 1988 the Bundespostminister published the draft Post Structure Law or *Poststrukturgesetz* (more properly entitled the 'Bill to Restructure the Post and Telecommunications and the German Bundespost' – *Gesetz zur Neustrukturierung des Post- und Fernmeldewesens und der Deutschen Bundespost*), together with the 'Government's Plan for the Reorganization of the Telecommunications Markets' (*Konzeption der Bundesregierung zur Neuordnung des Telekommunikationsmarktes*). On 11 May 1988 the cabinet approved the draft with a few minor modifications. The reform had two main emphases. Firstly, there should occur a considerable deregulation and liberalization of telecommunications markets. Secondly, the German Bundespost (DBP) should receive an entirely new corporate constitution with the aim that it should thereby be in a better position to hold its own against the increased domestic and foreign competition. However, it is most important to note that the bill did not plan to deliver the Bundespost into the hands of private interests, nor did it foresee the transformation of the Bundespost into a commercial joint-stock company (*Kapitalgesellschaft*), not least since such steps were expressly forbidden by Article 87 (Para. 1, Clause 1) of the Basic Law.

Yet the bill did aim to significantly reduce the influence of the state in favour of private enterprise in accordance with the government's slogan of 'more market, less state' (*Mehr Markt, weniger Staat*). The bill now foresaw the following measures of liberalization. The terminals markets were to be fully opened up by 1 July 1990 at the latest. The Bundespost's former monopoly was to be opened up to new private-sector entrants in all fields of telecommunications services. However, an important exception was the telephone service. It should be pointed out that the latter still accounted for about 90 per cent of the Bundespost's returns (although of course this percentage was due to fall as value-added services became increasingly important). In addition, the Bundespost's current network monopoly was to be reduced in order to allow for some low-bit-rate data transmission by satellite and also mobile radio telephony. Finally, the bill planned the reorganization of the Bundespost itself. It foresaw the separation of the Bundespost's regulatory function from its operational side and aimed to divide the latter into three more autonomous public enterprises – respectively for postal services (*Postdienst*), banking services (*Postbank*) and telecommunications (*Telekom*).

6. The Bill's Passage Through Parliament

In accordance with Article 76, Para. 2, of the Basic Law, the draft began its legislative passage through Parliament by being presented to the Bundesrat for its first reading. It then proceeded to the Bundestag for further readings, during which stage it was considered by the Bundestag's committee on post and telecommunications, before being passed back to the Bundesrat one last time (Southern and Paterson, 1991, p. 112). These various stages presented important hurdles even to a government with a disciplined Bundestag majority. The Bundesrat provided the *Länder* with an opportunity to present an 'opinion', propose modifications and even to obstruct the bill. The committee stage, the importance of which in the German system should not be underestimated, similarly presented considerable scope for criticism and amendments from a very wide range of social, economic and political actors. According to Schneider and Werle (1989, p. 43), more than fifty organizations participated in the Bundestag committee's hearings.

Faced with other very bitter battles over the proposed health reform and a tax reform, both of which were likely to involve hugely unpopular increases in consumer taxes and charges, the government was anxious to depoliticize the potentially explosive telecommunications issue as far as possible and to present it as a purely technocratic matter. The SPD opposition, on the other hand, sought to polarize the issue, almost seeming to question the very basis of the reform. According to the *Proporz* principle of proportional allocation of Bundestag committee chairmanships, their party's spokesman on media and telecommunications, Peter Paterna MdB, was the chairman of the parliamentary committee for post and telecommunications. Paterna voiced doubts as to whether the reformed Bundespost would be able to withstand competition from foreign multinational companies. He expressed reservations too about whether those services which the Bundespost would still offer after the reorganization would be capable of even covering their costs under the new circumstances. Emotively he predicted that there would be an inevitable rise in charges to the consumer. Most revealingly, Paterna alleged that the bill actually served the interests of big business: namely giant companies such as Siemens, which stood to continue to benefit first as suppliers, secondly as corporate customers. Supported by the Greens, the SPD raised fears about an expected decline in consumer services and a substantial laying off of Bundespost employees.

These criticisms were echoed, beyond the parliamentary arena, by the Postal Workers' Union (DPG), the German Trades Union Federation (DGB) and also the Association of Consumers' Organizations (*Arbeitgemeinschaft der Verbraucherverbände*). These groups anticipated negative effects of the bill for telecommunications employees and consumers. They played up to significant social reservations about deregulation, liberalization, and technological rationalization more generally. On the other hand, such fears were dismissed by the business associations and by many experts. Professor Witte lent his weight to the counter-argument that all categories of consumer, including those in rural areas, stood to gain considerably. Bundespostminister Schwarz-Schilling himself sought to popularize the case for the reform by emphasising the vital importance '... of not falling further behind in markets which according to all prognoses would within a few years amount to a sector of as great importance to the national economy as the automobile industry' (Jentsch, 1989, p. 8). It is already very clear, then, that the proposed reform was judged to be entirely compatible with the developing perceptions of strategic interest of German big business and certainly not a threat to very powerful vested industrial (Siemens) and organizational (Bundespost technocrats) interests.

In fact by themselves the SPD and Green opposition parties were in no position to overturn the bill since both houses of parliament had government majorities. Grounds for greater concern arose from the fact that for a while it appeared uncertain whether the government could rely on the sheer weight of its majorities to win the day. Within the ruling coalition itself the balance of forces for and against reform had not been entirely clear-cut. In the weeks following Schwarz-Schilling's publication of the reform proposals and the bill's adoption by the cabinet there arose some speculation that the reform might be obstructed by the *Länder* in the Bundesrat. The opposition of SPD *Länder* was stark, but the full support of the CDU/CSU *Länder* was not completely assured. There existed a distinct possibility at least that some of the CDU/CSU *Länder* might swing their weight behind the SPD opposition in the Bundesrat since the deregulatory reform proposals threatened the degree of influence which they, as provincial bodies, had been accustomed to enjoy in the Bundespost's management. According to the old structure, the *Länder* had delegated five representatives to the Bundespost's Administrative Council (*Verwaltungsrat*). Moreover, most of the *Länder* at least had an obvious interest in defending the public service principle of equitable infrastructural provision by the Bundespost (and no single *Land* was bold enough to risk breaking this consensus since even the 'sunrise' industrial *Länder* of Bavaria and Baden–Württemberg were also very rural).

In particular, the CDU's sister party, the CSU in Bavaria, could not be seen as an entirely reliable quantity. As already suggested, in the case of the CSU a major vested interest was at stake. Siemens was based in Bavaria and also the Bundespost's biggest supplier by far. It had been an understandable long-standing concern of CSU politicians that any reform should not undermine the privileged position which that firm had been accustomed to enjoy with the Bundespost. Accordingly, the CSU might be expected to be a source of attempts to obstruct or lame the reform. If so, the CSU would after all merely be acting true to form in seeking to use its leverage within the governing coalition to extract concessions for Bavarian interests. However, in the event, it turned out that such worries were misplaced.

In fact, due to its increasingly international orientation, Siemens was embracing the partial-liberalization option (Grande and Schneider, 1991, p. 36). It had already begun to feel embarrassed by the blatant degree of incestuous relations it had been accustomed to enjoy with the Bundespost. The company had become the main butt of US complaints about German protectionism in telecommunications markets. As already mentioned, these complaints had even been translated into threats against the Germans of retaliatory market closure in the US, a market of prime importance to the future plans of Siemens. Nor obviously did Siemens want to antagonize the European Commission (EC) since the company obviously had very major ambitions within the European 'internal market' as well. Moreover, Siemens itself was keenly diversifying into the computer sector (for example, acquiring Nixdorf) and consequently its perception about its interests in regulation was changing. Confident about its own ability to exploit new markets, particularly in post-1992 Europe, the company was amenable to the reform so long as the Bundespost's investment power from which it was accustomed to benefit remained high. The actual CSU stance reflected faithfully this position. After all, the reform proposals fell far short of a thorough-going privatization and liberalization and retained an important role for the Bundespost. Furthermore, parliamentary amendments were able to ensure an enduring important role for the *Länder* representatives within the latter's governing structures (see later).

The bill therefore received an easier ride through parliament than many had expected. Arguably, the most serious potential sources of opposition – the interests of the *Länder* and the CSU (representing Bavarian interests) – appeared to be satisfied by the moderate nature of the reform proposals and the guarantees of their continuing influence. The industrial lobby was clearly confident that the reform as actually constituted would not harm its vested interest in the survival of a powerful Bundespost. The political resources available to the opposition were weakened by the actual balance of parliamentary forces at the time (although in late 1989 – just too late – the SPD would have gained a brief window of opportunity to at least delay the reform when the Lower Saxony *Land* elections delivered it a short-lived majority in the Bundesrat, although not a blocking majority). The more fundamental objections from the parliamentary opposition were therefore swept aside. Finally, it might be suggested, the reform's moderation had itself been dictated by the Bundespost's own very central role in drawing up the legislation. Former Witte Commission member Wernhard Möschel (1988, p. 15) commented on the draft bill: '... the reform should not have been left to the overall control [*Federführung*] of the Bundespost.... A reform by the Post not primarily oriented to the Post's interests would have presupposed the mentality of sacrificial lambs'. SPD spokesman Peter Paterna is even alleged to have complained that consultation papers and reports were only made available when leaked and that amendments supported by the CDU/CSU appeared to stem directly from the Bundespost Ministry itself (Buchwald, 1989). According to detailed empirical research by Schneider and Werle (1989, pp. 46–7), the Bundespost Ministry was generally perceived to be the central policy actor in the reform process by the other relevant actors. Yet the central role of the Bundespost merely reflected the *Ressortprinzip* in the German governmental system and the resultant 'sectorization of policy-making' in the FRG (Bulmer and Paterson, 1987 and 1988). Moreover, the *Ressortprinzip* and sectorization worked against the more fragmentary pressures of the German political system and delivered a necessary coherence to an otherwise convoluted policy process.

7. A Critical Evaluation of the Reform

The bill was enacted in April, and the law came into effect from 1 July 1989. The actual extent of deregulation and liberalization was far more limited than, for instance, in Britain and the United States. The reform has been aptly described by Grande and Schneider (1991, p. 13) as a 'middle way' between the paths of countries with radical reforms like these countries and those which sought to retain their telecommunications monopolies. Firstly, the bill had contained no proposals to privatize the Bundespost. The West German constitution itself prevented any sell-off in the fashion of British Telecom since it stipulated that the Bundespost was an 'administration owned by the federation'. Secondly, no competition was introduced in the supply of the basic network, and the law did not adopt the Witte Commission's recommendation that this monopoly should be reviewed every three years. Thirdly, voice telephony remained a monopoly (in these latter two respects, British liberalization had presented British Telecom with significant competition in the shape of Mercury, – and most recently with the promise of further competition from other service providers). In the words of one British telecommunications analyst, '... the door to Europe's largest telecommunications market [was] being half-opened to competition' (Dixon, 1989, p. XII).

The law did open the way for free competition in the provision of terminal equipment and value-added services such as fax, data-transfer and other non-voice services. In the fast growing fields of radio paging and mobile radio/telephone networks there would be complete liberalization. Yet here there was a crying need anyway for change in Germany's own interests. In particular, Germany had been relatively backward in value-added services, which undoubtedly offered a large potential for private sector initiative and innovation. Even here, though, there remained cause for reasonable doubt as to whether the new regime would be able to guarantee entirely free competition in practice (Dixon, 1989, p. XII). Bundespost Minister Schwarz-Schilling had repeatedly emphasized that the Bundespost would continue to remain heavily involved in this promising field, inevitably as network provider and service carrier but also as likely co-partner. From the point of view of competition policy a strong case could be made for the exclusion of the Bundespost from these markets in view of its sheer size and strength together with its ability to use its remaining monopolies as a springboard for innovation in the field of value-added services. In particular, the Bundespost would still be able to draw on the massive resources that it derived from these monopolies in order to cross-subsidize its other existing and new services (it was in this spirit that the *Monopolkommission* had earlier called for the Bundespost's exclusion from the markets for terminal equipment). The Bundespost thus emerged from the reform with its in-built competitive advantage largely intact, which in turn might well be seen as a considerable deterrent to new market entrants – a matter which the EC Commission may yet be moved to rule more strongly on.

The mechanisms for approval and licensing of new services and equipment arguably provided even greater cause for doubting the likely extent of actual liberalization. The law did not provide for the institution of an unambiguously independent regulatory body – of the kind embodied in Oftel in Britain and arguably demanded by the spirit of the EC's '1992' programme. Instead, the matters of regulatory policy generally, and equipment approval and standard setting particularly, as well as the all-important field of licensing, all remained within the domain of the Bundespost Ministry. In this connection, it is entirely reasonable to question whether the Bundespost Minister can become a genuine 'referee' – as true liberalization implies – rather than a 'player', while he remains responsible for the largest state concern in Western Europe. This particular aspect of the reform has even been described as a 'façade' by a former member of the Witte Commission, the Tübingen academic jurist Wernhard Möschel (1988, pp. 14–15). In Möschel's words, '... the Post Minister remains the *Konzernchef*'. Moreover, nothing in the law's provisions suggested that the Bundespost would not continue to maintain its long-standing symbiotic relationship with leading West German electronic firms (for example, Siemens). Indeed, as suggested, CSU acquiescence in the bill's passage through parliament might be taken to be a useful indicator of the likely real limits of the reform package. As will be seen, very recent reports of Bundespost licensing plans for investment in the 'five new *Länder*' of the former GDR – if confirmed – would seem to testify to such limits.

Against this, the law did adopt the Witte Report's recommendations for a separation of the loss-making postal services, and of the Bundespost's banking services, from the telecommunications branch. The law divided the Bundespost into three businesses: *Telekom*; *Postdienst* (the postal service); and *Postbank* (the banking service). Apart from rationalizing these three areas of the Bundespost's activity, this structural component of the reform was intended to free the commercial side of the Bundespost's operations from close political control. However not too much should be read into even this aspect of the reform. On the one hand, according to the law each of these new enterprises would be managed by its own board of managers. On the other, the three businesses would remain legally and economically linked within the Bundespost. In addition, they would be responsible to a common directorate (*Direktorium*) which would answer in turn to the Bundespost Minister. Parallel to this was a special infrastructural council (*Infrastrukturrat*), composed of 11 political appointees each from the Bundestag and Bundesrat. This body retained an important say in matters such as new investment and tariff charges and therefore inherited important powers of the former Administrative Council (*Verwaltungsrat*).

This latter provision reflected the success of the *Länder,* represented in the Bundesrat, in imposing a significant amendment to the bill. Accordingly, each *Land* government would supply a representative to the *Infrastrukturrat* which itself had the competence to compel the three new corporations to provide services with a special 'infrastructural' significance regardless of the operations of the market. According to Schneider and Werle (1989, pp. 52–3), this modification of the bill by the *Länder* – including CSU Bavaria – is a clear illustration of how the reform process was influenced by political factors, rather than purely economic or technical rationales. In sum, it is very questionable how free Telekom was actually going to be from the timeworn practice of political tutelage – and by the same token from the *Kleinstaaterei* and thinly disguised industrial policy 'pork-barrel' politicking of *Länder* politicians.

Although the law allowed for a long overdue rationalization of the loss-making postal branch, it seems entirely reasonable to doubt '... whether Telekom will be run on a genuinely commercial basis' (Dixon, 1989, p. XII). The law did at least provide a clear imperative for the post-reform Bundespost to improve its marketing operations. According to Wolfhard Bender, director (*Ministerialdirigent*) responsible for public relations and marketing in the Bundespost Ministry, all three of the Bundespost's new enterprises would have to understand and treat '... marketing in future not merely as an instrumental function but increasingly as an attitude of mind [*Denkhaltung*], virtually as a corporate philosophy [*Unternehmensphilosophie*]' (Bender, 1989, p. 15).

It also is clear from Bender's statements that there will have to be considerably greater flexibility and market orientation in the work practices within the Bundespost's enterprises which have hitherto functioned according to a bureaucratic administrative logic. However, in the light of the Bundespost workers' determined struggle against the reform (described above), it is hardly clear that, as Bender maintains, the Bundespost's employees '... have less fear of competition, than apprehension about not receiving enough flexibility in order to be able to compete well' (Bender, 1989, p. 15). Moreover, the reform arguably did very little to provide the necessary instruments for a thorough-going de-bureaucratization of the Bundespost. There might now be provision for performance-related pay, yet all Bundespost managers, salesmen and employees alike remained civil servants – in other words, governed by a typically Germanic bureaucratic code of behaviour.

8.   German Unification and Revival of the Privatization Option

An interesting postscript of sorts is required by the unification of Germany in 1990 – an event that can in fact be seen as the effective takeover of the former GDR through the simple accession of the 'five new *Länder'* to the FRG. In late autumn of 1990 the international business community was excited greatly by German media reports that the Bonn government was giving serious consideration to the option of at least partially privatizing Telekom. It is obvious that such a development, if it materialized, would refute the central direction of the analysis that has been presented in this chapter. Apparently, the tremendous challenge of an entirely unpredicted national unification – in particular the huge problems of financing the integration and modernization of the 'five new *Länder'* – might now serve as the catalyst for exactly the kind of radical reform of telecommunications that the staid politics of Bonn and the provincialism of the West German state had thus far been unable to deliver.

According to an interview with the news magazine *Der Spiegel* in December 1990 Finance Minister Theo Waigel (CSU) admitted that the option was no longer being entertained by the small 'neo-liberal' FDP (Liberal) party alone. Both Chancellor Kohl (CDU) and most surprisingly Waigel himself (CSU) were now apparently giving the idea serious consideration. Reportedly a cabinet working party had even been established in order to examine the constitutional and legal issues raised by such a radical step. Moreover, the matter had become the object of intense discussions between those parties – namely the CDU, CSU and the FDP – which were almost certain to form a new coalition government following the first all-German elections of December 1990.

Despite doubling the rate of new connections since assuming responsibility for the Eastern network in 1990 (from 50 000 in 1989 to 100 000) Telekom had come in for the harshest kind of criticism yet levelled at the state telecommunications service – and this, ironically, because of the exceedingly poor state of communications with the Eastern part of the country. The immediate problem was that the volume of calls between the two parts of the reunited Germany was increasing far faster than Telekom could cope. Moreover, such was the state of the Eastern system that it needed to be completely rebuilt. For his part, Telekom president Helmut Ricke warned that the rewiring of the East would require Telekom to raise huge amounts of external capital. For a Bonn government that had promised 'no new taxes' (since reneged upon), this rewiring could be most easily achieved by privatizing the costs.

German unification momentarily appeared to have revived an option – privatization – that had been aired over the past few years but that had seemingly been definitively rejected by the very recent 'Reform Law to Restructure the Post and Telecommunications System and the Bundespost' which has been the subject of this chapter. Moreover, this new turn of events now gave powerful encouragement to those influential interests that had been disappointed by the limited extent and efficacy of this reform. Among the voices now demanding more liberalization and privatization were those of Tyll Necker, the president of the powerful German industrial association, the *Bundesverband der deutschen Industrie* (and former advocate of more 'radical' reform in the Witte Commission) and Hans-Karl Schneider, the chairman of the *Sachverständigenrat*, the Council of Economic Experts.

In fact, Waigel's interview provoked an immediate denial by Bundespost Minister Schwarz-Schilling (CDU) that there was any question of a British-style selling off of Telekom, although he did concede that the possibility of selling a minority stake had been discussed. The SPD opposition spokesman for media and telecommunications policy Peter Paterna was quick to scorn even the partial privatization proposal as a panic reaction of a government facing severe financial problems. Paterna let it be known immediately that his party's support for the constitutional change that would be required to enable even a partial privatization of Telekom was completely out of the question. Ominous warnings were quick to issue from the German Postal Workers' Union (DPG) that the very last thing a government faced with the enormous tasks ahead would welcome was the prospect of serious industrial unrest in a telecommunications sector already struggling to cope with the task of unification. Finally, in the German political system there always existed a further political–legal constraint. Given the dangerous potential for acute political polarization over the issue, described above, any such move in the direction of privatization was almost guaranteed to lead to legalistic opposition from the SPD most probably in the form of an appeal to the Federal Constitutional Court, the highest authority in the country. All these considerations seemed to ensure that the matter would be decided neither quickly nor straightforwardly. It was no surprise, then, that the government very soon announced that it had rejected the privatization option.

In any case, even the financial motivation for a partial privatization of Telekom should be placed in perspective. As things stood the highly profitable Telekom covered the considerable losses of its 'sister' postal services branch (around DM1.8 billion in 1990 alone) and also made a very large contribution to the public exchequer (around 10 per cent of its annual turnover and expected to be more than DM25 billion during 1990–3). In other words, there were compelling reasons for the financially hard-pressed government to keep the enterprise entirely in state hands. Selling a large minority stake in Telekom might have appeared at first sight to be an attractive one-off gain to the exchequer, but it would have entailed the significant diminution of the continuous flow of future funds from this particularly lucrative source. Moreover, the need to pay dividends on shares would probably have meant an end to the cross subsidies to the postal branch.

9.   The Likely Impact of German Unification

The post-unification political pressure on Telekom has at least appeared to have helped to shake up an organization already undergoing a profound reassessment of its past commitments and future tasks. As a legacy of past decisions made when the Bundespost was closely involved in governmental industrial policy, Telekom inherited a number of very expensive and hugely unprofitable projects. These were notably a television satellite the usage of which had had to be heavily subsidized; a national cable television plan for which the Federal Auditor-General's Office (*Bundesrechnungshof*) had estimated it would take 30 years to amortize the billions of Bundespost (now Telekom) investment involved; and also a commercially rather unsuccessful videotext programme (called *Bildschirmtext*). Now that Telekom is supposed to be operating more as a commercial enterprise, profitability (rather than simply industrial policy as before) is certain to become the main refrain of the future. Thus, the costs of these past commitments have assumed an entirely unexpected significance in view of the new burdens of German unification.

One solution will certainly be to share the costs of rewiring East Germany with the private sector. In July 1990 the Bundespost introduced a comparatively liberal satellite communication policy in order to help meet the exigencies of unification, relaxing its voice telephone monopoly for three years to permit private satellite links to the 'five new *Länder*'. What is more, for the first time ever, a non-German company, British Aerospace Communications (BAeCom), now gained a licence from the Bundespost to provide a private satellite network. Also, Telekom chief Ricke has recently announced a special crash programme for the former GDR. It appears that this too will involve the private sector – significantly, special contracts with the German firms SEL and Siemens were mentioned – in the construction of special networks in economically important cities, such as Leipzig and Dresden, and industrial regions, with the primary aim of responding quickly to the requirements of local business. At the same time, Telekom is to continue with its own public-service 'universal' rewiring programme, reaching a connection rate of more than one million connections in 1993.

According to the present law, the privately constructed networks would have to be entirely owned by Telekom. However, such a crash programme might be seen as the basis for an important first step towards the evolution of a mixed public–private network structure in the future (*Der Spiegel,* 48, 1990, pp. 141 ff).

There has been much speculation about the future involvement of foreign firms in the construction of the new telecommunications infrastructure in the five new *Länder*. However, fears have also been expressed that this will undermine the 'unity' of the German telecommunications system. Notwithstanding the award of a private satellite licence to a British firm, a cynic might still be tempted to suggest that there will be no prizes for guessing which firms will reap the lion's share of the Bundespost's contracts.

10. Conclusions

Nevertheless, it could not be gainsaid that by early 1991 it seemed that, having been one of the very worst past offenders against the principles of an open telecommunications market, the Germans were at last seriously embracing the liberalization option. It appears that unification is a significant domestic political factor for the introduction of a somewhat larger measure of liberalization (particularly of satellite communication) than was originally intended. However, it is also very clear that technological imperatives and the convergence of telecommunications and computing, combined with the external challenge from the US and Japan, had already together constituted the primary spur to reform. Manifestly, fear of loss of competitiveness and location policy (*Standortpolitik*) have been the main West German policy preoccupations since the mid 1980s.

These same imperatives were the stimulus to the EC's policies for Community-wide regulatory reform, placing deregulation and liberalization of telecommunications markets on the agenda of all the member states. EC policies were undoubtedly an important intermediate factor for German policy-making. Pressure from the European Commission had been exerted on the Germans on more than one occasion to open up their markets. This, and US threats of retaliatory market closure, had an undoubted impact on the strategic thinking of powerful German industrial interests including Siemens. At the same time, it should not be forgotten that when the Witte Commission was established, the EC was still a long way off from publishing its 'Green Paper' (European Commission, 1987). In fact, the latter appeared only a few months before the publication of the Witte report. Clearly, to an important extent, both documents reflected parallel thinking about global developments. Thereafter the EC's activism quickened, yet the European

Commission's important document 'Implementing the Green Paper' (COM/ 88/48) appeared only weeks before the draft *Poststrukturgesetz* in 1988. By this stage, the West Germans had apparently already moved into the pro-liberalization camp within the Community (see Woolcock et al., 1991, pp. 64–72). At the beginning of the 1990s, with the EC's 1992 deadline fast approaching, the Germans together with Britain, the Netherlands and Denmark are now aligned against France and certain other EC countries in full support of the European Commission's efforts to reform restrictive regulatory practices and to liberalize European terminal equipment and value-added service markets (Economist, 1989, p. 113.). Very clearly, regulatory reform in Germany has gone considerably further than – and has always been about far more than – merely seeking to minimally satisfy EC requirements.

Can it be described as a paradigmatic change though? This chapter has also suggested that there would still appear to exist distinct limits to de-regulation and liberalization in Germany arising from political–cultural, institutional and other domestic political factors. As Grande and Schneider (1991, p. 42) have recently concluded, despite a 'strong strategic will to reform' the actual reform process has nevertheless been characterized by a 'limited capacity of the state to act'. Moreover, the true extent of competitive openness has yet to be properly tested. As Grande and Schneider (1991, p. 36) have again suggested, throughout the reform process '… the symbiotic relations between the Bundespost and the [telecommunications] producers endured largely intact'. Above all, it is very evident that the social dimension of telecommunications remains a concern that is politically very important in Germany and still potentially explosive. Indeed this is even more the case after unification. It can be argued that the issue of the balance between (economic) 'efficiency' and (social) 'equity' has yet to be properly addressed by the European Community. Therefore there remains considerable scope for polarization among the member states over this particular aspect of regulatory reform. As Woolcock et al. (1991, p. 72) suggest, 'it is at this point … that the essential differences between the British and the German approaches to liberalization will become manifest'.

As regards the true extent of market liberalization, there continue to exist grounds at least for a modicum of healthy cynicism. The 1988–9 reform has produced some institutional re-design, and there has occurred a very important statutory loosening, even waiving, of market-restricting rules. However, it is equally clear that there remains considerable scope for an important degree of continuity as well. It would still be imprudent to interpret the German position as anything other than one of quiet confidence in the relative strength, within the European market at least, of their 'reor-ganized' – but certainly not unequivocally 'reconstructed' – telecommunications sector. Despite all this though, the discussion of the privatization option has not been entirely dispelled and the very latest signs are that unification has at least served to keep it alive.

References

Bender, W. (1989), 'Die Unternehmen der Post müssen neue Kräfte vom Markt gewinnen', *Medien Dialog*, (2), 9–15.
Bruce, P. (1987), 'Media man's place in history', *Financial Times*, World Telecommunications Report, October 19, IV.
Buchwald, H. (1989), 'Graue Post mit roten Zahlen und schwarzen Flecken', *Tageszeitung*, 1 February.
Bulmer, S. and Humphreys, P. (1989), 'Kohl, Corporatism and Congruence: the West German Model under Challenge', in S. Bulmer (ed.), *The Changing Agenda of West German Public Policy*, Aldershot: Dartmouth.
Bulmer, S. and Paterson, W. (1987), *The Federal Republic of Germany and the European Community*, London: Allen and Unwin.
Bulmer, S. and Paterson, W. (1988), 'The Federal Republic and the European Community: the Limits to Leadership', in Wessels, W. and Regelsberger, E. (eds), *The Federal Republic and the European Community*, Bonn: Europa Union Verlag.
Deutsche Bundespost (1988), *The Restructuring of the Telecommunications System in the FRG*, Bonn: Deutsche Bundespost.
Dixon, H. (1989), 'Radical reform of the Bundespost: West Germany now a leading advocate for more liberalization', *Financial Times*, International Telecommunications Survey, July 19, I–XX, at p. XII.
Dyson, K. (1982), 'West Germany: the Search for a Rationalist Consensus', in Richardson, J. (ed.), *Policy Styles in Western Europe*, Hemel Hempstead: Allen and Unwin.
Economist (1989), 'European telecommunications – O what a tangled web we weave', October 28, 113.
European Commission (1987), *European Communities Green Paper on the Development of the Common Market for Telecommunications Services and Equipment*, Brussels: European Commission.
Financial Times (1987), 'Survey: world telecommunications', October 19, p. IV.
Friebe, K. (1984), 'Industrial Policy in the FRG', in Friebe, K. and Gerybadze, A. (eds), *Microelectronics in Western Europe: the Medium-Term Perspective*, Berlin: Erich Schmidt Verlag.
Grande, E. (1987), 'Telecommunications Policy in West Germany and Great Britain – A Comparative Analysis of Political Configurations', Paper presented at the *Political Studies Association Annual Conference*, Aberdeen, April 7–9.
Grande, E. and Schneider, V. (1991), 'Reformstrategien und staatliche Handlungskapazitäten: Eine vergleichende Analyse institutionellen Wandels in der Telekommunikation in Westeuropa', *MPIFG Discussion Paper*, 3, June 1991, Cologne: Max-Planck-Institut für Gesellschaftsforschung.

Herrmann, E. (1985), 'Das Kräftespiel bei der Lenkung der Deutschen Bundespost', *Zeitschrift für öffentliche und gemeinwirtschaftliche Unternehmen*, **8**, 285–300.

Humphreys, P. (1988), 'The State and Telecommunications Modernization in Britain, France and West Germany', *Manchester Papers in Politics*, Government Department, Manchester University.

Humphreys, P. (1989), 'Policies for Technological Innovation and Industrial Change', in Bulmer, S. (ed.), *The Changing Agenda of West German Public Policy*, Aldershot: Dartmouth.

Humphreys, P. (1990), *Media and Media Policy in West Germany,* Oxford/New York/Munich: Berg.

Jentsch, P. (1989), 'Die Postreform: Auf den Prüfstand gestellt', *Das Parlament*, (6–7), 3/10 February, 8.

Katzenstein, P. (1987), *Policy and Politics in West Germany: the Growth of a Semi-Sovereign State*, Philadelphia: Temple University Press.

Leaman, J. (1988), *The Political Economy of West Germany 1945–85*, London: Macmillan.

Lehmbruch, G. and Schmitter, P. (eds) (1979), *Trends Towards Corporatist Intermediation*, London and Beverley Hills: Sage.

Lehmbruch, G. and Schmitter, P. (eds) (1982), *Patterns of Corporatist Policy Making*, London and Beverley Hills: Sage.

Lijphart, A. (1984), *Democracies – Patterns of Majoritarian and Consensus Government in Twenty-One Countries*, New Haven and London: Yale University Press.

Monopolkommission (1981), *Die Rolle der Deutschen Bundespost im Fernmeldewesen, Sondergutachten der Monopolkommission*, **9**, Baden-Baden: Nomos Verlag.

Morgan, K. and Webber, D. (1986), 'Divergent Paths: Political Strategies for Telecommunications in Britain, France and West Germany', in Dyson, K. and Humphreys, P. (eds), *The Politics of the Communications Revolution in Western Europe*, London: Frank Cass.

Möschel, W. (1988), 'Der Postminister bleibt Konzernchef', *Frankfurter Allgemeine Zeitung*, (270), 19 November, 14–15.

OECD (1983), *Telecommunications: Pressures and Policies for Change*, Paris: OECD.

OECD (1987), *Trends of Change in Telecommunications Policy*, Paris: OECD.

Scharpf, F. (1976), *Politikverflechtung: Theorie und Empirie des kooperativen Föderalismus in der Bundesrepublik*, Königstein: Athenäum.

Schmidt, M. (1988), 'The policy of the middle way', *Journal of Public Policy*, **7**, (2), 135–177.

Schneider, V. and Werle, R. (1989), 'Governance by Policy Networks: the German Telecommunications Sector', *Paper prepared for the conference on policy networks: structural analysis of public policy-making*, Max-Planck-Institut für Gesellschaftsforschung, Cologne, 4–5 December.

Schwarz-Schilling, C. (1987), 'Mittelweg für die Post', *Wirtschaftswoche* (39), 18 September, 49–55.

Snow, M. (1988), 'Telecommunications literature. A critical review of the economic, technological and public policy issues', *Telecommunications Policy*, June.

Southern, D. and Paterson, W. (1991), *Governing Germany*, Oxford: Basil Blackwell.

Spiegel (1982), 'Andere Umstände', *Spiegel* (45).

von Beyme, K. (1985), 'Policy-Making in the Federal Republic of Germany: A Systematic Introduction', in von Beyme, K. and Schmidt, M.G. (eds), *Policy and Politics in the Federal Republic of Germany*, New York: St. Martins Press.

Webber, D. (1987), 'The Assault on the "Fortress on the Rhine". The Politics of Telecommunications Deregulation in the Federal Republic of Germany', *Paper for the Conference of the Council of European Studies*, Washington D.C., 30 October–1 November.

Wilks, S. and Wright, M. (1987), 'Conclusion: Comparing Government–Industry Relations: States, Sectors and Networks', in Wilks, S. and Wright, M. (eds), *Comparative Government–Industry Relations: Western Europe, United States and Japan*, Oxford: Clarendon Press.

Witte, E. (1987), *Neuordnung der Telekommunikation*, Heidelberg: R. v. Decker's Verlag/G. Schenck.

Woolcock, S., Hodges, M. and Schreiber, K. (1991), *Britain, Germany and 1992: The Limits of Deregulation*, London: Pinter Publishers and The Royal Institute of International Affairs. Chatham House Papers Series.

Wright, M. (1991), 'The Comparative Analysis of Industrial Policies: Policy Networks and Sectoral Structures in Britain and France', *Staatswissenschaften und Staatspraxis*, (2), Winter.

6   Regulatory Change in German Financial Markets

Michael Moran

The oil crisis of 1973–4 marked the end of 'the long boom' in advanced capitalist economics. In the intervening years it has been perfectly possible for individual economies to achieve continuing growth; but a nation's capacity to sustain economic progress now depends, more than ever, on the ability to adapt in the face of an intensely competitive, and often unstable, international environment. That is why problems of structural adjustment have become central to policy argument and scholarly enquiry.

The capacity to achieve structural adjustment is in turn bound up with the potential for regulatory change, because the regulatory framework within which enterprises operate influences their ability to meet the challenge of changing competitive conditions. In debates about the conditions governing successful adjustment the Federal Republic occupies a particularly important place. On many indicators, notably inflation and export performance, the Federal Republic has shown an enviable capacity to cope with the problems of the 1980s – enviable, at least, when seen through British eyes. Yet compared with the adjustment capacities of Japan, its miraculous twin of the 1950s, Germany's performance has in recent years been unimpressive.

The debate about the origins of the Federal Republic's difficulties has a particular interest for political scientists, because the political system is itself now commonly seen as one of the chief culprits. Both Katzenstein (1987) and Bulmer and Humphreys (1989), have noted the weakness of central institutions charged with steering the system in a strategically enlightened way. 'Cooperative federalism' fragments authority territorially; *'Selbstverwaltung'* fragments it functionally. Fragmentation diminishes the institutional capacity to think strategically, while the need to solve problems consensually means that, even when strategically necessary choices are recognized, they can be blocked by territorial or functional interests.

Yet, as Katzenstein recognizes, there is also another side to the German policy coin. Practices like cooperative federalism are consensus-creating devices which can ensure that, when a decision is made, it will command widespread support and stand a reasonable chance of successful implementation. The recent history of British policy-making – of decisive actions taken without broad support – shows that consensus and cooperation have benefits as well as costs. The challenge of structural adjustment thus creates something more demanding than a need for strategic thinking and authoritative decision. It creates a dilemma where the capacity to respond authoritatively and swiftly has to be balanced against the need to create a consensus supporting the chosen course of action.

This dilemma is especially acute in the case of the area examined in this chapter, because in recent years the pace of competitive change in the world financial services industry has been rapid. Business practices, ownership structures and market organization – all have been transformed. The results are often summarized under the heading 'deregulation'; but deregulation is only part of a wider pattern of change, demanding adjustments in turn from policy-makers and from actors in markets. The Anglo–Saxon markets have been leaders in innovation. The German problem has consequently been twofold: how to formulate a response to change; and, once an appropriate response has been recognized, how to create a domestic coalition capable of pushing through reform.

The dilemmas faced by policy-makers in Germany have been sharpened by recent developments. The pressures for change emanating from the EC's Single Market project, and the extraordinary demands of German unification, have combined to put the consensus-seeking style under pressure. German financial regulation was characterized by a consensual and cooperative style, and by a suspicion of liberalization. Have the combined pressures of the world financial services revolution, the Single Market programme, and unification, produced a fundamental shift in regulatory style and substance?

These questions are pursued through an examination of three sets of institutions: insurance companies, securities exchanges and banks. This organization of the material gives neither full coverage of markets, nor a subtle distinction between institutions; but in the confines of a short chapter it provides some idea of where the system is changing, and where it is immobile. Behind the whole discussion, however, lies the canvas of the world financial services revolution – and we must begin with a sketch of that revolution.

1. The International Background: A Sketch

Three key regulatory features mark the changing international world of financial services: liberalization, harmonization and institutionalization (Moran, 1991). Only the first corresponds to deregulation (the dismantling of rules). Many barriers to competition are indeed tumbling. But at the same time existing regulatory regimes are showing growing *institutionalization*; rules are being codified, embodied in statute and enforced by state, or para-state, agencies. *Harmonization* of different national regimes is in principle neutral in its effect on the balance between regulation and deregulation; but in the German case, as we will see, it often leads to institutionalization.

Liberalization is the most widely noticed face of the world financial services revolution. It has involved the abolition, modification or circumvention of numerous barriers to competition. In the United States, for instance, the price cartel on the New York Stock exchange was abolished in 1975 and a range of administrative controls over interest rates, dating from the inter-war years, was phased out from the start of the 1980s. In Britain, administrative controls over bank lending were dismantled in 1971, and the price cartel on the London Stock Exchange went the same way after 1983. Barriers to market entry, although not so comprehensively dismantled, have also been lowered, removed or circumvented. For example in Japan, the United States and Britain administrative barriers against the entry of foreign firms into domestic banking and securities markets have been partially dismantled in recent years. In the UK the process has been especially radical: the 'Big Bang' after 1983 allowed foreign multinationals not only to become dominant members of the Stock Exchange, but also to acquire many leading British firms. In Japan and the United States, the two most important markets in the world financial services industry, there still exist legal barriers nominally prohibiting investment and commercial banks from entering each other's markets (Article 65 of the Japanese Securities Exchange Law and the American 'Glass–Steagall' Act). But these barriers have been widely circumvented, usually with the connivance or even encouragement of regulators. Finally, many of the characteristic instruments and markets associated with the financial services revolution – such as the booming markets in financial futures – owe their existence to the widespread removal of barriers to financial innovation.

Behind this process of liberalization lie struggles for competitive advantage. The biggest firms are represented in all the major world financial centres, and are integrating their operations between these different centres. National authorities are attempting both to advance the interests of their national champions, and to attract business to their own financial capitals.

In short, competitive struggles are now globally organized and involve coalitions of multinational enterprises and national regulatory authorities.

This in turn helps explain the pressure for regulatory harmonization. In the field of financial services, regulation is a shaper of economic outcomes, conferring competitive advantages or imposing handicaps. As markets become internationally integrated, regulatory variations between national systems thus acquire great importance. This is why the impending creation of unified EC markets in financial services has been accompanied by hard bargaining between member states over the terms of regulatory harmonization. But EC-wide moves towards harmonization are themselves only part of a wider pattern. The work of the committee of bank supervisors convened by the Bank for International Settlements in Basel, for instance, has substantially shaped the terms of the EC debate about how to harmonize capital standards in banking. Similarly, the harmonization of EC rules on insider trading is only in part a response to the unification of markets inside the Community; it is also the product of many years of pressure from the United States designed to impose American standards on foreign financial markets.

The 'harmonization' of insider trading regulation consists in large part in the diffusion of restrictive American regulations to other centres. As this example shows, there is an important connection between harmonization and the third feature of regulatory change identified earlier: the growing institutionalization of regulation. Institutionalization summarizes three different, though connected, phenomena: state intervention, legal controls and rule elaboration and codification. States have become central actors in the reform of regulatory regimes. In Britain, for instance, the crucial changes were imposed by the state; in Japan they are the result of negotiations in a joint committee of Japanese and American government regulators. In other words, even where change has actually involved dismantling regulations ('liberalization'), states have been key actors in the process. Commonly, however, regulatory change has meant increased legal codification, and the reorganization of institutions to allow more state control. The trend to greater legal control was pioneered by the Americans, notably in the 1975 Securities Amendments Acts, and in the American expansion of legal controls over insider dealing in the 1980s. Legal codification and state control are also the most striking features of the new British system, as embodied in the 1986 Financial Services Act.

Regulatory change in the world financial services industry is both complex and contradictory. It exhibits complex and contradictory features because it is shaped by forces working at very different systemic levels. On one level it is driven by the changing structure of the world economic and political system: by the competitive struggles unleashed following the breakup of the regulated international monetary order originally established at Bretton Woods; by the relative decline of American economic power; and by the consequent tugging and hauling between Japan and the United States for markets and for influence.

At the level of national regulatory systems yet another set of forces is at work. All the advanced capitalist economies have institutionally complex systems of financial regulation. Structures and rules are deeply shaped by the bureaucratic politics of these systems – by, for instance, the struggles for jurisdiction between and within Japanese ministries, or the battles for regulatory 'turf' that are endemic to American financial regulation.

Finally, regulatory struggles are meshed not only with bureaucratic politics but also with democratic politics. All the great financial centres are located in nations whose political systems show at least some features of pluralist democracy. The recurrent scandals over insider trading, in particular, are inexplicable outside the context of competitive democratic politics: the most obvious example is Japan where the Recruit insider trading scandal in 1989 was used to destroy Mr Takeshita as Prime Minister and to weaken the electoral strength of the ruling Liberal Democratic Party.

To note the obvious: the Federal Republic of Germany is a major actor in the international economic system; it has an institutionally complex system of financial regulation allowing ample scope for the struggles of bureaucratic politics; and it is a pluralist democracy. It is time to see how these features have shaped financial regulation – in the direction of liberalization, harmonization and institutionalization.

2. Insurance

The regulation of the insurance industry in Germany has a long history. The present regulatory structure is still based on legislation passed in 1901, strengthened in the 1930s after the collapse of a major firm, and reconstructed in the years following the end of the Second World War. The final reconstruction of the system was signalled by the law of 1961, which also established the main regulatory institution, the Federal Supervisory Office for Insurance (*das Bundesaufsichtsamt für das Versicherungswesen*), a freestanding agency of the Federal Finance Ministry located in Berlin (Krakowski, 1988). The regulation of the industry is marked by two important features. First, the Office practises a style of cooperative regulation with the industry: according to Krakowski (p. 459), for instance, it is common for changes in regulation to be informally negotiated between the federal supervisor and the trade associations before they are promulgated. Second, there are significant barriers to competition. justified on the grounds that ruinous competition would destabilize firms and damage the interests of the insured. The market is, true, quite open to the entry of foreign firms: there are 80 subsidiaries of firms from other EEC states already operating in the Federal Republic (Angerer, 1988). But the common rules under which companies operate place significant barriers against price competition, entry to new markets and product innovation. The Supervisory Office operates extensive controls over premiums, especially in life insurance. Instrument innovation – the creation of new kinds of contract – is also discouraged. Insurance firms are prohibited from entering some new markets: they may not, for instance, become members of stock exchanges, and there is an upper limit (20 per cent) to the proportion of their assets which life insurance firms can invest in shares (Kennedy and Bernstein, 1988). There are also important limits to competition inside the industry. The governing principle is *'Spartentrennung'*, the legally obligatory separation between firms operating in different insurance markets (life, health, and so on). The industry is also exempted from some of the requirements of the anti-cartel law, though the exact significance of that exemption is disputed (Buchner, 1988).

This restrictive regulatory system is now under pressure from three sources: from the changing structure of markets; from the impending impact of a single EC market; and from the play of politics between regulatory agencies and their allied interests in markets. As Stracke and Pöhl (1988) have shown, the companies' traditional markets will shrink because of population decline for the rest of the century (although this is counterbalanced by a long-term rise in saving via insurance at the expense of bank deposits). The insurance companies' response has been to try to move into new markets: the most competitively aggressive has bought a bank; others have formed alliances with individual *Sparkassen* (saving banks); and yet others have created holding companies to allow them to move into (prohibited) non-insurance markets. In 1989 the firms also lobbied hard – though without success – to be allowed to trade as members of stock exchanges.

The competitive pressures for change have been intensified because, while the firms' traditional markets are contracting through population decline, those very markets have been invaded by other financial institutions. In particular, as the restrictive structure of the retail banking system starts to break up (see section 5 below) banks have vaulted the traditional barrier separating banking and insurance. Since 1983 the Deutsche Bank (the biggest of the commercial banks) has marketed a savings plan with a life insurance cover. In 1989 it applied for permission to enter the life insurance market via a newly established subsidiary (Jones, 1989). In summary: competitive pressures in the market are destroying one of the characteristic features of the regulatory system, the separation of banking and insurance.

These pressures will be intensified after 1992, and have already prompted a campaign by German insurance interests to defend present restrictions against the threat of regulatory harmonization.

In the bargaining about harmonization the British are the main protagonists. The circumstances are the reverse of those prevailing in productive industry. The British are world champion exporters, the German industry a weakling: in the mid-1980s foreign premium income was 35 per cent of the value of the domestic premium income of British firms; the comparable German figure was 3.7 per cent (Krakowski, pp. 471–2). The market in Britain is perhaps the most permissively regulated in the EC. British companies believe they have a comparative advantage in price, and that the instruments they market are more varied and better adapted to different market segments than is the case in Germany. Their lobbying has concentrated on the demand that this diversity be preserved in any harmonized system. EC Commission proposals for life insurance have particularly alarmed the German industry. 'German life insurance must not be allowed to become a field of experiment for the useless deregulation plans of the EC Commission', writes a leading life insurer (Henning, 1989). Under the slogan '*Versicherungsschutz* "Made in Germany"' the industry argues that the German system delivers a higher-quality, safer product than is possible under the more free-wheeling British arrangements (Bremkamp, 1988).

German apprehension is probably justified. Although comparisons of costs and quality need to be made with caution, Krakowski's analysis (1988, pp. 474–7) indicates that over a wide range of insurance products the offerings on the British market are cheaper and better adapted to the demands of differing groups of customers. The German industry's own defence implicitly accepts this; it argues that controls deter ruinous competition and deliver a safer product to the consumer. This argument, while intuitively plausible, is unfortunately nowhere in my experience supported by comprehensive analysis – designed to prove, rather than merely assert, that the solvency of British firms is inferior to that of their German rivals.

It would be wrong to suggest that there is uniform resistance to liberalization among the firms in the insurance industry. The '*Spartentrennung*' principle has itself, after all, produced segregated and divided interests. Like most firms faced with complex market pressure, the companies have responded opportunistically: they defend themselves against the British challenge, and the threat of harmonization in a 'British' direction, by arguing that in foreign markets the barrier separating insurance from non-insurance has been destroyed; yet domestically in their struggles with banks, they are equally energetically contributing to that very process. This sort of contradictory opportunism is, of course, characteristic of the behaviour of business interests, and explains why the effective coalitions for change so often have to be organized by regulatory agencies operating at one remove from the daily pressures of the market. In other words, the eventual outcome will depend heavily on the play of agency politics, to which I now turn.

The most powerful ally possessed by the anti-deregulators is the *Bundesaufsichtsamt* itself. Here, institutional philosophy and institutional interests coincide. The President of the *Amt* has advanced two arguments in favour of present arrangements. First, he claims that the rates of entry and exit from the industry show that there already exists vigorous competition: in the ten years to 1988 129 new firms entered the market, and since the early 1950s about 270 have left. Second, he argues that in the mass market deregulation would damage consumer protection (Angerer, 1988) At the heart of the case offered by the *Bundesaufsichtsamt*, and by those in the industry opposed to liberalization, is a disbelief in the capacity of consumers accurately to estimate risks in competitive markets. In the case of the *Bundesaufsichtsamt* this institutional philosophy is powerfully supported by institutional self-interest, because deregulation involves an encroachment on its jurisdictional territory, not only from the supranational EC level, but from other actors in the state machinery. The Monopolies Commission has argued for extensive deregulation, while the Federal Cartel Office favours the modification of the present exemptions from the Cartel Law enjoyed by the insurance companies (Starke, 1988; Krause,˙1988). The forces shaping the intervention of the Cartel Office are a mirror image of those moulding the outlook of the *Bundesaufsichtsamt*: institutional philosophy (favouring competition); and institutional self-interest (an amendment to the Cartel Law would expand the jurisdiction of the Cartel Office into the insurance industry at the expense of the *Bundesaufsichtsamt*).

The regulation of the insurance industry in Germany is at an unclear, transitory stage. Two powerful pressures are working in the direction of liberalization: struggles in the domestic market, which are producing a familiar process of innovation and circumvention; and the impending challenge of harmonization, which offers the British firms the opportunity to lever open the rich German market. The most important members of the domestic coalition against change are the chief regulator, and the firms in the industry (although the latter certainly includes some who would fancy their chances in a more competitive environment, and a larger number whose actual market behaviour is opportunistic). How far this coalition can hold the line – or even remain united – is impossible to say. Circumstances are very different in the case of the securities exchange: there, as we will see now, the reforming coalition has won some striking recent victories.

3. Securities Exchanges

The organization of the securities exchanges has for over a decade been one of the most contentious issues in German financial regulation. After the banking collapses of the mid-1970s the leading world financial centres turned to 'securitization' (the denomination of assets and liabilities as instruments tradeable on securities markets). This encouraged the expansion in the United States and Britain of existing stock exchanges, and stimulated the development of new markets trading newly invented instruments, like financial futures. In a paper already published I have traced the history of the German reform debate to 1987 (Moran, 1989). Here, therefore, I will merely summarize conditions up to that point, and will then describe the important developments that have occurred in the past two and a half years.

Universal banking left the German securities exchanges with an unimportant role in the financial system. There are eight stock exchanges, and while Frankfurt and Düsseldorf command most business, the system has been fragmented and parochial. Each exchange enjoys considerable self regulation under the oversight of the respective state (*Land*) government. Some of the securities traded on the most rapidly growing and innovative Anglo–American markets (notably financial futures) were until recently prohibited by law in Germany. The organization of trading on the exchanges, their administrative resources and their use of technology have all been placed well behind Anglo–American institutions. This backwardness was also reflected in the organization of investor protection. While the United States and the United Kingdom extended their legal controls over insider trading in the 1970s and 1980s, German markets were until recently largely indifferent to the practice.

By 1987 an intense struggle was under way over the fate of the system. On the one side were ranged interests with a metropolitan outlook, sensitive to developments abroad and anxious to secure for '*Finanzplatz Deutschland*' a leading place in the world financial services industry. They encompassed the biggest commercial banks, the Frankfurt Stock Exchange, the government of Hesse (which has oversight responsibility for the Frankfurt Exchange) and the biggest foreign financial services firms established in Germany, which were anxious to integrate their securities operations worldwide. As the list shows, this was a 'Frankfurt' coalition, because it was recognized that if '*Finanzplatz Deutschland*' was to achieve and retain world status, it would have to do so by creating for Frankfurt a position akin to that enjoyed by capitals like London and Paris in their respective financial systems. On the other side stood the threatened small exchanges and their powerful institutional patrons in the other state governments, who in turn carried considerable weight in the federal politics of Bonn.

Reviewing this history in 1989, I concluded that the autonomy of the small exchanges, the federal structure of decision-making, and the power of economic interests at state level, would block any significant regulatory change. I was wrong. There have been rapid changes. Three are especially noteworthy: the assault by the 'modernizers' has intensified to the point where it is possible to say that a consensus favouring change has now been fashioned; there has been a major reform of the legal structure of the securities exchanges; and the system is poised on the brink of substantial reforms of the regulations governing insider dealing.

Two developments have powerfully strengthened the hands of the re-formers. Both are external to Germany, and both reflect the process of internationalization in the securities markets. The first is the loss of business to the innovative London markets. Already in 1985 the Deutsche Bank had moved its international banking operations to London. Then in September 1988 the London International Financial Futures Exchange (LIFFE) began trading a contract in German federal government long bonds. The contract was exceptionally popular because, in the absence until now of a financial futures market in Germany, it offered institutions their first opportunity to hedge risk in this large securities market (the government bond market is the fourth largest in the world) (Benke, 1988).

More threatening still is the second external development, the rise of Paris as an international financial centre (Cerny, 1989). London's role as one of the 'Big Three' (alongside New York and Tokyo) is acknowledged to be special. But this still leaves available the position of leading continental European financial centre. The rise of Paris as a centre for trading futures and options is thus especially challenging. Markets like these are obligatory for any financial centre that wishes to be in the world front rank, because the largest financial institutions now demand a full palette of instruments offering hedges against exchange rate and interest rate risk. The inroads made by London, and the rise of Paris, are therefore not just a threat to German securities exchanges; they threaten the whole future of Frankfurt as a major financial centre. The urgency of the challenge, and the determi-nation of the Frankfurt-dominated metropolitan elite to meet it, is shown by the blunt words of the Bundesbank President in June 1989. In a lecture widely reproduced in the newspapers of the financial elite he warned:

> We are in a backward condition and our backwardness threatens to become greater because the tempo [of change] elsewhere is higher (Pöhl, 1989).

He advocated a reformed stock exchange structure centralized in Frank-furt, and went on to attack the very constitutional basis of the regulatory system. In conditions where Frankfurt was the Federal Republic's obvious international financial centre, he noted, questions of exchange structure were no longer '*bundesrepublikanish-föderativ*'; they were international, turning on the relations between Frankfurt and other foreign centres. Herr Pöhl also expressed scepticism about another principle of exchange government, '*Selbstverwaltung*'. The arrangements for the new German futures exchange (see below) would be a serious test, he remarked, of the capacity of the system of *Selbstverwaltung* to achieve reform:

It remains to be demonstrated that the existing system of self-regulation can in future keep pace with other countries which will be efficiently and tightly directed from the centre. I think here above all of Paris.

This envious glance at French centralization shows that the process of regulatory change, even when it involves the abolition of regulatory restrictions, by no means necessarily implies a retreat by the state. The Bundesbank President's remarks convey a desire to exercise more state control over the stock exchanges in order to meet international competitive challenges (a lesson that he could as readily have learnt from London as from Paris).

The intensity of international competitive challenges helps explain the second major recent development in securities regulation: the amendment to the Stock Exchange Law which came into effect in August 1989. The amendment is the most important change to stock exchange regulation at least since the Nazi reforms of 1934, and perhaps since the original stock exchange legislation of 1896. The most important purpose of the new measure was to allow the establishment of a German (financial) futures exchange (the *Deutsche Terminbörse, DTB*). This began operating at the start of 1990, trading options contracts in 14 leading German shares, a futures contract in government bonds and a futures contract on the newly created DAX (German Stock Index) (Franke, 1989).

The DTB is, by German standards, an extraordinary innovation: it is a fully computerized marketplace in which participants are linked electronically rather than trading on an exchange floor; although centralized in Frankfurt, and under the supervision of the state government of Hesse, it breaks with the regional exchange principle because it is a Germany-wide exchange; and it is an exchange having only institutional members, the most important of whom are the big banks.

It is also in a political sense a breakthrough, because it represents a clear victory for the reforming coalition that for many years tried, without notable success, to break the power of the regional exchanges and their allies in the state governments. In the lobbying for the exchange, the core of the winning coalition was formed from the banks: the members of the company responsible for organizing the exchange are headed by the four biggest commercial banks, with the Deutsche Bank at the top.

Describing and explaining how this legislation survived the obstacle course of the Bonn legislative process, with its powerfully entrenched state (*Land*) interests, would be a study in itself. I tentatively suggest two factors to explain the reformers' success. The first is that the intensity of the international challenge mounted by London and Paris drove the reformers, and especially the biggest banks, to invest a large part of their considerable political resources in the success of the plan. Webber's accounts of the legislative process draw a picture of intense lobbying right up to Chancellor level (Webber, 1989). In other words, they won because this time the pressure of international competition made them desperate to win.

The second factor behind the reformers' success is institutional, and augurs well for their longer-term reform strategies: it is the role now played by the Association of Stock Exchanges in both developing financial innovations and pressing for organizational reform. In 1989 I described how the Association had been reconstituted to strengthen the hand of the Frankfurt reformers; but noting the way voting rules had been constructed to allow the smaller exchanges a veto over Frankfurt, I doubted whether it could be an effective instrument of change. What this conclusion neglected was the capacity of the Frankfurt interests to control the everyday workings of the Association. Under Rudiger van Rosen (a former aide of Bundesbank President Pöhl) the Association has become a major propagandist for change and – for instance through its role in the creation of the *Deutsche Aktienindex* (DAX) – an important source of the financial innovations needed to create the new financial futures exchange.

The intensification of the reformers' campaign, and their breakthrough with the creation of the new futures exchange, are plainly both linked to international pressures. The same is true of the third major recent change, concerning the regulation of insider trading. In this case the German system is being pressed in the direction of what I earlier called institutionalization – the codification of rules, their incorporation into statute and their enforcement by the state.

A number of changes have taken place. First, there has been an incremental growth in the scope and detail of the non-statutory rules operated by individual exchanges. In 1988, for instance, Düsseldorf widened the range of individuals covered by its insider-dealing rules (to include journalists and large shareholders) and created a system for publicly identifying those firms which had declined to commit themselves to its voluntary code (Schubert, 1988) This piecemeal change reflects a more general movement of opinion. In May 1988 a working group on insider-dealing problems, composed of leading figures in the business community, proposed a package of reforms, the most important of which would have widened the existing German definition of insider dealing (*Wertpapier,* 6 May 1988). The group stopped short, however, of recommending legal controls – abstention from which has made the Federal Republic distinctive among leading capitalist nations. Such is the pace of regulatory change that, in a year, this opposition was abandoned. The new directive on insider dealing, agreed by the EC's Finance Ministers at their meeting in Luxembourg on 20 June 1989, in effect juridifies German insider-dealing law for the first time.

The precise extent of the German concession is not yet clear, for much will depend on implementation. In the bargaining over the original Commission proposals the Germans managed to extract important concessions: for instance, the sanctions against insider dealing will be decided by each separate member. This plainly leaves open the possibility of a merely symbolic German enforcement regime. Nevertheless, the acceptance of the principle of a common Community-wide definition of, and ban on, insider dealing is a significant development in a nation that, until recently, viewed the practice with indifference. It is a striking instance of how the pressure for harmonization has produced more, not less, regulation.

The experience of the German stock exchanges in recent years shows, yet again, how inadequate is 'deregulation' as a summary of what has been going on in German financial markets. Certainly there has been some abolition of restrictions on competition, but the forces driving the system are not primarily pressures to deregulate: they arise from external competitive challenges, the impact of these challenges on the position of the (chiefly Frankfurt-based) modernizing coalition, and the (rearguard) action being fought by more parochial economic interests and their allies in the state governments. Similar themes reappear when we examine the changing regulation of banks, the concern of the next section.

4. Banking

Regulation of the banking system developed comparatively late in Germany: the first important American law was passed in 1863 and in Japan the key legislation was passed between 1882 and 1890. In Germany, by contrast, the development of a significant system of state oversight had to await the crisis of the Great Crash of 1931. The Nazi reforms of 1934 created what is still the modern framework – governing admission, capital and liquidity rules. This was reconstructed in the Credit System Law of 1961, which also centralized bank supervision in the Federal Supervisory Office for the Credit System in Berlin (Reszat, 1988). This suggestion of a comparatively unfettered banking regulatory culture is strengthened by the experience of recent regulatory history. In the banking systems of the other great capitalist nations regulatory struggles within the banking industry have turned on two regulatory barriers: against price competition (controls over interest rates on loans and deposits, administrative rationing of credit) and against market entry (until the 1980s there were *de facto* barriers separating commercial and investment banking in Britain, and there still exist such legal barriers in the USA and Japan).

In the Anglo–American world the endeavour to break through or to circumvent those barriers has been one of the main causes of financial innovation; it is not too exaggerated to say that banking regulatory history in the last two decades has been conditioned by the efforts of banks and their competitors to adapt these restrictions to their own competitive advantage.

The most striking feature of recent regulatory history in Germany is the absence of many of these regulatory barriers – and the consequent absence of many of the market innovations designed to break the barriers. Thus, the German 'universal' banking system embodies precisely that principle – the unification of commercial and investment banking – which the Glass–Steagall Act in the United States, and Article 65 of the Japanese Securities and Exchange Law, prohibit. The Federal Republic also has a liberal history on interest rate controls: the last administrative restrictions disappeared in the late 1960s (OECD, 1986). By contrast, controls in Britain lasted until 1971, the Americans phased out legal restrictions in the 1980s and Japanese liberalization is only now beginning. But while the two great sources of regulatory struggle in the banking industries of other advanced capitalist nations have been missing, immense strains nevertheless exist in both retail and wholesale banking.

In retail ('high street') banking the forces for change resemble those elsewhere in the banking markets of other advanced capitalist economies: the entry into markets by firms offering near substitutes (like credit cards) for the payment services traditionally offered by banks: the development of technologies allowing existing banks to expand beyond the traditional geographical boundaries of their markets; the growing competition from nonbank financial institutions, especially insurance companies, for savings; and the growing sensitivity of customers to costs, yields and quality of service.

This growing competition is destroying established divisions, between the commercial banks, the saving banks, the cooperative banks and the specialized institutions like the *Bausparkassen*. The single most important regulatory consequence of these intensifying competitive struggles is the large question mark they have placed against public ownership in banking. About half the banking system in the old, pre-unification Federal Republic was in the public sector, mostly controlled by the individual states in the federation. The savings banks (*Sparkassen*) pose particular problems. They still account for a substantial volume of all banking business, but their share has fallen in the last decade and, partly in response, there has been a wave of defensive mergers between banks. Their potential for geographical expansion is limited and – more serious still – their access to the capital needed to provide a base for expansion is also restricted. Indeed, some *Sparkassen* claim that without an injection of capital they will be unable to conform to the impending EC common capital requirements (see below). In Rhineland–Palatinate, as a consequence, the savings banks have pressed the state government for legislation allowing them to raise private capital. They have a receptive audience: in 1988 the state's economics minister was advocating extensive privatization of the savings bank system. Developments in retail banking show how difficult is the task of arriving at any estimate of the changing balance between 'regulation' and 'deregulation'; on the one hand, clear erosion of barriers to competition and powerful pressures for privatization; on the other hand, privatization pressures themselves result partly from the need to meet new capital adequacy standards produced by the process of Community-wide harmonization.

Similar contradictory features are evident in wholesale banking, especially in the regulation of investment banking. Some key liberalization measures carried out elsewhere (like the abolition of restrictions on capital movements implemented in Britain and Japan at the end of the 1970s) had already been accomplished in Germany by the early 1960s (a few remaining residual restrictions went at the start of the 1980s). In 1984–5 a further round of liberalizing measures were introduced: a coupon tax discriminating against foreign bond holders was abolished; in underwriting, a 'gentlemen's agreement' barring foreign banks from lead-managing bond issues was modified to allow German subsidiaries of foreign banks to perform that role; and prohibitions on a wide range of financial instruments – Certificates of Deposit, bonds with exotic interest-rate arrangements, swaps – were lifted. Since the mid-1980s there has been a steady drip of further liberalization measures.

The changes summarized here, though undoubtedly of a liberalizing character, should not be equated with a process of state withdrawal from the regulatory arena. On the contrary: they represent tactical choices by regulatory authorities in an environment of intense international competition in financial services. The lifting of restrictions on innovative financial instruments, for example, is connected to the need to defend Frankfurt's attractiveness as an international financial centre. The changes in rules governing foreign participation in bond issues was on a reciprocity basis – in other words, the subsidiaries of foreign banks were only allowed to 'lead manage' when their home regulatory authorities offered reciprocal terms to German institutions. This was part of a 'financial services trade war' that broke out between the most advanced capitalist states in the mid-1980s. The Japanese were a particular object of German attack: the 'reciprocity' clause is part of the campaign to open up the Japanese markets to German institutions.

It should be plain that regulatory developments in retail and investment banking involve complex tensions between liberalization and institutionalization. By contrast a third recent element in policy debates – the revival of the 'bank power' thesis – threatens the big commercial banks with significantly increased legal restrictions. The bank power thesis is in essence a claim that 'universal banking' gives a few banks a stranglehold over capital markets and an excessively strong presence in industrial boardrooms. The thesis was given renewed life by Pfeiffer's analysis (1986) of the web of interlocking shareholdings involving the big three commercial banks – an analysis taken up and publicized by the trade unions, the banks' chief competitor for influence over industrial managers. Despite a strenuous defensive campaign by the banks, there is now a formidable coalition which supports an amendment to the Cartel Law, the object of which would be to curb bank holdings of shares and participation in company boards. This coalition unites the SPD, the present leadership of the FDP, the Cartel Office and even some members of the CDU. There is, in the present Bundestag, almost certainly a majority for legislation. More important, there are signs of the emergence of an all-party consensus on the issue with the emergence of leading CDU critics of bank power.

Some of the contingent reasons for this campaign are readily understandable: the Cartel Office wants to expand its jurisdiction; the CDU wants to avoid being isolated in defence of a potentially electorally unpopular interest. But the deeper reasons behind the campaign for increased regulation are unclear, especially because the decline of the housebank and the intensified competition for customers have probably already reduced bank power. My own guess is that the banks, as key managers of industrial change in German capitalism, have been forced to make many enemies in trying to manage the process of industrial adjustment in the 'post-miracle' era. The enemies made in pushing for reform inside the financial services industry itself undoubtedly helps explain the position of one influential critic, Otto Graf Lambsdorff of the FDP. In its drive to modernize the stock exchange system the Deutsche Bank has come into serious conflict with the less internationally minded interests defending the federal stock exchange structure. Lambsdorff, as President of the Association for the Defence of Shareownership, has been a vocal defender of the regional exchange principle, and has linked his attacks on bank power to a defence of the federal stock exchange system in general, and of the small exchanges in particular (Lambsdorff, 1988).

The 'bank power' debate threatens to produce a major change in banking regulation; but the process of harmonization in the Community already has produced commitment to change. The EC Finance Ministers in June 1989 agreed a major liberalization measure which was adopted by the Council of Ministers in December 1989. This involves the creation of a single Community banking licence from January 1992 which will allow banks licensed in one member state free entry to the markets of other members (Woolcock, et al., 1991). But this undoubted step towards liberalization has had two other consequences whose full implications for the German regulatory system are unclear. First, the creation of a common licence necessarily also involves the specification of common prudential rules, in order to create a 'level playing field'. Germany unsuccessfully opposed the liberalization measures on the grounds that it was unhappy with the effects of proposed solvency ratios on some West German banks. It is at the moment simply unclear how far the harmonization of prudential rules will create a stricter or a more permissive regulatory regime in Germany. Given the complexities of prudential regulations it may be that we shall have to wait for the practical implementation of rules before we make any judgement. A second consequence is even more unclear. The creation of a common banking market also entails the creation of a common Community system for licensing banks from non-EC states. The June agreement offers the familiar principle of reciprocity: a licence will be available to non-EC banks whose states offer reciprocal terms to Community members. But the detailed implementation of this arrangement still has to be worked out, and it is the detailed implementation of regulation, not a general principle, which is crucial in determining outcomes. It is, in other words, unclear whether in the 1990s the German market will be less or more open than at present to the competitive challenge of non-EEC banks.

5. Conclusion: Why Was There No 'Big Bang' in Frankfurt?

The version of the German question that I pose here asks how we can account for the absence of large-scale policy change in the face of changes in the composition of government (Katzenstein, 1987, p. 4).

In the 1970s and 1980s regulatory change in financial markets was typically inaugurated by a 'Big Bang' (New York, London, Paris). In other words, there occurred a self-consciously dramatic change in the regulatory regimes, produced by decisive state intervention on the side of reforming coalitions. The Federal Republic has witnessed no such dramatic events. The development of financial regulation is consistent with the evidence from the very different policy fields examined by Katzenstein (1987), by Bulmer and Humphreys (1989) and by Webber (1988): there are powerful institutional obstacles to change in the Federal Republic. Authority is dispersed: through the federal structure, through the different local power bases of the Bonn political elite, through the network of free-standing federal regulatory agencies, and through self-regulation. Creating and mobilizing a winning coalition for systemic change has to overcome these institutional obstacles: and the absence of a 'Big Bang' in Frankfurt shows that this successful winning coalition has not been created. The process of German unification has made this more difficult still. The Bundesbank, the core of any reforming coalition, suffered significant set-backs in the debates over the financial arrangements for unification. In 1991 Herr Pöhl, the most powerful and prestigious of the reformers, stepped down as Bundesbank President. And, more generally, the task of integrating the old GDR into the financial system has meant that the energies of key actors and institutions have been absorbed by the reunification process.

It would be wrong, however, to conclude that German regulation is sclerotic. In the absence of a 'Big Bang' there has been a series of more minor explosions – the loudest being the opening of the German Futures Exchange in 1990. Despite the considerable institutional obstacles there has, as the preceding pages show, been considerable change. Four sources of change are worth noting.

First, the institutional structure has not been able to suppress the process of adaptation and innovation in markets. New technologies, changing demographic patterns, the example of other financial systems, the entry of foreign competitors into German markets: all these have prompted firms to treat the regulatory structure in an opportunistic way. Failure to do so is a recipe for decline and, as the cross-entries into insurance and banking markets show, the more ambitious firms have been unwilling to accept that recipe.

Second, the very institutional structures that have stood in the way of a 'Big Bang' have helped the process of piecemeal change. The dispersed structure of power means that, just as conservative coalitions can block comprehensive reform, reforming coalitions have the independence to achieve change in those parts of the system under their control. It has been plain that those who are most interested in Frankfurt's future – a group uniting state politicians, regulators in the Bundesbank and firms in the market – have simply gone ahead with their own innovations.

Third, while the opponents of change have powerful institutional advantages, a reforming coalition that can encompass the Bundesbank, the biggest commercial banks, and some state governments also commands considerable resources. In conditions where the opposing domestic coalitions both occupy positions of strength, external pressures can be crucial. In financial services, the progress of the world financial services revolution has created external pressures in favour of change. The breakthrough with the creation of the German Futures Exchange shows how the threat from external events can galvanize reformers into using their resources to the full. The Exchange has both a substantive and a symbolic importance. Substantively, it equips Frankfurt with the kind of market now demanded by powerful financial interests in all great centres. Symbolically, it breaks with federal principles, thus taking a step towards a more centralized system – a direction in which, as Herr Pöhl's June 1989 lecture showed, the reformers would like to move.

The phenomenon of innovation in the marketplace; the opportunities offered to reformers for piecemeal regulatory change; the advantages conferred on coalitions by the pressure of external events: all these help explain why regulatory change is indeed taking place in the Federal Republic. To this we must add a fourth, obvious factor: the Single European Act, and its implementation, has enlarged the cast of actors on the policy stage. As the creation of a common banking licence, Community-wide prudential banking standards and EC rules on insider dealing show, the new actors are decisively reshaping the German system. But the uncertainties in this reshaping process also exemplify the uncertain general character of regulatory change in the German financial markets. The Community is a source of irresistible pressure in the direction of harmonization. Whether the net result will be more or less liberalization, and more or less institutionalization, will only become clear into the 1990s.

Notes

This paper was originally given at the Workshop on 'The Politics of Regulation' convened by Kenneth Dyson at the University of Bradford, 5–6 October 1989. I am grateful to the participants for the helpful comments offered on that occasion.

References

Angerer, A. (1988), 'Versicherungsaufsicht und Wettbewerb der Versicherer', *Das Wirtschaftsstudium*, 8–9 August.
Benke, H. (1988), 'Terminhandel mit Bundesanleihen – London', *Die Bank*, **10**, October.
Bremkamp, D. (1988), 'Versicherungsschutz "Made in Germany" – ein internationaler Qualitätsvergleich', *Versicherungswirtschaft*, **43**, (1), January.

Buchner, G. (1988), 'Die Versicherungswirtschaft in der Wettbewerbsordnung', *Versicherungswirtschaft*, **43**, (6), 15 March.

Bulmer, S. (ed.) (1989), *The Changing Agenda of West German Public Policy*, Aldershot: Dartmouth.

Bulmer, S. and Humphreys, P. (1989), 'Kohl, Corporatism and Congruence: The West German Model under Challenge', in Bulmer (1989).

Cerny, P. (1989), 'The "Little Big Bang" in Paris: financial market deregulation in a *dirigiste* system', *European Journal of Political Research*, **17**.

Cooper, W. (1987), 'The financial services trade war', *Institutional Investor*, November.

Franke, J. (1989), 'Options und Terminmarkt in Deutschland', *Blick durch die Wirtschaft*, 7 June.

Henning, W. (1989), 'Kein Experimentierfeld für untaugliche Dereguliersπläne der EG-Kommission', *Handelsblatt,* 6 June.

Jones, C. (1989), 'A more productive relationship', *The Banker*, May.

Katzenstein, P. (1987), *Policy and Politics in West Germany: The Growth of a Semi-sovereign State*, Philadelphia: Temple University Press.

Kennedy, S. and Bernstein, G. (1988), 'Sind Aktien geeignete Anlagen für Lebensversicherungsgesellschaften?', *Zeitschrift für das gesamte Kreditwesen*, **41**, (10), 15 May.

Krakowski, M. (ed.) (1988), *Regulierung in der Bundesrepublik Deutschland*, Hamburg: Verlag Weltarchiv.

Krause, J. (1988), 'Die Deregulierungsdiskussion – theoretische Grundlagen und Bedeutung für die Versicherungswirtschaft', *Versicherungswirtschaft*, **43**, (6), 15 March.

Lambsdorff, O. (1988), 'Banken und Unternehmenskonzentration – Muss der Bankeneinfluß zurückgeschraubt werden?', *Zeitschrift für das gesamte Kreditwesen*, **41**, (2), 15 January.

Moran, M. (1989), 'A State of Inaction: the State and Stock Exchange Reform in the Federal Republic of Germany', in Bulmer (1989).

Moran, M. (1991), *The Politics of the Financial Services Revolution: the USA, UK and Japan*, London: Macmillan.

OECD (1986), *Economic Survey: Germany*, Paris: OECD.

Pfeiffer, H. (1986), 'Grossbanken und Finanzgruppen', *WSI Mitteilungen*, 7 July.

Pöhl, K. (1989), 'Frankfurt im Konkurrenzkampf der Finanzplätze', *Frankfurter Allgemeine Zeitung*, 24 June.

Reszat, B. 'Regulierung der Banken', in Krakowski (1988).

Schubert, W. (1988), 'In die Enge Getrieben', *Wirtschaftswoche*, 29 April.

Starke, O.E. (1988), 'Umfassende Deregulierung in der Versicherungswirtschaft und Versicherungsaufsicht gefordert', *Versicherungswirtschaft*, **43**, (18), 15 September.

Stracke, G. and Pöhl, M. (1988), 'Financial Services in Deutschland', *Die Bank*, April.

Webber, D. (1988), 'Krankheit, Geld und Politik: Zur Geschichte der Gesundheitsreformen in Deutschland', *Leviathan*, **16**, (2).

Webber, D. (1989), 'All quiet on the West German front', paper to Workshop, University of Bradford, October.

Wertpapier (1988), 'DSW setzt Neufassung der Insider-Regeln durch', 6 May.

Woolcock, S., Hodges, M. and Schreiber, K. (1991), *Britain, Germany and 1992*, London: Pinter, Royal Institute of International Affairs.

7 Vorsprung durch Technik? The Politics of German Environmental Regulation

Albert Weale

When the wave of environmental concern rose and broke over industrialized liberal democracies in the 1960s, the passions it aroused were as strong in Germany as anywhere else. Its effects cut deep into the fabric of German politics, increasing public participation in the policy process, reconfiguring patterns of interest-group representation and restructuring the party system. The politics of environmental protection disproportionately engaged the increasing segment of the population with high educational status who were sensitive not only to reports of environmental damage, for example fish poisoning in the Rhine, but also to international currents of opinion represented by the widespread attention paid to the publication of Rachel Carson's *Silent Spring* (1962). By the beginning of the 1970s awareness of environmental concerns quickly spread. Between September 1970 and November 1971, the proportion of interviewees in public opinion polls reporting that they had not heard of environmental protection decreased from 59 per cent to 8 per cent (Magedant, 1987, pp. 15–28). In response to local issues of traffic and town planning, citizens' initiatives mushroomed. The *Bundesverband Bürgerinitiativen Umweltschutz* (Association of Citizens' Initiatives in Environmental Protection) was formed in 1972 and with the challenge to particular construction projects, for example the building of a nuclear power station at Whyl am Kaiserstuhl in 1975 or the west runway at Frankfurt airport, the oppositional role of the citizens' initiatives took on national significance (Scott, 1990, p. 83). By 1980 the Greens had been founded as a new political party and three years later, in 1983, entered the Bundestag. By the 1980s, not even the most established political party could afford to ignore environmental issues. The political

159

agenda of Germany had been decisively changed. Some commentators have even claimed to see environmental protection as one of the main elements in the transformation of politics in Germany to a new agenda of 'post-materialism' in which the traditional issues of politics, the economy and the welfare state in particular, are supplanted by an overriding concern with questions involving the quality of life.

Yet, if the public concern with environmental protection represented a new phase of politics, its pursuit and implementation in public policy built upon traditional approaches, institutions and instruments. Unlike many other countries in the 1970s Germany did not create a ministry or equivalent administrative structure devoted primarily to environmental policy, and the creation of an environment ministry (the *Bundesministerium für Umwelt, Naturschutz und Reaktorsicherheit*) had to wait until 1986 when it was established rapidly in the wake of the Chernobyl incident. Although new legislation was passed in the 1970s in the field of air pollution, the model followed had already been pioneered in North-Rhine Westphalia in 1962. The primary instruments of environmental policy remained legal regulation and pollution charges based on administrative costs, with relatively little attention paid to economic instruments like tradeable permits or to strategies of self-regulation. Moreover, environmental protection through regulation exemplifies many of the themes that are found in other sectors of regulation: the Roman law use of general principles; the juridification of politics; the concern for norms of constitutional propriety according to the principles of the *Rechtsstaat*; and the cult of expertise.

In the course of policy developments, new thinking emerged about the role and purpose of environmental regulation. This thinking was expressed in the *Vorsorgeprinzip*, or principle of precaution, and it stressed the need to anticipate, rather than simply react to, environmental problems. This is not to say that German environmental policy conformed to the principle of precaution. Indeed, on two major issues of environmental protection, namely forest damage (Boehmer-Christiansen, 1989) and pollution of water by nitrates (Conrad, 1988), German policy was clearly reactive rather than anticipatory with public policy following the identification of environmental damage rather than preventing it. Even so, the principle of precaution has become an important premiss of justificatory strategies in policy discourse, and it has proved important in Germany's attempt to secure protection of the environment through international action, both in the context of the European Communities and in relation to the regime of international protection for the North Sea. It can also be argued that the *Vorsorgeprinzip* forms part of a wider set of ideas that found favour with some German and other policy elites in the 1980s, in the form of an ideology of 'ecological modernization'. According to this ideology, environmental protection does not rival the demands of economic development but forms a necessary condition of such development. Thus, high standards of environmental protection can form the basis for greater international economic competitiveness, and pollution control technologies and environmentally sound products are means by which improved performance could be secured against competition from Japan and the United States. These ideas, as we shall see, stand in a complex and subtle set of relationships with the institutions and processes of German environmental regulation.

In what follows I shall seek to examine these relationships, firstly, by identifying the main features of the legacy created by the historical development of environmental regulation in Germany and, secondly, by examining policy developments since the inauguration of the modern phase of environmental policy at the end of the 1960s. I shall then examine the likely effects on environmental regulation from German unification, as well as Germany's role in international regimes of pollution control, before going on to examine more general questions about style, process and policy learning in German environmental regulation.

1.   Historical Background of Environmental Regulation

Three factors conditioned the early development of environmental regulation in the nineteenth century: the decentralization of the political system in matters other than defence policy; the ethos of public authority playing a developmental role in relation to economic activity; and the high priority accorded in public policy to economic growth as measured by the level of industrial output. The combination of these factors meant that there was little pressure to develop a structure of environmental regulation at national level, as Great Britain had developed its national Alkali Inspectorate in the 1860s. Instead, the pattern of environmental regulation sprang from the sub-national patterns that had been developed by the *Länder* prior to unification, of which the most important were the Prussian General Trade Ordinances (*Gewerbeordnungen*) of 1845. These ordinances enabled local authorities to place conditions on manufacturing methods where emissions were likely to cause a problem of air pollution. This precedent was taken up by the North German Confederation in 1869, but the legislation remained permissive in character, and the degree of concern about pollution was limited by the so called 'duty of toleration' (*Duldungspflicht*) in the Civil Code of 1873, by which individuals were required to tolerate a certain amount of nuisance if this was necessary for the promotion of public welfare, interpreted as economic development (Wey, 1982, p. 109).

By the time of the First World War, the machinery and process of pollution control that was to remain in place until the 1950s was already established. In the case of air pollution control, the machinery comprised trade inspectors who had power to control emissions for a limited range of pollutants, notably smoke, particulates and sulphur dioxide. Within the legislative framework it was possible for the pollution control authorities to issue Technical Instructions (*Technische Anleitungen*) and in 1895 these allowed authorities to insist that operators conformed to the existing state of technology (*Stand der Technik*) in meeting emission limits. Although the Reich had established the Royal Prussian Office of Research for Air and Soil Hygiene in 1901, the role of the Reich was in practice limited to technical advice (Wey, 1982, p. 69).

The decentralized nature of environmental regulation meant that local standards varied considerably, a trend that was vividly illustrated in the case of water pollution. When in 1878 the *Deutsche Landwirtschaftsrat*, an organization of agricultural chambers and large landowners, protested about river pollution in a report to the Reich Chancellor, it met with the excuse that it was impossible to lay down a common standard for water cleanliness, and it was up to the confederate states to legislate in their own area (Wey, 1982, p. 38). In this context, what would now be termed 'transboundary' pollution became a serious issue when, in 1902, the BASF plant at Ludwigshafen discharged dye into the Rhine, making the river run red and creating anxiety in Worms, only 15 kilometres away but with its own distinct political administration. It was this incident which prompted the formation of the *Emscher Genossenschaft,* an association of local authorities and producers who banded together to regulate discharges and prevent excessive pollution. The Emscher precedent was followed by similar associations for the Wupper, the Lippe and the Ruhr. These *Genossenschaften* still remain in place with membership drawn from the owners of businesses operating in a river basin, communities within the area and representatives of the water industry. Like the system of air pollution control the essential structure of water pollution control was untouched by the political turbulence that preceded the creation of the Federal Republic in 1949.

The early years of the Federal Republic were the years of the *Wirtschaftswunder*, and concern about pollution was lost amid visible symbols of economic growth. After the Second World War and the 'hungry years', there was satisfaction that the 'chimneys were smoking again' (Spelsberg, 1984, p. 205). Economic growth not only obscured economic problems, but it also intensified them. This was clearly true with the growth of mass car ownership, but it also applied to new forms of pollution, for example from detergents. Moreover, because the legislative and administrative framework of the Trade Ordinances provided for protection from the effects of harm from trade, it was generally assumed that no special anti-pollution measures were necessary (Dreyhaupt et al., 1979, p. 1).

The first assault on these assumptions came in North-Rhine Westphalia, where it was estimated that during the 1950s some 600 000 tons of dust alone were discharged into the atmosphere every year. The issue was brought on to the agenda by Herr Sturm-Kegel, the Director of the *Siedlungsverein*, or neighbourhood association, in the Ruhr. He argued the need for a regulatory organization on the model of the *Genossenschaften* for water (Wey, 1982, p. 182). Although Sturm-Kegel's proposal did not get very far because of opposition from the Federation of German Industry (*Bund der Deutschen Industrie* – BDI), among others, the issue was taken up by Dr Schmidt, a *Landtag* deputy, who argued the need for more information and research. The campaign was also taken up by the Social Democratic Party at the federal level. The reports that resulted from this political pressure acknowledged that air pollution was a problem, particularly in relation to dust and the sulphur compounds, and argued that emission limit values ought to be applied for specified substances and that surveys of air quality should be undertaken.

The main legislative response to these ideas took place in North-Rhine Westphalia in 1962. The legislation covered not only smoke and gaseous emissions but also noise and vibration. Its method of control was to specify emission limits for certain processes in the context of ambient air quality standards. At the federal level the Clean Air Maintenance Law of 1959 extended the list of facilities which required a permit in order to operate and adopted other measures to strengthen implementation. After 1961 the Ministry of Health took over the responsibility of regulation from the Ministry of Labour; it developed new Technical Instructions for air which were issued in 1964. Modelled on the approach adopted in North-Rhine Westphalia, these Technical Instructions specified the licensing procedures for facilities requiring a permit. They also detailed air quality standards for five pollutants (dust, chlorine, sulphur dioxide, nitrogen dioxide and hydro-sulphide) and stipulated that emitting facilities should use the principle of *Stand der Technik* for controlling emissions.

In the case of water pollution the pressure for change came from industrial users, worried about the quality of supplies as inputs to manufacturing processes. Early in the 1950s the BDI ran a campaign for a 'usable environment' which resulted in the Federal Water Resources Act of 1957, which required that users of water resources should obtain an official permit for its use and set norms for discharges among those whose permits allowed them to use water for effluent purposes.

Despite these changes, the structure and functioning of the control system by 1964 was only partially modified from the Prussian system of trade regulation dating back to the middle of the nineteenth century. There was no national administrative body with prime responsibility for environmental standards and, although there were calls for further research, there was no administrative capacity or resources to undertake such work. Only a limited range of pollutants was controlled and the federal government possessed only framework powers of legislation. It was to take the wave of concern about environment quality that swept through the developed world in the late 1960s and early 1970s to begin the process of modification to the regulatory system. Even now the process is incomplete.

2.   Structure and Functioning of Environmental Regulation

The late 1960s and early 1970s saw a dramatic wave of concern about environmental deterioration, both at the level of mass public opinion and at the level of policy elites. The first stirring of environmental politics in Europe was symbolized by the Council of Europe's Year of Nature Protection in 1969. Domestically the general public in West Germany was alerted to the dangers of pollution in 1969 by fish poisoning in the Rhine resulting from the dumping of toxic waste and by subsequent scandals involving private waste removal firms. Policy developments in the United States, especially the establishment of the Council on Environmental Quality and the Environmental Protection Agency in 1970, significantly affected West German policy-makers (Hartkopf, 1988, p. 667). The United Nations' Conference on the Human Environment in Stockholm in 1972 brought about an improvement in international cooperation and also provided a stimulus to policy action through the United Nations' Environmental Programme. In its wake the EC Heads of States and Government initiated the Community's environmental policy, thus setting off a process of policy development that was to have significant repercussions on Germany's international bargaining about environmental regulation in the 1980s (see pp. 174–6)

In September 1970 the cabinet issued the *Sofortprogramm* (Immediate Programme) drawing attention to the need to develop environmental policy which was followed up in 1971 by the publication of the *Umweltprogramm* (*Umweltschutz*, 1972). The *Umweltprogramm* stated some basic principles in relation to environmental policy, including a commitment to the 'polluter pays' principle and to the principle of cooperation. Written in the early years of the Social–Liberal coalition, it also reflected the coalition's commitment to planning as a method of public policy. In his introduction, Hans-Dietrich Genscher (*Umweltschutz*, 1972, p. 11) wrote:[1]

Environmental policy means environmental planning over the long term.... Environmental planning must depend upon an environmental law that makes protection and development of nature an urgent matter of public precautionary concern.

The Programme also referred to the Cabinet committee that had been created on environmental affairs and detailed a list of action points aimed at controlling pollution.

In the wake of the establishment of environmental policy a number of changes in the machinery of government were introduced. On the model of the US Council of Environmental Experts the *Rat der Sachverständigen für Umweltfragen* (Council of Experts on Environmental Questions) was established, publishing its first report, on 'The Automobile and the Environment', in 1972. Containing a mixture of social and natural scientists, the 12-member Council produces regular reports on environmental questions. Sometimes these are on special topics, for example on automobiles or the state of the North Sea, and sometimes they represent a general evaluation of the state of the environment. On some occasions their work has led to specific policy developments: for example, the 1980 report on the North Sea was part of the process by which Germany convened the first Inter-Ministerial Conference on the North Sea (see below p. 176), whilst at other times their work has raised more general issues, for example in relation to the problem of the so-called implementation deficit or tendency for environmental regulations to be only weakly applied in practice. It was the Council's report in 1983 that first identified forest damage and acid rain as 'probably the greatest problem for environmental policy' in the Federal Republic (Boehmer-Christiansen, 1989, p. 102).

As part of the same process the *Umweltbundesamt,* or the Federal Agency for the Environment (UBA), was created in 1974. Despite its name and inspiration, UBA does not perform the same function as the US Environmental Protection Agency (EPA). EPA is responsible for the writing and implementation of pollution control regulation. Research and advice are part of EPA's tasks, but only a part. UBA, by contrast, is purely concerned with research and advice. It provides research assistance and advice to the ministry responsible for constructing and formulating regulations. It also summarizes more general research, and provides an information capacity for identifying environmental problems. Because of historic concerns about the development of unaccountable bureaucratic agencies, it would be politically and constitutionally impossible for UBA to develop a direct regulatory role. That role is performed with federal government ministries.

Despite other organizational reforms, there was no attempt in the 1970s to create an environment ministry. In 1969 the *Bundesministerium des Innern*

(BMI), the Federal Interior Ministry, was given responsibility for the air, noise and clean water sections transferred from the *Bundesministerium für Gesundheitswesen,* a change which involved the shifting of 14 sections (Müller, 1986, pp. 545–7). However, the creation of a central ministry for the environment was not on the political agenda until the mid-1980s, partly because the creation of a new ministry would have raised awkward questions about the allocation of cabinet portfolios among coalition partners, and partly because of some serious organizational doubts about the extent to which environmental functions should be concentrated in one ministry or integrated with the structure of a number of ministries (Müller, 1985, passim). In June 1986 the *Bundesministerium für Umwelt, Naturschutz und Reaktorsicherheit* (BMU), the Federal Ministry for Environment, Nature Protection and Reactor Safety, was created by Chancellor Kohl after there had been a demonstrable failure by the German environmental protection system to cope with the consequences of Chernobyl (Weale, O'Riordan and Kramme, 1991, pp. 122–35).

In Germany the primary task of an environment ministry is to develop policy and formulate legislation or regulations. In a system in which the emphasis is upon uniform emission standards for specified types of plant, for example the specification of allowable emissions of sulphur dioxide per square metre for electricity furnaces of a given megawattage, the task of formulating regulatory standards is a time-consuming and difficult one. Legal and engineering competence is given high weight, partly because Germany's constitutional system and concern for the principles of the *Rechtsstaat* mean that administrative regulations can be challenged in the courts and partly because the principle of *Stand der Technik* presupposes considerable familiarity with technological options. Technical instructions, which according to strict constitutional principle are only binding on the administration, are extremely detailed and complex, in order to ensure that all contingencies are covered and to provide grounds for resisting challenges in the administrative courts. In this respect, the German system resembles closely that found in the US, but Germany has managed to avoid the sort of costly litigation over proposed federal regulations that has led to the search for new regulatory strategies in the US (Bingham, 1986; Susskind and McMahon, 1985). Even so, there have been some significant court challenges, for example in 1984 when the operators of a district heating scheme appealed to the Federal Administrative Court over a change in the terms of their licence (see below, p. 171).

One particular aspect of the German system of rule-making is its dependence upon a specialized division of labour within sections of the ministry. As Mayntz and Scharpf (1975, chapter 7) have noted, the organization of the section tends to discourage lateral thinking outside the area of specialist expertise with which the section is concerned. This has implications for the technical effectiveness of pollution regulation. Since the environment is an interrelated system through which substances undergo cycles of changes, it is possible that the solution to a problem of pollution in one medium, for example emissions to the air, may be solved only at the expense of creating increased liquid discharges to water or a solid waste disposal problem to land. This insensitivity to problems of cross-media pollution has been identified as one of the shortcomings of the system of environmental regulation in Germany (Weidner, 1986, pp. 31–3). However, it may be argued that to a certain extent this deficiency is compensated for by developments that are occurring at the *Land* level.

Germany's system of federalism imposes a break in the policy cycle between policy formulation and policy implementation. Whilst the federal authorities have the responsibility for formulating policy and writing the appropriate regulations, the 'horizontal' federation of Germany means that it is the *Land* authorities that have responsibility for their implementation. Moreover, the *Länder* differ considerably in themselves, in terms of their susceptibility to environmental problems, their organizational structure and the ideological commitments of their governing parties. *Land* governments initiated experiments at different times in new forms of environmental administration, including the formation of a Ministry for State Development and Environmental Questions in Bavaria in 1970 – an innovation that was subsequently followed by other *Länder* over the years until May 1988 when the incoming SPD government in Schleswig–Holstein, the last in the chain, created an environment ministry.

For the historic reasons already identified, Germany lacks a comprehensive environmental protection act. However, its air pollution legislation, the *Bundes-Immissionsschutzgesetz (BImSchG)*, Federal Emission Control Act, provides some basis for regulating not only air pollution but also other sources of pollution as well. This is of particular importance at the level of implementation. The processes for granting a permit under the *BImSchG* enable regulators to control the permitting process for noise, worker safety, accident hazards, waste management, and building permits in addition to air since the administrative decisions for all these processes are included in the *BImSchG* permitting procedure. Moreover, other aspects of the *BImSchG* mean that the *Land* authorities can now include water treatment facilities in their permitting provided they are part of a plant that comes under the relevant legislation (Bennett and von Moltke, 1990, pp. 123–5).

Empirical work in Hamburg on the operation of the permitting system reveals that the process of regulation is transformed in the course of implementation, taking enforcement beyond the mechanical application of rules to a more subtle process by which optimum discharges are sought within the confines of legally specified emission limit values: 'it is apparent that identifying ways to reduce releases, taking into account technical and economic feasibility, below federally set standards is an essential element of the permitting process' (Bennett and von Moltke, 1990, p. 129). An example is provided by a furnace that was required to retrofit flue-gas desulphurization equipment, and where a process was agreed with the regulators by which the air pollution control objective could be achieved before the legislatively mandated timetable at the cost of some increase in landfill waste. Thus, even within a tightly regulated system of environmental protection, the negotiation of professionals within federally determined constraints still provides room for manoeuvre and opportunities for the exercise of administrative discretion.

One aspect of the German approach that deserves mention concerns the difficulties of tightening regulatory controls on emissions in the face of an industrial structure that is highly concentrated. The logic of the German environmental regulation is to observe the emergence of new technologies of pollution control as they are developed by industry, and then to set new and more stringent limits as these emerging technologies reveal new possibilities. Some regulators have claimed to observe a process by which industrialists refrain from introducing new technologies, as part of a collective response intended to slow down the need to introduce new technology, thereby reducing regulatory uncertainty. These 'cartels of refusal' (Wagner, 1991, p. 142) are leading to new regulatory counter-strategies, for example the allocation of targeted public funding to develop specialized innovations, but at present this type of response is still in its infancy.

3.   Policy Development and Policy Principles

The most important legislative development of the 1970s was the *Bundes-Immissionsschutzgesetz (BImSchG)*, the Federal Emission Control Act, which the Social–Liberal coalition passed in 1974, having obtained concurrent powers with the *Länder* in the field of air pollution in 1972. The act gives the federal government the competence to develop specific measures of pollution control in the form of ordinances and their associated technical instructions. Since 1974 a whole series of ordinances have been developed, of which the most important is the Large Combustion Plant Ordinance (*Grossfeuerungsanlagenverordnung*) of 1983. The general trend under the legislation is to strengthen (that is, lower) emission limit values in the light of a judgement about what is technically possible according to the principle of *Stand der Technik,* and to extend the range of emissions that are controlled. In general, German air pollution control is not technology-forcing in the strict sense. That is, it does not require operators of polluting equipment to install specific devices to reduce emissions. Instead, it sets emission standards in the light of the available technology and allows operators freedom to decide how to meet those standards. Among the exceptions to this general principle is the requirement that cars be converted with catalytic converters to reduce emissions of nitrogen oxides, but this exception can partly be explained by the technical difficulties of meeting tight emission standards by devices other than catalytic converters (in the present state of understanding at least) and partly by the desire of Dr Friedrich Zimmerman, the federal minister responsible for the environment in 1985, to be able to make a dramatic gesture on environmental affairs at a time when public attention was high.

The passing of the Large Combustion Plant Ordinance in 1983 represented a decisive shift in the intensity of environmental regulation. After the first burst of legislation and organizational restructuring in the early 1970s, German environmental policy passed from what Edda Müller has termed an 'offensive' phase to what she terms a 'defensive' phase (Müller, 1986, p. 45). In the wake of the 1973–4 oil crisis, a more reactive policy style was established (Richardson and Watts, 1985, p. 8), and in 1975 a meeting at Gymnich, between party, bureaucracy and social interest representatives, marked the beginning of a period in which traditional economic considerations prevailed over environmental protection. The transition was aptly symbolized in 1974 by the creation of a special unit within the Federal Ministry of Economic Affairs whose task was to check the costs of environmental policy measures (Hucke, 1985, p. 161). In the early 1980s public concern and awareness over *Waldsterben*, forest death, or *Waldschäden*, forest damage, (the terms themselves became elements of discursive strategies in a political game) led to rapid policy developments, as did the increase in the political organization of environmental groups, most notably the emergence of the Greens as a potentially pivotal political party in the formation of *Land* and federal governmental coalitions. In this context, the new Christian Democrat–Liberal coalition sought to meet the policy and political challenge by adopting the Large Combustion Plant Ordinance.

The Ordinance was the thirteenth in the list of ordinances issued under the *BImSchG*, and it introduced mandatory emission values on a range of pollutants both for new and for old plant that used combustion furnaces. The exact limits depend upon the size of the furnace and the type of fuel used and the emission limits apply not only to sulphur dioxide but also to nitrogen oxides, dust, heavy metals, halogen compounds and ozone. As a measure it had been brewing in the federal bureaucracy since 1978. Thus, although it was not originally conceived as a measure against *Waldsterben*, the public concern over forest death provided the catalyst for action, and the Ordinance rapidly came to be described as concerned with that problem (Boehmer-Christiansen, 1989, p. 131).

Undoubtedly the most significant innovation, in policy terms, under the Ordinance was the requirement that *existing* plant meet the standards within a five-year period, namely by 1 July 1988. To meet the standard required the retrofitting of flue-gas desulphurization equipment, which is expensive in itself and particularly expensive for older plant where the pay-back period for new investment is shorter than for new plant. Moreover, the scientific evidence linking forest damage with the range of pollutants controlled is by no means clear (Boehmer-Christiansen and Skea, 1991, pp. 38–41; Pearce, 1987, chapter 2), so that it was not possible to establish clear environmental benefits from a dramatic clean-up of emissions. There is no doubt that the control of emissions has been a success as a result of the policy. OECD (1991, p. 21) figures show a 59 per cent drop in total emissions of sulphur compounds between the beginning and the end of the 1980s (the USA recorded a 12 per cent drop and the UK a 24 per cent drop for the same period); but the environmental benefits of this change are difficult to estimate. Moreover, as Boehmer-Christiansen (1989, p. 33) stresses, the political coalitions favouring the policy development had mixed motives. Bavarian politicians, in particular, favoured the development both as an opportunity to embarrass the SPD in North-Rhine Westphalia, where much fossil fuel burning was concentrated, and as a device to enhance the promotion of nuclear power which they favoured on other grounds.

However, it is possible to argue that broader conditions were required in order to enable this policy development to take place. One of these conditions is that an ideology of 'ecological modernization' was beginning to find favour with certain policy elites in Europe in the 1980s, and that Germany provided fertile ground in which the seeds of this ideology could be planted (Weale, forthcoming). The central tenet of this ideology is that environmental protection should no longer be seen as standing in an antagonistic trade-off relation with the demands of economic growth with a trade-off to be made between the two. Instead, the development of pollution control equipment and technology could be a potent source of economic gain in global markets, so that by requiring high standards of pollution control the state had a device by which it could steer the economy on a new path. The implementation of the Large Combustion Plant Ordinance accorded well with Shonfield's (1969, pp. 239–64) characterization of Germany as an economic system of 'organized private enterprise'. Research and development investment was carried out by the government on environmentally friendly technologies, and there was concerted discussion on how to handle the problems associated with the disposal of gypsum created as a result of flue-gas desulphurization technology (Weale, O'Riordan and Kramme, 1991, pp. 184–200). The German gypsum industry has taken the initiative in extending its operations to the UK to take advantage of the British government's decision to implement flue-gas desulphurization as a technique of air pollution control, thus showing the export potential of being in the forefront of stringent environmental policy developments.

The legitimacy and public rationale of more stringent environmental regulation was developed by appeal to the so-called *Vorsorgeprinzip*, or principle of precaution. The origins of this principle arguably go back to the development of environmental policy in the 1970s and Genscher's insistence that environmental protection required far-sighted planning. However, the term itself clearly appears in the *BImSchG* (Chapter 5, sections 1–2) where precautionary measures are made a requirement of action in accordance with the principle of *Stand der Technik*. Shortly after this legislation in 1976 the Supreme Administrative Court of North-Rhine Westphalia confirmed the decision of the Düsseldorf Administrative Court that the extension of a coal-fired power station at Voerde ought not to be allowed because the area was already one of high air pollution (Müller, 1985, p. 272).

Subsequently the courts have used and developed the principle. On one occasion the Federal Administrative Court refused to accept a clear distinction between hazard protection and the risks inherent in nuclear power in its decision on the Wyhl nuclear power station. The principle of protection from danger (*Gefahrenabwehr*) is well established in German law, and the Federal Court argued that known hazards, falling under the principle of *Gefahrenabwehr*, and potential hazards, falling under the *Vorsorgeprinzip*, were on a continuum, so that the dangers associated with nuclear power should be reduced in the best possible way, taking into account the state of science and technology (Rehbinder, 1988). In 1984 the Federal Administrative Court heard an appeal against the Large Combustion Plant Ordinance from the operators of a district heating scheme, who argued that their furnace should be allowed to operate under the terms of a licence granted in 1976. The Court rejected the appeal arguing that the *Vorsorgeprinzip* contained in the *BImSchG* applied not only to the determination of air quality standards in the immediate location of a plant but also carried implications for the control of long-range pollutants. Moreover, the cost of control had to be considered in relation to the whole economy and not just in relation to one particular sector (Bundesverwaltungsgericht, 1984).

In a useful discussion of the *Vorsorgeprinzip*, Rehbinder (1988) has identified no less than 11 different meanings that the term can have in different institutional contexts. They involve the following ideas: preventing future damage that arises indirectly from certain sources; environmental quality improvements that allow a margin of protection for environmental restoration; the reduction of hazards that cause knowable, but very unlikely, damage; the reduction of hazards where the damage is unknown; minimizing environmental stress, even when there is no identified hazard or possible risk; choosing the best possible environmental option; stopping things getting worse; preventing contamination of the environment, even when there is no proof it is polluting; enforcing zero emission levels; avoiding the imposition of conflicting requirements in the pursuit of preventive environmental protection strategies; and forbidding the permanent use of certain environmental resources. Although there is this great diversity in the different senses that the *Vorsorgeprinzip* can bear, a common thread in all of them is the need to regulate for environmental protection where the benefits cannot be directly and tangibly related to the costs of the measures adopted.

In domestic policy terms, some of the implications of this idea were spelt out by the federal government in its discussion document published under the title *Leitlinien Umweltvorsorge* (1986). The implication of the *Vorsorgeprinzip,* according to this document, is that stringent emission limits are insufficient by themselves and need to be complemented through specific environmental quality standards not only in the case of air, where they currently apply, but also in the cases of soil and water. Such a development of policy in line with the *Vorsorgeprinzip* would undoubtedly have wide-ranging implications. However, it can be argued that an even greater challenge confronts German environmental regulation, namely what to do about the legacy of environmental degradation it has inherited from the former German Democratic Republic as a result of unification.

4.   Environmental Regulation and German Unification

One of the sights that symbolized the collapse of the former German Democratic Republic was a queue of young Germans in their *Trabis* waiting to travel to the west. Yet the *Trabi* also does duty as another symbol, namely of an inefficient and unmodernized system of production that was unable to manufacture goods to a high environmental quality. Whatever it did for the flight to freedom, the *Trabi* did little for the atmosphere into which its exhaust gases were emitted.

Even before unification became a practical political possibility it was clear that environmental protection in the Democratic Republic was of a low standard. In the early 1980s, for example, it experienced average monthly sulphur depositions of 77 800 metric tons, nearly 70 per cent of the West German level for a country with about one-third of the population.

Moreover, by comparison with West Germany, a much higher proportion of sulphur (64 per cent as distinct from 48 per cent) was domestically produced (Weidner, 1986, p. 16). These levels of pollution reflected low levels of investment, the failure to implement regulations to restrain the production imperatives of the state and the lack of political influence and power by which members of civil society could protect their interests. These factors combined made Article 15 of the GDR's constitution, by which clean water and clean air were guaranteed to citizens (Paucke, 1987, p. 150), little more than a paper promise.

The period since unification has revealed the seriousness of environmental degradation in the former German Democratic Republic and the size of the clean-up costs that will be necessary in order to make the environment habitable by any reasonable standards. A striking example of the problem is provided by a border area between Thuringia and Saxony, where huge masses of radioactive earth have been dumped above ground which are regularly deposited by winds on surrounding villages. The former East German government allowed the Soviet Union to dump the material from its atomic weapons programme. The total clean-up costs are currently reckoned to be some DM15 billion. The human cost is indicated by the exceptionally high incidence of cancer among residents and workers (Douglas and Kleine-Brockhoff, 1991).

In the closing months of the communist regime, the West German government had begun moves to improve environmental protection in the Democratic Republic in fields where the two political systems had joint concerns. In July 1989 there was a joint agreement on six environmental projects, to which the Federal Republic contributed DM300 million and of which the most urgent was the establishment of a smog alarm system in East Germany. The programme was subsequently developed to include 15 more projects at a cost of DM600 million from the German Federal Ministry of Environment. In the run-up to unification, the pace of developments quickened. By February 1990 a joint commission had been established to look into specific policy problems, with three working groups covering the fields of legal/organizational arrangements, ecological restoration and energy and the environment. The following month, in March 1990, a similar agreement was signed covering nuclear matters (BMU, 1990, pp. 158–61).

Since unification the smog alarm system has been integrated into that of the former West Germany and is now run by UBA, although there are continuing problems with the transmission of the data due to the operational deficits of the former East German telephone network (Lersner, 1991, p. 237). However, the most important action has been the development of an immediate environmental programme for the *Länder* of the former GDR, including Berlin, concluded on 17 May 1991 between the federal ministry and representatives of the *Länder*. The immediate programme contains a promise of DM800 million over the period 1991–2, to be devoted to the improvement of drinking water quality, making waste sites safe, the conversion of incinerator plants and the improvement of environmental administration, particularly in respect of licensing processes (Bundesministerium für Umwelt, 1991, pp. 238–40).

It is difficult to predict how the process of unification will relate to the development of environmental regulation. Environmental clean-up costs present a potentially large demand on an economy that already has to absorb other financial burdens flowing from unification. On the other hand, since much new investment will be required to bring the economy of the former Democratic Republic up to date, there is an argument to say that production processes can be quite quickly adapted to the high environmental standards that West Germany was beginning to achieve. Certainly nothing reveals more clearly the kernel of truth in the thesis of ecological modernization that in an advanced economy environmental standards are a precondition of economic health than the collapse in demand for goods from the East German *Länder*. The federal government currently intends to apply the standards from West Germany by the middle of the 1990s. If this goal is accomplished, it will be a striking demonstration of the centrality of environmental protection to the German political agenda.

5. The International Dimension

At the time of the second oil-price explosion in 1979 an observer of international environmental policy would have concluded that the Federal Republic of Germany took a cautious and conservative attitude. It opposed the further reductions in sulphur dioxide emissions under international agreements like the 1979 Convention on Long-Range Transboundary Air Pollution, and it did not use other international fora to push a pro-environmentalist line. From the summer of 1982 onwards, however, there was a sharp reversal of attitude, after the Social–Liberal coalition reversed its previous policy stance, and the German government made clear its conversion in June 1982 at the Stockholm Conference on the Acidification of the Environment.

One of the first effects of this conversion was felt in the European Community, where by coincidence the Commissioner responsible for environmental affairs was German. After the passage of the Large Combustion Plant Ordinance, the German government came under strong pressure from industrialists to take action to even out the cost burdens that German industry now suffered. Officials within the Directorate-General XI of the

EC Commission were instructed to prepare an EC equivalent to the Large Combustion Plant Ordinance. Despite warnings that such an approach would be politically unacceptable, it was hardly surprising given the context that the proposed draft directive bore a close resemblance to its German original. The essence of the proposal was to set limit values for all plants in the Community over 50 megawatts and to stipulate a timetable for the reduction of a specified range of pollutants. By 1995, it was proposed, sulphur dioxide emissions should be reduced by 60 per cent, and 40 per cent reductions in nitrogen oxides and dust were to be achieved, relative to a base-line of 1980.

The response to these proposals was predictably varied. Haigh (1989) suggests that it fell into four groups. The Netherlands and Denmark joined Germany in being enthusiastic. France and Belgium were able to be relatively indifferent given the development of nuclear power. A group of less developed countries, led by Spain, rejected as draconian the burden of cost control at a phase of their development where they were expanding energy consumption. Finally, Italy and the UK were both large emitters dependent upon coal. The UK, in particular, emerged as a key opponent of the draft directive and its successors, influenced partly by an elite of scientific advisers who were sceptical of the ecological benefits of large reductions of sulphur dioxide and partly by the investment cycle of the Central Electricity Generating Board, which together with the Treasury, doubted the wisdom of the spending necessarily involved.

Successors of the original German proposals underwent five years of tortuous bargaining at official and ministerial level before an acceptable compromise emerged in the form of the Large Combustion Plant Directive (Commission of the European Communities, 1988). The eventual agreement differed markedly from the original proposal. Belgium, Denmark, France and the Netherlands joined Germany in accepting target reductions of sulphur dioxide by 2003 at or around 70 per cent of 1980 levels. Other countries, including the UK, had target reductions of around 60 per cent by 2003 implying a significantly slower timetable for reductions than the original proposals. Three countries (Greece, Ireland and Portugal) were even allowed increases in their emission ceilings.

Although the focus of the most intense environmental diplomacy in the 1980s, it can be argued that the struggle over the Large Combustion Plant Directive was important because it symbolized a broader shift of influence in the relation between Germany and the EC, and the wider world, rather than for its intrinsic aspects. During the course of the 1980s the notion that European environmental policy and regulation needed a precautionary principle, akin to the German *Vorsorgeprinzip*, steadily gained ground. Such an approach was embodied in the ECs statement of its *Fourth Environmen-*

tal Action Programme (CEC, 1986) and, indeed, by 1990 even the UK government formally adopted the principle (UK Government, 1990), although in a form so qualified as to give reason to doubt that the government fully understood what it was saying. The *Vorsorgeprinzip* has also played an important role in Germany's attempts to establish an international regime for the protection of the North Sea. In its 1980 report on the North Sea, the *Rat für Sachverständigen Umweltfragen* had argued the need for precaution in the North Sea, claiming that the principle of precaution warranted action in advance of clear evidence of environmental damage. In response, the German government convened an Inter-Ministerial Conference on the North Sea in Bremen in 1984, which has subsequently met on two occasions, once in London in 1987 and once in The Hague in 1990. Standing in a rather uneasy relationship to two international organizations for the protection of the North Sea (Hayward, 1989), namely the Oslo and the Paris Commissions, the Inter-Ministerial Conference has none the less developed extensive regulatory policies, with an explicit acknowledgement of the *Vorsorgeprinzip*.

It can be argued that the German style of environmental regulation translates well into an international context. The legal formalism of the German approach favours uniform emission standards and minimizing the discretion to be exercised in specific situations. Because problems of compliance and verification loom large in international agreements, uniformity of approach is attractive in terms of international regulation. Thus the 1990 Inter-Ministerial Conference on the North Sea agreed to phase in a complete ban on sewage sludge dumping at sea for all countries. Environmental scientists in Britain, educated in a regulatory culture that favours a piecemeal approach to problems on a scientifically informed basis, argue that this approach ignores the environmental problems that alternative disposal routes encounter, and prefer the principle of optimally balancing protection of the North Sea with the need to dispose of pollution. But one country's optimal use of a common resource is difficult to verify in an international context, whereas the rigorous application of a common rule, which so naturally arises from a German regulatory culture, has an obvious appeal in the context of international agreements and the search for compliance. As European integration develops, the German style of regulation is likely to become more prevalent rather than less. But what are the essential elements of this style, and of the regulatory culture and institutions that underlie it?

6. Style, Process and Policy Learning

German environmental regulation instances many of the features that are common to regulation of other policy issues in Germany: the juridification of politics; the deference to technical expertise; the shared consultation among policy elites in industry and government about the development of industry; and the limited opportunity structures for public participation.

The juridification of environmental regulation is expressed in various ways of which one of the most important is the use of general principles in legislation and policy within a policy system in which constitutional norms of due process have high status. These policy principles are not simply a rhetorical veneer, but provide a means by which participants in the policy process orientate their perceptions and actions. At any one time there will be a set of regulatory policies or programmes; but behind these stand the general principles of which the policies or programmes are an expression. Participants in the policy process are often concerned with the 'concretization' of principles, and this is natural in a policy belief system in which general principles are basic and individual policies or programmes a consequence of their application. Although this stylistic feature of the belief system underlying the regulatory system can seem highly abstract and formalized (at least to the non-native German, and perhaps to many native Germans as well) it can be argued that it is essential to the ideas of a *Rechtsstaat,* the requirements that state action be conducted in a publicly justifiable manner through legal processes, to which the state itself is subject (Ellwein, 1965, pp. 420–1).

A consequence of this approach is that the courts, and in particular the administrative courts, play a role in the setting of regulatory standards in their review of appeals against administrative rule-making. The use of general principles becomes important in this context, as was revealed in the Federal Administrative Court's decision over the *Grossfeuerungsanlagenverordnung,* and the administrative courts are always potentially important in regulatory decision-making because of the general German constitutional principle of *Verhältnissmässigkeit,* or proportionality, by which the burdens imposed by regulation have to be brought into relation with the prospective advantages.

One particular implication of the high importance given to due process within the tradition of the *Rechtsstaat* is provided by the question of the choice of policy instruments. There has been a great deal of interest in economic instruments at the level of policy discussion. In particular, the question has been raised as to whether it is possible to substitute pollution taxes for uniform regulations, because of the putative efficiency properties of the former by comparison with the latter. Thus, a damage-based taxation scheme would imply that manufacturers in areas of heavy pollution should face higher costs than manufacturers in areas where marginal damage was less. Yet, as Michael Kloepfer (1990) has pointed out, this type of proposal runs into difficulty from considerations of due process. Regulations, it may be argued, impose uniform burdens on all manufacturers; pollution taxes imply differential burdens, and so run up against problems of due process and constitutional propriety.

The stress upon the cult of expertise in German politics is illustrated by the appointment of Professor Klaus Töpfer as Federal Minister for the Environment. An academic environmental economist by background, he succeeded Walter Wallmann, whose task had been to steer the new ministry through its early and difficult months. Professor Töpfer has been able to solidify and strengthen the administrative structures of the new ministry and consolidate its regulatory strategy. Since his appointment the ministry has steadily extended and strengthened the scope of its regulatory activity. An important recent example is provided by an ordinance under the waste law which makes producers and retailers responsible for the disposal of their packaging. Professor Töpfer himself remains an active participant in the academic discussion of environmental regulation, and regularly gives papers at academic and other conferences organized for members of the policy community.

There is also the question of the type of expertise that is incorporated into the regulatory process. Legal and engineering expertise has traditionally been given a central role in a system in which the legal codification of uniform standards is important. The advisory part of the regulatory process has seen broader types of expertise drawn upon, although lawyers and engineers remain powerful. For example, Professor Fritz Scharpf, an expert in the administrative sciences, has held a place on the *Rat für Sachverständigen Umweltfragen,* and the Council itself has undertaken work on such topics as implementation deficit in a way that its British equivalent, the Royal Commission on Environmental Pollution, has not done.

This combination of constitutional orientation and structured expertise has implications for the political opportunity structures (Kitschelt, 1986) that confront environmental activists. As Paterson (1989, pp. 278–80) points out, the political opportunity structure on the input side of policy-making is generally closed in Germany, whereas on the output side environmental groups can use the legal review process to slow down or reverse the implementation of policy. In consequence there have been no experiments with what in North America is termed 'regulatory negotiation' (cf. Amy, 1990; Doern, 1990). Regulatory negotiation involves a process by which regulatory standards are set by negotiation between representatives of industry, public agencies and non-governmental organizations, where the purpose is to seek to evolve a consensus about rule-making. This type of participatory approach is entirely absent from German practice and arguably it reflects the political and cultural gap that still exists between environmental activists and members of the policy-making elite.

The character of the environmental regulation that emerges from this mixture of elements is defined by a strong emphasis upon constitutional formalism, on the one hand, embedded in the preferences for uniform emission standards, and technical expertise on the other, reflected for example in the thoroughness of the reports from the Council of Experts on Environmental Questions. *Vorsprung durch Technik* would not be an inappropriate motto for the process of policy-making. Within this context key ideas within the ideology of ecological modernization have found a receptive context in which to develop. Once leading members of the political and economic elite came to see the export and growth potential inherent in the development of new pollution control technologies, the simple antagonism between economy and environment in decision-making was broken down. This does not mean that worries about the costs of stringent environmental regulations are absent in German policy discussions, either in terms of the direct costs of higher electricity prices, for example, or in terms of the indirect costs attributable to a movement of capital to countries in which regulatory standards are less strict. It does mean, however, that problems of economic feasibility have to be accommodated within a generally acknowledged commitment to improve the environment to meet popular expectations about the quality of life.

Does this mean that there has been a paradigm shift in the character of German environmental regulation? The answer here is ambiguous. To the extent to which since 1982 the balance of argument has shifted from economic feasibility to environmental protection the answer must be yes. Germany is now legislating some of the most stringent environmental standards in western Europe and, just as importantly, is maintaining its momentum for improvement. Yet the majority of what has been accomplished has been done using traditional modes of regulation by ordinance. The legitimating principle of greater stringency has derived from the *Vorsorgeprinzip,* which, though innovatory, could be regarded as an extension of a complex body of ideas about the responsibility of the state to ensure the conditions for social development (Dyson, 1980), and the courts have felt able to apply the notion of *Vorsorge* partly because they have seen it as being continuous with other well-established principles.

It can be argued that the successes of German regulation, most notably the reduction in sulphur emissions, have been those which its orientation in terms of technical rationality find most easy to achieve. Since a high proportion of sulphur emissions come from larger stationary sources, an approach in terms of legally induced engineering controls is likely to be rapidly effective. The same approach applied to the non-point sources of pollution looks less plausible. Nitrate pollution from farmers provides one example and nitrogen oxide emissions from fast driving speeds on the *Autobahnen* provide another. Behavioural changes have been induced by public policy, for example the separation of household waste for recycling, but such changes look more difficult when the behaviour has significant economic consequences for private individuals, as is the case with farming controls, or impinges upon a complex psychological attachment to fast cars. Moreover, among those groups who draw their inspiration from the ideology of new social movements and who are concerned to protect the environment, the dominance of technical rationality within a bureaucratic and industrial complex is part of the problem rather than part of the solution.

The issue is important because new environmental problems, most notably the issue of climate change, look as though they will require behavioural as well as technological change. Germany has committed itself to the ambitious target of reducing its carbon dioxide emissions by 25 to 30 per cent by the year 2005. Considerable progress towards this target can undoubtedly be made by improvements in the energy consumption of appliances and products. However, significant reductions in energy use are also likely to involve less use of the private car and a reversal in the growth of regional airports. These behavioural and social changes look more difficult to achieve, and they are certainly not amenable to the types of intervention that have dominated hitherto. Such policy problems will raise complex issues about the relationship between the state and civil society, which is not a novel theme in German history. In this context, *Technik* may well be revealed by its limits.

Acknowledgement

This chapter draws upon research material from two research projects: 'Change and Choice in Environmental Regulation' financed by the Anglo–German Foundation for Industrial Society and 'The North Sea: International Regimes and Environmental Policy' financed by the European Science Foundation. As well as acknowledging this support, I owe special thanks to Louise Kramme and Andrea Williams for research assistance. David Goodhart proved a valuable informant and Ken Dyson, as editor, was both patient and insightful in his comments.

The Politics of German Environmental Regulation 181

Note

1 'Umweltpolitik bedeutet Umweltplanung auf lange Sicht.... Umweltplanung muss auf einem Umweltrecht beruhen, das Schutz und Entwicklung der Naturgrundlagen zu den dringlichen Aufgaben staatlicher Daseinvorsorge macht' (*Umweltschutz*, 1972, p. 11).

References

Amy, Douglas (1990), 'Decision Techniques for Environmental Policy: A Critique', in Robert Paehlke and Douglas Togerson (eds), *Managing Leviathan*, Peterborough, Ontario: Broadview Press, 59–79.

Bennett, Graham and von Moltke, Konrad (1990), 'Integrated Permitting in the Netherlands and the Federal Republic of Germany', in Nigel Haigh and Frances Irwin (eds), *Integrated Pollution Control in Europe and North America*, Washington D.C.: The Conservation Foundation, 105–45.

Bingham, Gail, (1986), *Resolving Environmental Disputes: A Decade of Experience*, Washington D.C.: The Conservation Foundation.

Boehmer-Christiansen, Sonja (1989), *The Politics of Environment and Acid Rain in the Federal Republic of Germany: Forest versus Fossil Fuels?*, Science Policy Research Unit, University of Sussex: SPRU Occasional Paper, Series No. 29.

Boehmer-Christiansen, S. and Skea, J. (1991), *Acid Politics*, London and New York: Belhaven Press.

Bundesministerium für Umwelt (1990), *Umwelt '90: Umweltpolitik, Ziele und Lösungen*, Bonn: BMU.

Bundesministerium für Umwelt (1991), 'Sofortprogramm zum Umweltschutz angebufen', *Umwelt*, Nr 6, 238–40.

Bundesverwaltungsgericht (17 February 1984) 7C 8/82 (Mannheim).

Carson, R. (1962), *Silent Spring*, Harmondsworth: Penguin, 1983 reprint.

Commission of the European Communities (1986), *Fourth Environmental Action Programme 1987–92 Com (86) 485 Final*, Luxembourg: Office for Official Publications of the European Communities.

Commission of the European Communities (1988), 'Directive on the Limitation of Certain Pollutants into the Air from Large Combustion Plants' (88/609/EEC), *Official Journal of the European Communities* L336/1.

Conrad, Jobst (ed.) (1988), *Wassergefährdung durch die Landwirtschaft*, Berlin: Sigma.

Doern, G. Bruce (1990), 'Regulations and Incentives: The NOx – VOCs Case', in G. Bruce Doern (ed.), *Getting It Green: Case Studies in Canadian Environmental Regulation*, Ottawa, Ontario: C.D. Howe Institute, 89–110.

Douglas, H. and Kleine-Brockhoff, T. (1991), 'Heisse Erde aus dem kalten Krieg', *Die Zeit*, **24** (7 June), 15–17.

Dreyhaupt, Franz Joseph et. al. (1979), *Handbuch zur Aufstellung von Luftreinhalteplänen*, Köln: TÜV Rheinland.

Dyson, K. (1980), *The State Tradition in Western Europe*, Oxford: Martin Robertson.

Ellwein, Thomas (1965), *Das Regierungssystem der Bundesrepublik Deutschland*, Köln and Opladen: Westdeutscher Verlag.

Haigh, N. (1989), 'New tools for European air pollution control', *International Environmental Affairs*, 1.

Hartkopf, G. (1988), 'Umweltpolitik', *Handwörterbuch des Umweltrechts*, Berlin: Frich Schmidt Verlag.

Hayward, Peter (1989), 'The Oslo and Paris Commissions', *International Journal of Estuarine and Coastal Law*, 91–100.

Hucke, J. (1985) 'Environmental Policy: The Development of a New Policy Area', in K. von Beyme and M.R. Schmidt (eds), *Policy and Politics in the Federal Republic of Germany*, Aldershot: Gower.

Kitschelt, H. (1986), 'Political opportunity structures and political protest: Anti-nuclear movements in four democracies', *British Journal of Political Science*, 14, (1), 57–85.

Kloepfer, M. (1990), 'Rechtsstaatliche Probleme und gesamtwirtschaftliche Effekte', in Gerd Rainer Wager (ed.), *Unternehmung und ökologische Umwelt*, München: Franz Vahlen, 241–61.

Lersner, Heinrich von (1991), 'Das Smog – Frühwarnsystem im vereinten Deutschland', *Umwelt*, Nr 6, 237–8.

Magedant, K. (1987), 'Die Entwicklung des Umweltbewusstseins in der Bundesrepublik', *Aus Politik und Zeitgeschichte*, 29, 15–28.

Mayntz, Renate and Scharpf, Fritz (1975), *Policy-Making in the Federal German Bureaucracy*, Amsterdam: Elsevier.

Müller, Edda (1986), *Innenwelt der Umweltpolitik*, Opladen: Westdeutscher Verlag.

OECD (1991), *The State of the Environment*, Paris: OECD.

Paterson, William E. (1989), 'Environmental Politics', in Gordon Smith, William E. Paterson and Peter H. Merkl (eds), *Developments in West German Politics*, Basingstoke: Macmillan, 267–88.

Paucke, Horst (1987), 'The German Democratic Republic', in Gyorgy Enyedi, August J. Gijswijt and Barbara Rhode (eds), *Environmental Policies in East and West*, London: Taylor Graham, 148–65.

Pearce, Fred (1987), *Acid Rain*, Harmondsworth: Penguin.

Rehbinder, Eckard (1988), 'Vorsorgeprinzip im Umweltrecht und präventive Umweltpolitik', in U.E. Simonis (ed.), *Präventive Umweltpolitik*, Frankfurt/New York: Campus Verlag.

Richardson, J. J. and Watts, N. (1985), '*National Policy Styles and the Environment: Britain and West Germany Compared*', Berlin: Internationales Institut für Umwelt und Gesellschaft.

Scott, A. (1990), *Ideology and the New Social Movements*, London: Unwin Hyman.

Shonfield, Andrew (1969), *Modern Capitalism*, London: Oxford University Press.

Spelsberg, G. (1984), *Rauchplage: Hundert Jahre Saurer Regen*, Aachen: Alano.

Susskind, Lawrence and McMahon, Gerald (1985), 'The theory and practice of negotiated rulemaking', *Yale Journal of Regulation*, 3, 133–65.

UK Government (1990), *This Common Inheritance*, London: HMSO.

Umweltschutz (1972), Stuttgart: W. Kohlhammer.
Wagner, Gerd Rainer (1991), 'Entrepreneurship and Innovation from an Environmental Risk Perspective', in L. Roberts and A. Weale (eds), *Innovation and Environmental Risk*, London and New York: Belhaven Press, 138–48.
Weale, Albert (forthcoming), *The New Politics of Pollution*, Manchester: Manchester University Press.
Weale, Albert, O'Riordan, Timothy, and Kramme, Louise (1991), *Controlling Pollution in the Round*, London: Anglo-German Foundation.
Weidner, Helmut (1986), *Air Pollution Control Strategies and Policies in the Federal Republic of Germany*, Berlin: Wissenschaftszentrum Berlin für Sozialforschung.
Wey, Klaus-Georg (1982), *Umweltpolitik in Deutschland: Kurze Geschichte des Umweltschutzes in Deutschland seit 1900*, Opladen: Westdeutscher Verlag.

8 The Politics of Nuclear Regulation

Stephen Padgett

Currents of liberalization and deregulation have made no impact upon the nuclear energy sector in the Federal Republic. In fact the last two decades have witnessed a tightening of the grip of regulation on the sector, to a point where the economic viability of commercial nuclear energy has become marginal. In no other major industrial country, with the possible exception of the United States, has the nuclear industry been subjected so heavily to regulatory pressures. The insulation of the sector from deregulatory initiatives can be partially explained by the inherent characteristics of nuclear technology. Since energy supply is network-bound it is less susceptible to the forces of international competition and the globalization of markets which have driven deregulation in other sectors. Moreover, the unique hazards of nuclear technology, and the intensification of public perceptions of these risks, have led all democratic states to acknowledge a regulatory duty. However, in contrast to the flexible and centralized regimes in France and Britain, nuclear regulation in Germany is bound by legal rigidities, fragmented, and susceptible to political conflict. In the last decade it has severely limited the commercial potential of the sector.

The singular impenetrability of the network of nuclear regulation in the Federal Republic, and its resistance to simplification or relaxation can be explained with reference to three characteristics of the regulatory regime. Firstly, the regulatory regime is very heavily conditioned by the historic tradition of legalism. The parameters of nuclear regulation are anchored in the 1959 Nuclear Energy Act, *Gesetz über die friedliche Verwendung der Kernenergie und den Schutz gegen ihre Gefahren* (Federal Act on the Peaceful Uses of Nuclear Energy and Protection against its Hazards). The regulatory regime is thus ordered with reference to legal norms about which policy is orientated in an attempt to derive authoritative answers to the ethical and social dilemmas inherent in nuclear technology. The result has been the *juridification* of regulation, or regulation by legal norm, an effect which has been observed in a number of other sectors (Peacock, 1984, p. 118; Hancher and Ruete, 1987, pp. 171–3). Juridification has served to open up the regulatory process to broad participation through the courts. Moreover, the intertwining of the legal and political processes has resulted in labyrinthine complexity and a rationality deficit.

Secondly, nuclear regulation in Germany is subject to the syndrome of *Politikverflechtung* – the interrelation of multiple agencies and levels of government. The institutional framework of the federal system encourages policy formation and implementation by bureaucratic negotiation between the two levels of government resulting in sub-optimal policy outcomes lacking in strategic direction (Scharpf, 1988, pp. 139, 149). *Politikverflechtung* has bred a pluralistic regulatory regime and a fragmentation of authority, leading to inconsistencies of regulatory practice and, since the breakdown of the nuclear consensus, outright conflict between federal and state authorities.

Thirdly, the regulatory regime is very heavily marked by the ethos of *Sachlichkeit* (objectivity). A basic legal principle of regulation is the *Schutzpflicht* of the state. The state thus carries the ultimate responsibility for nuclear safety, and has pursued a safety philosophy based on objective standards contained in a hierarchical code of technical guidelines and norms, drafted and administered by independent bodies of technical experts. These practices differ sharply from the regime in the UK, where the Nuclear Installations Inspectorate has resisted the specification of rigid technical standards in favour of flexibility and operator responsibility (Smellie, 1988, pp. 190–3). The emphasis on formalized rigid standards and independent expert bodies in the Federal Republic has led to the proliferation of the bureaucracy surrounding the licensing of nuclear installations, and a progressive escalation of safety requirements. Moreover, 'as the controversy between incompatible positions within the scientific community widened, and as the conflict became more political, the guiding function of scientific argumentation was completely lost' (Kitschelt, 1980, p. 213).

These three factors combine to inhibit change in the regulatory regime. Regulatory objectives are defined in the Nuclear Energy Act, and interpreted by the courts. Juridification has removed the major questions of nuclear regulation from the political arena. *Paradigm change* – the redefinition of the ground rules of regulation – would require an overhaul of the Act, politically inexpedient in the face of social opposition. Regulatory procedures are encased in the Nuclear Energy Act, and are frequently contested in the courts with reference to their compatibility with the Act. Without amendments to the law, even incremental changes in the practice of regulation are impossible to achieve. The fragmentation of the regulatory apparatus between federal government and the *Länder,* and its bureaucratization, present a further obstacle to change. In so far as regulatory change has occurred at all, it has been towards an ever narrower interpretation of the law, and a more restrictive application of existing instruments. The nuclear industry recognizes that a prerequisite of the relaxation or simplification of the regulatory regime is the formation of a positive public attitude towards the industry, hardly to be expected under present circumstances.

1. Regulatory Culture: Some Cross-National Comparisons

The destructive potential of nuclear technology means that in almost all countries its exploitation is subject to rigorous national and international regulation. From the outset there was a broad consensus, at least amongst scientific and political elites, over the potential (civil and military) benefits of nuclear power. It was recognized, however, that in the interests of national security and in order to secure the legitimacy of the nuclear project, some form of regulation was necessary. The main objective of policy-makers in Britain was to exert control over nuclear activity by establishing something close to a state monopoly. No provision was made for control over government or the regulation of the design, construction, or operation of government plants. 'It seems to have been assumed that the government could keep its own house in order ... government scientists were assumed to be able to operate systems of self-supervision' (Smellie, 1988, pp. 58, 61).

Subsequently the primary action of the government in relation to the control of nuclear hazards was 'to create a responsible body of official experts [the Atomic Energy Authority] which it was felt could be trusted to get on with the job' (Smellie, 1988, p. 356). The impetus for independent oversight, formal regulation and licensing came later in response to the Windscale fire of 1957 and the recommendations of a succession of official advisory committees, the result of which was the Nuclear Installations Inspectorate.

The role of the NII took shape through subsequent, piecemeal legislation, on the basis of the recommendations of Royal Commissions and Commons Select Committees. However, despite a succession of administrative exercises in reorganization the relationship between the Inspectorate, government, the AEA and the Health and Safety Executive remained ill defined and loose jointed. In terms of status, resources and independence the Inspectorate remained weak. In defiance of criticism from official sources it has maintained an essentially flexible and informal system of safety criteria based on 'reasonably practicable' safeguards. Nuclear regulation in Britain thus conforms uncannily to Hayward's model of the British policy style. 'Firstly, there are no explicit, overriding medium- or long-term objectives. Secondly, unplanned decision-making is incremental. Thirdly, humdrum or unplanned decisions are arrived at by a continuous process of mutual adjustment' (Hayward, 1974, pp. 398–9).

In France nuclear policy and regulation was located within a coherent and centralized apparatus. A cohesive technocratic elite emerged, based on the state-run electricity generating concern Electricité de France, the Atomic Energy Commission, and the relevant government departments. Its personnel exercised a virtual monopoly over the sector, coordinating all aspects of nuclear energy, including the regulation and licensing of plant. Appointees of government, these officials rarely challenged government policy and 'the government never rejected a licensing request despite vigorous opposition from citizens' (Campbell, 1988, p. 140–1).

In both Britain and France, then, the development of civilian atomic energy programmes was accompanied by the growth of cohesive nuclear elites, reinforced by a centralized state apparatus. In neither country was there any formal recognition of the potential for conflict between the promotion of nuclear energy and its regulation. Authorities avoided rigidly formalized codes of practice in favour of flexible guidelines. The adoption in the Federal Republic of a comprehensive and rigorous legal code in the form of the Nuclear Energy Act can be partially explained with reference to the sectoral context. Whilst in most countries early nuclear development fell within the domain of the state, in the Federal Republic it was designated to the private sector. However, an important element in the explanation is the historic tradition of legalism with which the German state is imbued, and which permeates the regulatory culture.

2.   The Legal and Political Framework

In terms of rigour and scope the Nuclear Energy Act goes far beyond legislative provisions in Britain and France. The main purposes of the Act are defined in terms of the promotion of research, development and utilization of nuclear energy, and to protect life, health and property against its hazards. In fact practically the entire text of the law is devoted to the latter purpose. An elaborate framework of controls is set out, embracing the whole spectrum of activities related to nuclear energy and the nuclear fuel cycle. The principal instrument of control is the practice of licensing. The compliance of the licensing procedure with the precepts of the Nuclear Energy Act, and ultimately the Basic Law, is enforced through the

Bundesverwaltungsgerichte (Federal Administrative Courts) or the *Bundesverfassungsgericht* (Federal Constitutional Court). The Act is deliberately framed in terms of broad skeletal principles rather than detailed prescriptions. It is not an instrument of regulation but rather an enabling act for the creation of regulatory instruments and the establishment of legal norms to govern their operation. Provision is therefore made for delegated legislation, to give substance to the abstract principles contained in the Act through the promulgation by Federal Government of ordinances (subject to Bundesrat approval), general administrative regulations, guidelines and directives, and technical standards.

Implementation is designated to the *Länder* under the concurrent powers provision of the Basic Law (Art. 87c), in accordance with which the *Länder* act in the commission of the Federal Government. Accordingly, they are responsible for the execution of the Act, including the conduct of the licensing procedure. However, the Federal Government retains the power to issue binding instructions and to exercise a supervisory role. These functions fall within the remit of the Environment Ministry, *Bundesministerium für Umwelt, Naturschutz und Reaktorsicherheit* (Federal Ministry for the Environment, Nature Conservation and Nuclear Safety). Established in 1986 in the aftermath of Chernobyl, the new Ministry inherited responsibilities which had previously passed through a succession of federal ministries. Under the new regime the Environment Ministry shadows the *Länder* in their conduct of licensing. Each case is considered by technical experts acting for the Ministry, and on the basis of their report the Ministry issues a statement, which the *Länder* authorities must 'take into consideration' in reaching their decision. Coordination between the *Länder* and mediation between Bonn and the *Länder* is carried out by a committee of representatives of the competent *Länder* authorities and the Environment Minister. Until 1986, relations were relatively harmonious, and the exercise of the directive powers of the Federal Government in licensing matters was not an issue. However, with the breakdown of interparty agreement which accompanied the SPD's adoption of a non-nuclear position, the potential for conflict between the regulatory authorities in Bonn and those in the SPD-governed *Länder* has increased.

Scientific and technical aspects of the regulatory process such as the drafting of technical standards and norms, the approval of plant construction designs, supervision of technical practices and the scrutiny of licence applications, are designated to bodies of technical experts. Thus the Ministry is advised by the Nuclear Safety Standards Commission (*Kerntechnischer Ausschuße*, KTA), the Reactor Safety Commission (*Reaktor Sicherheitskommission*, RSK), the Radiation Protection Commission (*Strahlenschutzkommission*, SSK), and the Company for Reactor Safety

(*Gesellschaft für Reaktorsicherheit*, GRS). The *Länder* designate the technical aspects of the licensing procedure to the Technical Inspection Agency (*Technische Überwachungsverein*, TÜV). These bodies differ in status (public or private), terms of appointment, remit and composition. However, they share a common 'philosophy of nuclear safety' which gives a coherence to the technical sphere of regulation which is often lacking at other levels.

With German unification the legal framework of nuclear regulation was extended to the new eastern *Länder*. The Nuclear Energy Act was enforceable in the east from 1 July 1990 in accordance with the State Treaty on German Economic and Monetary Union. The BMU assumed overall authority for the licensing of nuclear plant in the east, in line with its existing responsibilities in the west. Doubts about the technical competence of the supervisory authorities in the east meant that the scientific and technical aspects of licensing here were vested in the bodies of technical experts in the west. In contrast to the practice in the west whereby nuclear plants are licensed for an indefinite period of operation, East German plants are to be licensed for a limited period of five years. This provision was an attempt to reconcile concerns over the safety of nuclear plant in the east with the imperative of reducing dependency upon environmentally noxious brown coal.

3.   The Juridification of Regulation

The legal framework within which nuclear regulation was located was heavily conditioned by the circumstances of its origins. The industry emerged at a time when nuclear activity in the Federal Republic was a question of some international sensitivity. The Allied ban on research and development was lifted in 1955, but the exploitation of nuclear technology for military purposes remained (and still remains) prohibited. The designation of a civilian nuclear programme to the private sector was a means of defusing international resistance to the revival of nuclear development in Germany. Moreover it was in accordance with the market economy orientation towards reconstruction:

> ... in contrast to France, domestic and foreign policy considerations in Germany called for a cautious and fragmented approach to nuclear policies.... Not surprisingly, therefore, the nuclear effort in Germany began in the private and local sector and only gradually acquired a national or public character (Nau, 1974, p. 73)

In view of the destructive potential and political sensitivity of nuclear technology, it was inevitable that its development within the private economic sector would be tightly circumscribed by state regulation sanctioned by law.

These circumstances accentuated a persistent feature of national policy style which has been observed across a wide area of public policy. 'At a very generalized level the importance of legality and legal problem-solving is widely noted in the Federal Republic.' This has been traced to a legal and administrative tradition which emphasizes 'the importance of allegiance to state priorities, and the requirement for the state to lead or authorize major economic developments' (Wilks and Wright, 1987, pp. 286, 279). Policy objectives, and the role of the state in their promotion, are set out in laws which serve to orientate and circumscribe the subsequent actions of the public authorities.

Moreover, in accordance with the Roman Law tradition, legislation is often set out in terms of normative principles instead of simple statutes. The practice of *Rechtsordnung* (the ordering of a sphere of activity according to legal norms) has been identified in another context as one of the dominant characteristics of West German public policy. 'As is generally true of politics in a Roman Law country, legal categories were part of the texture of political life. The term economic order suggested a requirement to relate conduct in a rationalist manner to economic first principles' (Dyson, 1981, p. 40).

Imbued with the German tradition of legalism, the Nuclear Energy Act represents an attempt to furnish authoritative legal solutions to the ethical, social, and scientific dilemmas of nuclear power. The ground rules of regulation are derived not from simple statutory instruments, but from broad, categorical imperatives expressed in the form of legal norms. Article 7 of the Act contains a 'state of the art clause', requiring operators to incorporate ultimate safeguards 'in the light of existing scientific knowledge and technology' at every stage of plant design and construction. Article 9 obliges operators to make provision for the re-utilization of spent fuel wherever that is scientifically possible and economically viable. Alternatively, provision must be made for the safe and orderly disposal of radioactive residues in the form of waste. This part of the Act also requires that the choice of plant location must not conflict with overriding public interest particularly in regard to the danger of water, air and soil contamination, and that land use planning must ensure that there is no impairment of the 'common welfare'.

The practice of interpreting laws in conjunction with the Basic Law accentuates the normative character of the law surrounding nuclear regulation. Read alongside the right to life article in the Basic Law, the Nuclear

Energy Act offers a legal solution to the inherent conflict between the promotion of nuclear power and protection against its hazards, allocating priority to protectional over and above promotional objectives, and defining the responsibilities of the state to ensure adequate protection (*Schutzpflicht*).

The juridification of nuclear regulation is compounded by the West German legal system. Public law is dispensed by a hierarchical system of administrative courts (*Verwaltungsgerichte*) which provide an elaborate system for the redress of grievances arising out of the actions of public bodies. The conduct of licensing procedure relating to nuclear installations is thus subject to a form of judicial review, based on the precepts of the Nuclear Energy Act. Decisions of local courts are subject to challenge in the Upper and Federal Administrative Courts (*Oberverwaltungsgerichte* and *Bundesverwaltungsgeriche*). Moreover, the actions of the licensing authorities and decisions of the administrative courts are ultimately subject to adjudication by the Federal Constitutional Court.

With the breakdown of the nuclear consensus in the early 1970s, the legal instruments of regulation (particularly the procedure for plant licensing) were drawn into the wider conflict over the social acceptability of nuclear energy. With increasing frequency, decisions of the regulatory authorities were contested before the courts. 'The courts effectively took over ultimate responsibility for making final decisions over questions of economic policy and national economic security of the highest order' (Michaelis, 1986, p. 1016). The Nuclear Energy Act thus assumed a significance, and a function, which it had never been intended to fulfil. A framework law, setting out the *principles* of regulation, became instead a regulatory *instrument*. In accordance with the tradition of positive law, the judiciary often derived judgements directly from a literal and absolute reading of the Act. Whilst the expert bodies advising and acting for the political authorities applied essentially practical safety criteria based on commonly accepted standards, the judiciary executed regulation by legal norm. In view of the ambiguity and open-endedness of the Act, interpretation was bound to be acutely problematical. Manufacturers and operators drew attention to the vagaries of interpretation in the courts, and called for a clarification of the purposes of the Act on the part of Government.

Judicial interpretations of Article 7 (the obligation to incorporate safeguards according to the existing state of scientific and technical knowledge), and Article 9 (the obligation to make provision for the disposal of spent fuel) were particularly significant for the nuclear industry. Literal interpretations of Article 7 led the Freiburg Administrative Court in 1975 to annul licences on technological grounds with reference to plant designs which had previously been approved by expert bodies (*Handelsblatt*, 15 March 1977). A similarly rigid interpretation of Article 9 by the Lüneburg Upper

Administrative Court in 1977 precipitated a major crisis in the nuclear industry. This judgement meant that the progress of the nuclear programme was dependent upon the formulation of a coherent and viable plan for the final storage (*Endlagerung*) of spent fuel. Regulation thus became inextricably tied up with wider policy issues, tightening the Gordian knot between law and politics in the nuclear field.

The Lüneburg decision was a thinly veiled attempt on the part of the court to pressurize the nuclear industry to fulfil its long-standing but hitherto abortive plans to build an integrated spent fuel storage, disposal and reprocessing complex capable of servicing the entire nuclear industry (Patterson, 1984, pp. 69–70). It represented a sequel to Chancellor Schmidt's attempt the previous year to move the sector (and the licensing authorities) forward by threatening to suspend reactor licensing until Federal and *Land* governments made decisions about the location of storage and reprocessing facilities, and issued construction permits to enable construction to go ahead (Campbell, 1988, p. 174). For the next decade, the provision for spent fuel disposal or reprocessing (*Entsorgung*) was the Achilles' heel of the nuclear industry as licensing law and fuel cycle policy became inextricably entwined. The legal threat of the suspension of plant operating licences in the absence of *Entsorgung* provisions, was reiterated by a Declaration of Principles on the part of Federal and *Land* Ministers in 1979, and was only warded off by a series of temporary expedients on the part of the industry.

Subsequently, plans for the integrated *Entsorgungskomplex* were shelved in favour of a less ambitious reprocessing plant at Wackersdorf in Bavaria. Although licensing proceeded more smoothly than might have been expected, the project began to ship water in 1989 with conflict over the magnitude of financial backing from Federal Government. The industry was stunned in 1989 by the conclusion by the VEBA energy concern – one of the largest parties to the consortium behind the Wackersdorf project – of a long-term reprocessing contract with the French reprocessing company COGEMA. This development, and the failure of the government to reaffirm unequivocally its commitment to Wackersdorf, led to the abandonment of the project. Major operators followed VEBA in concluding arrangements for reprocessing in France or the UK. It remained a matter for legal speculation whether these arrangements met the *Entsorgung* requirement of the Nuclear Energy Act.

The juridification of an essentially political conflict field has its corollary in the politicization of the law. This issue was raised by a bizarre judgement of the Münster Upper Administrative Court in 1977 relating to the fast breeder reactor project SNR 300, in the course of which the court expressed misgivings concerning the conformity of Article 7 of the Nuclear Energy Act with the Basic Law. The Court held that inasmuch as it enabled the licensing of potentially uncontrollable fast breeder technology, and designated ultimate authority to the courts, the Article contravened the constitutional principles of the *Rechtsstaat* and parliamentary democracy which formed the basis of the separation of judicial from political authority. The extraordinarily far-reaching importance of the issue for the common welfare demanded a concretization of the provisions of Article 7 on the part of the legislature. Moreover, it fell to the executive to define the extent of the state's duty of protection against potentially hazardous technology of this nature. Although the Federal Constitutional Court dispatched this argument with unusual and unexpected decisiveness, it reflected a wider view that reliance on the law as *Ordnungsfaktor* in an area of acute political conflict, was ultimately bound to undermine the authority of the law. 'To the extent that there is a question mark ... over the acceptability of nuclear energy, the credibility of nuclear energy law will suffer in equal measure' (Michaelis, 1986, p. 1037).

As has been observed in another context, juridification serves to open up the regulatory process to broader participation (Hancher and Ruete, 1987, p. 175). In the context of nuclear regulation this meant that there were multiple opportunities for anti-nuclear groups to intervene (Kitschelt, 1986a, pp. 157–85), stalling nuclear programmes for lengthy periods. Between the late 1960s/early 1970s and the late 1970s/early 1980s, the timescale of project completion (from construction start to commercial operation) practically doubled from an average of six years to one of over 11 years (Rinke, 1980). Given the magnitude of capital investment involved, delays of this order carried very significant implications for the commercial performance (and ultimately viability) of nuclear energy.

4.   The Politicization of the Administrative Regime

Bureaucratic fragmentation and the decentralization of authority combined with the openness of the system to challenge in the courts makes the regulatory regime unusually unwieldy. Indeed, a report of the US regulatory agency in 1982 cited the West German system as the only one in the world more cumbersome than its own (Campbell, 1988, p. 145). Politicization has served to accentuate this syndrome. These features also have implications for the relationship between the regulators and the industry. Although discoveries of malpractice have been accompanied by allegations of *Verfilzung* (interpenetration) between the regulatory authorities and the industry, there is no easily identifiable network of relations which would suggest a systematic process of 'regulatory capture'. It might be supposed that bureaucratic fragmentation and the dispersal of authority, along with the political sensitivity of the issues, have inhibited the onset of such a process.

The fragmentary nature of the administrative machinery for plant licensing has been recognized as a potential threat to the vitality of the nuclear programme since the early 1970s. Three features of the licensing procedure were identified as sources of bureaucratic proliferation and delay. Firstly, a system of partial licences meant that there were up to 18 stages to negotiate, corresponding to successive phases of plant construction and operation. Secondly, procedural and organizational diversity between *Länder,* and the multiplicity of authorities within a single *Land*, compounded the bureaucratic complexity of the licensing process. The competent *Land* ministry varied from one *Land* to another and, in some states, licensing and supervision were carried out under two different ministries. Moreover, in addition to nuclear licensing, plant construction was subject to licensing under a range of land use, building, emissions, and water authorities. Thirdly, reactor design and construction was submitted to full-scale technical examination by the authorities, even when it was closely related to a reactor family for which licences had already been granted.

With the politicization of nuclear power in the 1970s, the licensing procedure became more demanding, with a corresponding escalation of documentation. The manufacturers of the Biblis B plant in 1975 were required to submit 42 items of documentation; three years later the authorities demanded some 270 items for the licensing of the Grafenrheinfeld plant (Rinke, 1980, p. 838). Manufacturers and operators urged the government to carry out an overhaul of procedure, and Chancellors Brandt and Schmidt accepted the necessity of streamlining. However, the political and legal sensitivity of the issue, not least within the SPD, inhibited the government, and it was not until 1982 that positive steps were taken. An amendment to the Nuclear Licensing Procedure Ordinance (*Atomrechtliche Verfahrensverordnung*) met most of the requirements of the industry, consolidating the processes and coordinating the competent authorities. Above all, the amendment included provision for the practice of convoy licensing by which installations of a standard type could be licensed simultaneously in a single process.

Convoy licensing represented a particularly significant breakthrough for the industry. A prerequisite of its introduction was the standardization of reactor design on the part of the manufacturers. A lack of coordination within the industry itself, and a tendency amongst the electricity utilities to foster competition amongst manufacturers, militated against concertation along these lines. 'The short-term imperatives of a competitive reactor manufacturing industry prevented the development of a single reactor concept' (Campbell, 1988, p. 155). Ultimately, convoy licensing was a product of cooperation between the industry (in the form of the sectoral association, the *Deutsche Atomforum*) and the Federal Interior Ministry which was responsible at the time for the overall supervision of nuclear licensing. Its relatively late conception is indicative of the difficulty which a weakly articulated sector can experience in coming to terms with the regulatory authorities. With a competitive industry lacking the solidaristic traditions of, for instance, the chemicals sector, and a regulatory regime in which authority was dispersed to an unusually high degree, it is perhaps not surprising that a fully articulated network of relations between industry and regulatory authorities failed to emerge.

Ironically, the streamlining of the licensing procedure occurred after sectoral activity had reached its peak. Only three plants – Emsland, Isar II and GKN III – were built under convoy licence. Thereafter, the commercial nuclear energy programme was curtailed, due firstly to an unforeseen overcapacity in electricity supply and secondly to extremely unfavourable developments in the political landscape in consequence of the nuclear reactor accident in the Ukraine (Roser, 1986, pp. 842–5; Popp, 1987, pp. A7–A23). Chernobyl effectively destroyed an already fragile nuclear consensus. In its aftermath, the SPD moved decisively towards an anti-nuclear stance. The party's commitment to a phased withdrawal (*Ausstieg*) from nuclear power had far-reaching implications for regulation. Although the SPD was in opposition in Bonn, its governing role in a number of the *Länder* meant that it had a powerful lever in the licensing process.

Formally, the relationship between the Federal Government and the responsible regulatory authorities in the *Länder* is quite clearly defined. The latter are responsible for the implementation of regulation acting in the commission of Federal Government, and under the terms of federal laws and ordinances. In practical terms, however, relations are much more complex than this, and there is considerable potential for conflict (Bauer, 1987, pp. 230–6). The delegation of authority to the *Länder* was unproblematical in the era of consensus but had begun to show signs of strain in the late 1970s and early 1980s. With the SPD in opposition in Bonn since 1982, the divergence of regulatory practices under different party administrations widened considerably. This state of affairs was reflected in a marked unevenness in the development of nuclear power between the SPD and CDU/CSU *Länder* as the utilities based plant location on political calculations.

From 1986 licensing practices were subject to overt party politicization and continual conflict between the competent federal ministry and the SPD *Länder*. Conflict centred on the operations of the Hannau-based fuel manufacturer *Reaktor-Brennelement Union* (Hesse, 1986), the restart after routine shutdown of the *Preußen Elektra* Brokdorf reactor (Schleswig–Holstein, 1988), and the long-running issue of an operating licence for the *SNR 300* fast breeder reactor project at Kalkar (North-Rhine Westphalia). In each case, an SPD administration withheld the grant of a licence on legal or safety grounds in defiance of the federal ministry and the technical expert bodies. Although *Land* ministers defended decisions with reference to *Recht und Gesetz,* or technical safety criteria, the licensing issue was merely symbolic of the wider conflict over the social acceptability of nuclear energy.

It was within the power of the federal minister to issue binding instructions to the authorities in the *Länder* obliging them to issue licences. However, in the political climate after Chernobyl such a course was highly sensitive, particularly after competence passed from the Interior Ministry to the Environment Ministry, the creation of which was an attempt to restore public confidence in nuclear power. Instructions were ultimately issued in the cases of *RBU* and Brokdorf, and *Land* administrations complied (in the case of Hesse the SPD's compliance precipitated the collapse of the coalition with the Greens).

Over the SNR 300 the Minister was much more circumspect. After Chernobyl the CDU/CSU had reaffirmed their commitment to nuclear power, but with the qualification that it was regarded as a transitional energy source. Since the SNR 300 was, in terms of commercial viability, a long-term programme Environment Ministry support was bound to be less than totally wholehearted. Rather than issuing instructions to the North-Rhine Westphalia authorities, the Minister merely set out directives which stated the law in relation to licensing and called upon the *Land* authorities to comply. This exercise in political expediency did not escape the criticism of the nuclear industry, which was becoming increasingly resigned to the demise of the fast breeder programme.

The creation of the Environment Ministry itself added a new dimension to the complex problem surrounding nuclear regulation. In contrast to the Interior Ministry, where reactor safety had been marginal to the mainstream of ministerial activity – 'ministers wanted us to keep quiet and not make any trouble for them' – the Environment Ministry was much more purposeful. Under Töpfer, especially, the Ministry has become markedly more activist in orientation, with a rather broader interpretation of the supervisory role than that which prevailed in the Interior Ministry. Safety *concepts* have been subject to a more or less continuous process of review. Major studies have been launched in risk assessment and accident management and moves made to reinforce the supervision of nuclear transport and to establish a new directorate within the Ministry to oversee fuel cycle operations. Overall, Töpfer's performance is assessed extremely positively by officials in the Ministry (author's interview, Environment Ministry officials, 27 April 1989).

The impetus for a more dynamic approach to questions of nuclear safety derived largely from political pressures generated by Chernobyl, and by a series of scandals which broke in 1987, concerning malpractice in firms engaged in fuel cycle operations. Investigations into the activities of the fuel processing undertaking *Alkem* (a Siemens subsidiary) and the nuclear transport concern *Transnuklear* exposed irregularities in licensing procedures, flagrant breaches of regulatory codes governing the transportation of fissionable material, and widespread bribery and corruption. Three officials of the Hesse licensing authorities and two *Alkem* executives (one of whom was also a CDU Bundestag deputy) faced criminal charges. Amidst allegations of *Verfilzung* between regulatory authorities and the industry, it was revealed that successive Interior Ministers had turned a blind eye to malpractice, and that attempts had been made by the Ministry (under Friedrich Zimmermann) to arrange a legal amnesty for those involved. In the course of the *Transnuklear* affair it became apparent that significant quantities of weapons-grade plutonium had been illegally diverted to destinations which the authorities were unable to identify. The breakdown of regulation in so sensitive an area of nuclear activity seriously undermined the credibility of the regulatory regime.

Cleaning-up operations after the *Transnuklear* and *Alkem* scandals fell to the BMU. Minister Töpfer announced a *Neuordnung* of the fuel cycle sector which involved the creation of a new directorate within the Ministry and a new office, the *Bundesamt für Strahlenschutz,* to strengthen state control over the sector. (According to the Nuclear Energy Act, fuel cycle operations fell within the competence of the Federal Government, but had subsequently been delegated to the private sector.) For its part, the industry carried out some internal restructuring in an attempt to pre-empt more drastic state intervention in the sector. However, damage limitation along these lines was only partially successful. 'The plutonium industry' came under increasing political pressure, with implications for related projects like the *SNR 300* fast breeder, and the reprocessing plant under construction at Wackersdorf.

The self-proclaimed objective of the Environment Ministry in the aftermath of the disaster in the Ukraine and scandal in the Federal Republic was the restoration of public confidence in nuclear energy and the rebuilding of the nuclear consensus. An activist approach to regulation was part of the Ministry's strategy for restoring the legitimacy of the sector. The new activism inevitably meant a reorientation of relations between the Ministry and the nuclear industry. Since the function of the Ministry is primarily supervisory and therefore not directly involved in the day-to-day issues of regulation, the relationship is characterized by a certain distance. On the other hand there appears to be a standing dialogue which brings together

Ministry officials and *Fachleute* from the industry. These circles share a common background in nuclear science – the Reactor Safety Division of the Environment Ministry is comprised predominantly of scientists and lawyers – and a common understanding of nuclear safety. Dialogue takes the form of persuasion, with officials pressing the industry to adopt safety-promoting design refinements. The Ministry is inevitably influenced by the wider political environment, and has been known to take up issues which have been raised by the anti-nuclear lobby. In this sense it could be regarded as the Trojan horse of nuclear regulation. However, the industry is acutely aware of the politics of nuclear energy and is capable of appreciating the symbolic importance of the Ministry.

The reorientation of the Ministry under Töpfer also had implications for interministerial relations, increasing the potential for conflict between the protectional (and legitimizing) objectives of the Environment Ministry and the promotional goals of the Federal Ministry for Research and Technology (*Bundesministerium für Forschung und Technologie*). Conflict came to a head over the licensing procedure for the *SNR 300* fast breeder project. Research and Technology Minister Riesenhuber was openly critical of Töpfer's reluctance to employ his powers of instruction to compel the North Rhine Westphalia authorities to grant an operating licence. By way of retaliation, Töpfer was equally critical of the alleged failure of the manufacturers to submit the required documentation and of the Research and Technology Ministry to use its influence with the industry to remedy this state of affairs. The exchanges which ensued exemplified the tension which can arise between the state's promotional and regulatory functions, and illustrates the ambivalent character of relations between the state and the industry.

5. Politicization of the Technical Domain

In accordance with the German tradition of *Sachlichkeit* in the public policy process, the ethos of scientific objectivity and independence is embedded in the culture of nuclear regulation. Strenuous efforts are made to promote the formal appearance of independence in the expert consultative bodies which advise the licensing authorities. A regulatory regime based on scientific objectivity is an important element in the machinery for legitimizing nuclear energy. However, in the highly specialized field of nuclear science, expertise is inevitably concentrated in the industry itself, and in state-sponsored nuclear research establishments, the primary function of which is promotional. The formal independence of expert bodies, then, is somewhat questionable in practice, and is derided by the anti-nuclear lobby. Divisions within the scientific community, moreover, concerning technical questions of nuclear safety, and the social acceptability of nuclear energy, have had the effect of further eroding the credibility of scientific objectivity.

At the peak of the expert consultative apparatus is the Reactor Safety Commission (*Reaktorsicherheitskommission*, RSK), an advisory body answering to the Environment Ministry and appointed by the Minister. It is composed of around 20 *independent experts* appointed in a personal capacity (that is, not as representatives of particular interests). The two criteria for appointment are expertise, and 'a certain measure of institutional independence' (author's interview, Environment Ministry, 27 April 1989). The remit of the RSK is to investigate the generic problems of reactor safety, to formulate basic principles, and to draft the guidelines within which technical standards are subsequently set. RSK guidelines are of considerable practical importance, since licensing authorities usually demand proof of their fulfilment. Moreover, the guidelines very often serve as criteria for Court decisions in cases relating to licensing procedures.

The Nuclear Safety Standards Committee (*Kerntechnischer Ausschuße*, KTA) also acts in an advisory capacity to the Environment Ministry. In contrast to the RSK, the KTA is conceived of as a representational body. Its strength of 50 is drawn equally from five sectoral interests – manufacturers, operators (electricity utilities), *Länder* and Federal authorities, technical experts, and 'other' involved interests (trade unions, insurance companies, banks). The KTA draws up safety standards within RSK guidelines. Draft standards are published for comment and opinion before being put to a ratifying vote which requires a 5/6 majority (so that no single group within the KTA can be outvoted).

The Technical Inspection Agency (*Technischer Überwachungsverein*, TÜV) is an independent, regionally organized body originating in the nineteenth century as an industrial initiative in self-regulation. Subsequently it has been co-opted by the state and given quasi-official status (under government supervision) for the purposes of verifying compliance with technical norms across a wide range of sectors. Regional TÜVs act in the commission of the *Länder* conducting the assessment and testing involved in the licensing procedure, and carrying out the routine inspection of plant. The 11 TÜVs are in turn shareholders, along with the Federal Government, the governments of Bavaria and North-Rhine Westphalia, and a consortium of insurance companies, in the Company for Reactor Safety (*Gesellschaft für Reaktorsicherheit*, GRS), a non-profit making consultancy which carries out safety assessments on behalf of the federal and *Land* authorities.

The membership of the official and quasi-official bodies responsible for drafting, applying and enforcing the guidelines governing nuclear safety is drawn from nuclear science (bio-physics, radio-chemistry, electrical engineering, and so on). Members of the RSK, for instance, are distinguished

scientists with national and very often international reputations (a considerable number have worked extensively in the USA). Analysis of career
histories reveals a network of interlocking affiliations which embraces the
state-run nuclear science research establishments at Karlsruhe and Jülich,
the KTA and GRS, the TÜVs, and the Federal Office for Scientific and
Technical Standards (*Physikalisch- Technische Bundesamt*). Officials in the
Reactor Safety Division of the Environment Ministry have connections
with the nuclear science establishment. (One interview subject in the Min
istry had studied under the present Chairman of the RSK.) This is not to
imply any sinister undercurrents of conspiracy. Rather it indicates the existence of a policy community surrounding nuclear regulation, with a common background in nuclear science.

Members of this policy community appear to share a common philosophy
of nuclear safety, based on a scientific assessment of the inherent risks of
nuclear technology, and a concept of risk limitation through the application
of codified standards. Members of the community subscribe to the ethos of
scientific objectivity and independence, which is the source of their authority in the regulatory process. On the other hand they are aware of the
commercial implications of safety requirements. Hence they take a practical
rather than an absolute view of reactor safety, in particular in relation to the
'state of the art' safety technology requirement of the Nuclear Energy Act.

A distinction is often made between a narrowly defined and cohesive
policy *community* on the one hand, and a wider and more diffuse *policy
universe* on the other (Wright, 1988, p. 605). This distinction can usefully
be employed here. There is a recognizable boundary between the *regulatory
policy community* and the wider *nuclear policy universe* which embraces the
state, science and industry. Members of formally independent bodies like
the RSK and GRS are principally concerned specifically with nuclear *safety*
as opposed to mainstream research and development. They do not, in
general, have a background in the industry. The idea that these bodies are in
some sense 'independent' is not, therefore, too fanciful. However, this
assertion requires qualification on two points. Firstly, members of the independent regulatory bodies are often drawn from the state-sponsored nuclear
R&D establishments at Jülich and Karlsruhe. Secondly, there appears to be
a fairly close relationship between the regulators and *Fachleute* employed
directly in the industry. Indeed, a certain intimacy is inevitable in a regulatory regime in which cooperation is a basic principle, and which is geared
to the 'harmonization of the participating authorities, utilities, vendors and
technical agencies' (BMU, 1987, p. 5).

Since the politicization of nuclear energy issues, the point at which
cooperation begins to infringe on the independence of expert bodies has
become the focus of conflict. The Greens have alleged, for example, that

the TÜV is no more than an 'association of the big [nuclear] concerns, through which they can exercise self-regulation' (*Frankfurter Allgemeine Zeitung*, 5 March 1988). Criticism of this sort has arisen out of the practice of appointing one or two nuclear industry practitioners to independent regulatory bodies like the RSK and TÜV.

The industry has opposed initiatives to place regulation entirely in the hands of 'outsiders'. In one instance, the reactor manufacturer *Kraftwerk Union* (KWU) clashed sharply with Environment Minister Wallmann over his proposal to allow outside independent experts to conduct the International Atomic Energy Authority's OSART (Operational Safety Review Team) programme. KWU maintained that IAEA teams should be made up of 'highly qualified career people drawn from the operators, manufacturers and scientific bodies'. In response Wallmann argued that it was important to avoid giving the impression that reactor safety was in the hands of '*interessengebundenen Experten*' (interest-related experts) (*Kölner Stadtanzeiger*, 3 July 1986). The politicization of scientific opinion has made the authorities highly sensitive to allegations of this kind.

6.   State/Sector Relations

It is not easy to arrive at a clearly defined picture of relations between the nuclear industry and the state. Although at the overall level of *sectoral coordination* the state plays only a distant role, 'allowing the market and private groups to coordinate sectoral activity' (Campbell, 1988, p. 147), it is nevertheless possible to identify at least a skeletal network of relations between government, science and industry. Given the strategic importance of the sector this could hardly have been otherwise. In the regulatory regime also relations are characterized by cooperation between the authorities and the manufacturers and operators. However, as will be evident from the above, there are a number of factors which set limits to the intimacy of relations. Firstly, licensing is subject to legal norms and technical standards which are outside the control of the political/administrative authorities and which do not encourage a bargaining style between the authorities and the industry.

> In West Germany ... the design of licensing procedures for industrial (nuclear) plants reflects the arm's length relationship between the state and business. The state symbolically assumes the position of a neutral arbiter who settles disputes between the proponents and opponents of industrial projects. Although state agencies have clearly been sympathetic to nuclear manufacturers and utilities in licensing hearings, the nature of the procedures compels the regulatory agencies

to reason with anti-nuclear groups and to examine their arguments (Kitschelt, 1986b, p. 93).

The juridification of regulation has increased the pressure on the authorities to act strictly in accordance with *Recht und Gesetz*. Federal Government, though broadly sympathetic to the industry, has shown an increasing tendency to allow the courts to act as the ultimate arbiters of regulatory policy, even when the outcomes have been unfavourable to the industry. The politicization of nuclear issues reduced still further the scope for a permissive regulatory regime.

Secondly, the fragmentation of the state in its dealings with the nuclear industry has militated against the emergence of a 'client' relationship and the 'capture' of the regulatory authorities by the industry. In particular, the formal separation, enshrined in the Nuclear Energy Act, between the promotion of nuclear energy and protection against its hazards, has led to a role separation between the Economics and Research and Technology Ministries on the one hand, and the Environment Ministry on the other. Whilst the promotional ministries are close to the industry, the Environment Ministry is obliged, for political reasons, to maintain a certain distance. Fragmentation is compounded by the dispersal of authority between Bonn and the *Länder*. With the politicization of the nuclear issue, the coordination of licensing procedures became impossibly difficult to achieve. The tone of relations between the *Land* authorities and the industry became dependent upon the political composition of the *Land* government.

Thirdly, there are reasons to believe that the industry itself may be less cohesive than is commonly supposed by proponents of the *Atomstaat* argument. The diversity of nuclear-related activities – reactor manufacture, fuel cycle operations, electricity generation – militated against cohesive sectoral organization. Moreover, the industry is dominated by very large concerns, often with their commercial centre of gravity outside the sector. It may not therefore be surprising that the emergence of a sectoral association in the accepted sense did not occur until 1976 with the establishment of the *Wirtschaftsverband Kernbrennstoff-Kreislauf* (WKK) (Industry Association for the Nuclear Fuel Cycle). As its title suggests, the Association is principally concerned with fuel cycle operations, although the reactor manufacturers are amongst its members. Previously sectoral interests had been represented by the *Deutsches Atomforum,* a loosely organized body of technical specialists in the industry, research and technical bodies like the TÜV. For their part the electricity utilities were represented by the *Vereinigung Deutscher Elektrizitätswerke.* The utilities' customer relationship with the manufacturers and their status as mixed public/private undertakings meant that, although they shared certain common interests in relation to nuclear licensing, their wider interests often diverged from those of the rest of the sector. In the absence of a cohesive industrial association, sectoral coordination was highly personalized, conducted in an informal and *ad hoc* manner by the leading figures of the biggest concerns.

7.   The Impact of Regulation on the Sector

In an era of nuclear consensus (at least at the level of the elites) it was possible to steer nuclear projects through the regulatory process, although with a much longer planning and construction schedule than in other countries. However, with the collapse of an already fragile societal consensus, and the party politicization of the nuclear issue in the aftermath of Chernobyl the regulatory process was drawn into the wider conflict over the social acceptability of nuclear energy. The political opponents of nuclear energy were able to exploit licensing procedures to stall nuclear projects, creating uncertainty over their commercial future. The industry faced a slow death by regulatory strangulation. The retreat from future-orientated projects like the *SNR 300* fast breeder project at Kalkar, the Wackersdorf reprocessing plant and the experimental High Temperature Reactor project is indicative of sectoral decline and is attributed by the industry to the political environment. In each case, licensing problems compounded the already uncertain economic viability of the projects, leading to the withdrawal of the principal commercial sponsors.

The sector itself is resigned to a virtual moratorium on nuclear development for the medium-term future. A defensive posture has been adopted in which the promotion of nuclear energy and earlier demands for the streamlining of the regulatory regime have been shelved. Priority is now placed on the restoration of public confidence in nuclear technology, and there is a recognition that this entails a more positive attitude towards nuclear safety on the part of the regulatory authorities and the industry itself.

German unification was initially seen as a window of opportunity for the nuclear industry in the Federal Republic. Nuclear electricity offered a 'clean' alternative to the environmentally toxic brown coal commonly used in electricity generation in the GDR. However, nuclear plant in the new German *Länder* falls far short of meeting western safety standards. Although plant in the east will not be subject to the full rigours of the Federal Republic's technical specifications until 1995, safety concerns have already resulted in plant closures. The first casualty was the Greifswald plant where all operational capacity had been closed by the end of 1990. Plant under construction at Greifswald, and elsewhere, conformed more closely with west German standards, and upgrading is being undertaken by the west German nuclear industry. Electricity generation in the new German *Länder* has been taken over by a consortium of west German utilities. Their plans for the future include a substantial nuclear component, but they emphasize that this depends upon the existence of the political will to cut through the regulatory morass.

The main consequence of the deadlock in nuclear regulation concerns the electricity supply industry. Whilst the reactor manufacturers can turn abroad for new orders, the utilities face the prospect of potentially damaging competition with the French state concern EdF, anxious to unload its surplus capacity of nuclear electricity. This threat assumes greater proportions in view of the European Community's programme for a single European energy market (Commission of the European Communities, 1988) and mounting pressure on the German government to liberalize the heavily regulated electricity supply industry. The disparity between Germany and France in terms of the regulatory regime surrounding nuclear energy places the German utilities at a competitive disadvantage which is unlikely to be significantly offset by the opportunities arising in the new German *Länder*.

8. Conclusion

In contrast to pragmatic and flexible regulatory regimes in Britain and France, nuclear regulation in the Federal Republic is based on a single, comprehensive legal instrument and is rooted in a culture of legalistic formalism. It has been argued that the result is regulation by legal norm, or the juridification of regulation. The syndrome can be defined as a tendency to express ethical, social and economic issues in the form of legal or constitutional precepts, and to resolve those issues through the judicial process. It carries with it a number of consequences. Firstly, there is a fusion of law and politics, as legal conflict acts as a surrogate for wider forms of social conflict. Secondly, this fusion of political and judicial processes has implications for conflict resolution; there is a tendency for informal bargaining to be replaced by recourse to highly formalized legal procedures. Thirdly, there will be a tendency for policy debate to be conducted in legal terms. 'Law does not only provide the "technical rules of society" ... but also the language in which policy debates are often couched. ... Legal arguments over the interpretation and application of constitutional principles are thinly disguised policy debates' (Hancher and Ruete, 1987, p. 173). The resulting entanglement between the law and the policy process can lead to distortions in the latter. The issues of spent fuel storage and reprocessing, and the collapse of the fast breeder reactor project, illustrate the complexity and loss of rationality which can result from the interplay of legal, political and economic forces in the decision process.

The decentralization of the political and bureaucratic apparatus of regulation in the Federal Republic has severely limited the capacity of the state to reconcile nuclear safety and the promotion of nuclear energy in a rational manner. In this sphere, the Federal Republic conforms to models of the 'weak state' in which 'authority is dispersed and no one group of officials can take the lead in formulating policy. Under these circumstances authority is typically diffused among several bureaux and between levels of government resulting in overlapping jurisdictions and bureaucratic competition' (Atkinson and Coleman, 1989, p. 51). Politicization increased the potential for interministerial conflict (between the promotional and protectional ministries) and between federal government and the *Länder*. *Politikverflechtung* along these lines has militated against the 'capture' of the regulatory authorities by the nuclear industry, as has the relatively weak coordination of the sector itself.

Nuclear regulation in the Federal Republic is permeated by the German tradition of *Sachlichkeit* (objectivity) in the public policy processes. The independence of the expert bodies responsible for drafting technical standards and norms, and for ensuring compliance, is an important element in the regulatory philosophy. In the closed world of nuclear science, the independence and objectivity of expert regulatory bodies is bound to be questionable, but it has been argued above that it is possible to distinguish a regulatory policy community from the broader nuclear policy universe. The operational procedures governing the setting and application of technical standards are much more formalistic and inflexible than in most other countries. Authoritative scientific opinion assumes a major role in the legitimation of nuclear energy, intensifying the pressure on the authorities to maintain the ethos of independence and procedural rigour. However, the politicization of scientific opinion has eroded the authority of officially accredited expert bodies. A proliferation of scientific institutes hostile to nuclear energy now contest the findings of the official bodies, questioning their independence.

It has been argued above that the regulatory regime in the nuclear sector in West Germany shows some singular characteristics in relation to nuclear regulation in other countries which can only be fully explained with reference to a national regulatory culture, and to the institutional framework of the federal state. Lacking the pragmatism and flexibility of nuclear regulation in Britain, and the cohesion and centralization observed in France, the German regime has proved stubbornly resistant to liberalizing change of either a paradigmatic or incremental nature. The changes which have taken place – notably the relocation of overall authority within the Federal Environment Ministry – have failed to make any significant contribution to streamlining. Indeed, the Environment Ministry is particularly sensitive to societal and political attitudes to nuclear energy. The creation of the new ministry merely exacerbated the openness of the regime to social opposition, without cutting through the legal and administrative rigidities which are the hallmarks of nuclear regulation in the Federal Republic.

Note

The author wishes to acknowledge the support of the Nuffield Foundation in the form of a research award which enabled this work to be conducted.

References

Atkinson, M.A. and Coleman, W.D. (1989), 'Strong states and weak states: sectoral policy networks in advanced capitalist economies', *British Journal of Political Studies*, (19), 47–67.

Bauer, J.F. (1984), 'Rechtliche Voraussetzungen und Folgen der energie-politischen Aufgabenverteilung im föderativen Staat', *Zeitschrift für Energiewirtschaft*, (4), 230–36.

Bundesministerium für Umwelt, Naturschutz und Reaktorsicherheit (1987), *Nuclear Power Plant Licensing and Supervision in the Federal Republic of Germany*, Bonn: BMU.

Campbell, J.L. (1988), *Collapse of an Industry: Nuclear Power and the Contradictions of US Policy*, Ithaca and London: Cornell University Press.

Dyson, K.H.F. (1981), 'The politics of economic management in West Germany', *West European Politics*, **2**, (4), May.

Hancher, L. and Ruete, M. (1987), 'Legal Culture, Product Licensing, and the Drug Industry', in Wilks, S. and Wright, M. (eds), *Comparative Government Industry Relations: Western Europe, United States and Japan*, Oxford: Clarendon Press.

Handelsblatt (1977), 'Richter machen die Energiepolitik; eine Moratorium für die deutsche Kernkraft', 15 March.

Hayward, J. (1986), *The State and the Market Economy: Industrial Patriotism and Economic Intervention in France*, Brighton: Wheatsheaf.

Kitschelt, H. (1980), *Kernenergiepolitik: Arena eines gesellschaftlichen Konflikts*, Frankfurt/New York: Campus Verlag.

Kitschelt, H. (1986a), 'Political opportunity structures and political protest: antinuclear movements in four democracies', *British Journal of Political Science*, **1**, (16), 157–85.

Kitschelt, H. (1986b), 'Four theories of public policy making and fast breeder reactor development', *International Organisation*, (40), 65–104.

Michaelis, H. (1986), *Handbuch der Kernenergie: Kompendium der Energiewirtschaft und Energiepolitik, Band 2*, Düsseldorf: Wien Econ Verlag.

Nau, H. J. (1974), *National Politics and International Technology: Nuclear Reactor Development in Western Europe*, Baltimore and London: Johns Hopkins University Press.

Patterson, W. (1984), *The Plutonium Business and the Spread of the Bomb*, London: Paladin.

Peacock, A. (1984), *The Regulation Game: How British and West German Companies Bargain with Government*, Oxford and New York: Blackwell.

Popp, M. (1987), 'Kernenergie 1987: Im Schatten des Unfalls von Tschernobyl', *Jahrbuch der Atomwirtschaft*, A7–23.

Rinke, W. (1980), 'Notwendige Verbesserungen für das Genehmigungverfahren zur Errichtung neuer Kraftwerke', *Energiewirtschaftliche Tagesfragen*, **11/12** (30).

Roser, T. (1986), 'Die Politische Landschaft nach Tschernobyl; Bürger und Parteien nach dem Unglück', *Energiewirtschaftliche Tagesfragen*, **11**, (36).

Scharpf, F.W. (1988), 'The joint decision trap: lessons from German federalism and European integration', *Public Administration*, (66), Autumn.

Smellie, R.L. (1988), *Political and Governmental Aspects of Major Technological Risks*, Unpublished Thesis, University of Manchester.

Wilks, S. and Wright, M. (1987), *Comparative Government–Industry Relations: Western Europe, United States and Japan*, Oxford: Clarendon Press.

Wright, M. (1988), 'Policy community, policy network and comparative industrial politics', *Political Studies,* (XXXVI), 593–612.

9 The Politics of Regulatory Change in the German Health Sector

Douglas Webber

1. Introduction

The health sector was the location of some of the fiercest controversies in German domestic politics in the 1980s. The Christian–Liberal coalition's attempts to reform the statutory health insurance scheme in particular served drastically to raise the temperature of political debate. The Federal Labour and Social Affairs Minister likened himself to a valiant Saint George, upholding the public interest in a titanic struggle with a host of 'dragons' of particularistic producer and service provider interests. The lobbies of the latter portrayed themselves as the defenders of time-honoured and cherished principles which the government was prepared to sacrifice on the altar of political expediency.

Once the political dust had settled following the debate over the health insurance reform which raged especially in 1987 and 1988, the health system structures which became visible once again looked remarkably similar to those which had existed when the centre-right coalition assumed office in Bonn in 1982. In short, in international comparison and also as compared with some other policy sectors in West Germany, the extent of regulatory change in the health sector seemed to have been very modest. The purpose of this chapter is to portray the nature of the regulatory changes which occurred in the Federal Republic in the 1980s, to analyse the forces and actors which tried to put 'deregulation' on the health policy agenda, and to try to explain why their impact remained so limited.

The analysis is divided into nine parts. In the first the history of health sector regulation until the 1980s is summarized. The second explores the background to the debate over health insurance reform under the Christian–Liberal coalition. The third contains an analysis of the forces which militated or campaigned in favour of health sector deregulation. In the fourth part we assess the extent of the changes in the methods and instruments of regulation at the sub-sectoral level. In the fifth part the obstacles to radical regulatory changes in the health sector are investigated more systematically. The following three parts are devoted respectively to a comparison of the German with the British experience in the field of the health sector regulation in the 1980s and an assessment of the implications of the European Community's 1992 project and German reunification for the (formerly West) German health sector. In the conclusion an attempt is made to sum up the argument and assess the likelihood of major changes in health sector regulation in the foreseeable future.

We distinguish between three essential modes of regulation: between market regulation, in which patterns of resource allocation are the product of the spontaneous interaction of individual consumers and suppliers in the market-place; state regulation, in which decisions concerning resource allocation are made by government organizations or agencies; and collective self-regulation, in which such decisions are reached in bargaining between organizations representing the interests of suppliers and consumers. Furthermore, a distinction may be drawn between procedural regulation, the stipulation of the 'rules of the game' which lay down how decisions are to be reached in the sector, and substantive regulation, the making and implementation of the concrete decisions concerning the funding and delivery of health care.

2.   A Brief History of Health Sector Regulation in Germany

The history of health sector regulation in Germany may be summed up as one of the expansion of procedural regulation by the state and of substantive regulation by the joint self-administration (*gemeinsame Selbstverwaltung*) of health insurance funds and organized health care providers. The combined impact of these two processes has been to narrow the scope for the operation of market mechanisms in health care provision.

The modern history of health sector regulation began not with Bismarck's social insurance legislation in the 1880s, but, before then, with the self-organization of Social Democratic workers in voluntary sickness insurance funds. With the establishment of first the voluntary and later the compulsory health insurance funds, doctors were confronted by collectively-organized bargaining partners who could exploit the doctors' disunity to obtain more favourable terms for medical care delivery. The doctors' bargaining weakness precipitated the formation of doctors' unions, most notably the Hartmannbund at the turn of the century. The decade up to the First World War and the Weimar years were punctuated by a series of bitter conflicts between health insurance funds and doctors' organizations – conflicts which are still stored in the institutional memories of the doctors' organizations, which frequently oppose health care 'deregulation' on the grounds that it could divide the doctors and weaken their bargaining power *vis-à-vis* the insurance funds.

The escalation of conflict between the doctors and insurance funds in turn prompted greater state intervention in the health sector. In 1923, as the statutory health insurance was on the verge of collapse, the government intervened to give the existing collective agreements between doctors and insurance funds – which determined doctors' fees – the force of law. The onset of the Depression in the early 1930s produced a fresh health insurance crisis. After the Labour Minister had threatened the doctors with socialization if they did not contribute to containing health care spending, the government enacted by emergency decree a compromise package which admitted more doctors to the statutory health insurance, provided for an overall ceiling on ambulatory health care spending, and established associations of health insurance doctors (*kassenärztliche Vereinigungen*) to which all private-practising doctors who wished to treat insurance fund members had to belong, which negotiated fees with the funds and then paid their members according to the services they had rendered. The creation of such quasi-public institutions had been a long-time demand of the doctors' groups, which aimed thereby to replace regulation of the doctors by the insurance funds with professional self-regulation minimizing the funds' control over doctors' behaviour.

Essentially, this Weimar Settlement has survived all subsequent changes of political regime in Germany as well as German reunification. The Nazi dictatorship implemented a number of measures which increased the degree of state control of the system and changed the balance of power between the doctors and the funds in favour of the doctors, but did not destroy the institutions for the regulation of health care which it had inherited from the final administrations of the Weimar Republic. One of the advantages of the Weimar Settlement for the doctors was that they were organized as a bargaining monopoly, whereas their negotiating partners were divided into several different kinds of funds: local insurance funds (mainly for manual workers), white-collar employees' funds, artisans' and craftsmen's funds, and company-based funds. In the immediate post-Second World War period, the local funds, the unions and Social Democrats campaigned for the creation of a single social (health, pension and unemployment) insurance fund. A monopolistically-organized financer of health care would then have confronted a monopolistically-organized supplier. However, the formation of a Christian Democrat-led coalition after the first West German elections crushed such ambitions. In 1955, the government enacted legislation which basically confirmed the Weimar Settlement, guaranteeing the private-practising doctors a monopoly of ambulatory health care provision in exchange for the doctors' forfeiting the right to strike.

Over the following 30 years rising health care spending prompted a series of governmental attempts to reform the statutory health insurance. The first were undertaken by Christian Democratic-led governments in the early 1960s and were singularly unsuccessful. Plans to introduce hefty patients' charges for doctors' visits and to increase state control of doctors' fees failed on the combined opposition of the doctors' organizations and the trade unions as well as on the disunity within the Christian Democratic Union, with Chancellor Adenauer confessing that it was 'extraordinarily difficult' to enact a law against the wishes of 70 000 doctors who each saw 30 patients a day (Rosewitz and Webber, 1990, p. 182). Rapid economic growth in the late 1960s and early 1970s even facilitated an expansion of statutory health insurance coverage and services by the Social–Liberal coalition. The most important Social–Liberal innovation was a reform of hospital financing which strengthened the influence of the federal government on hospital building and, more so, that of the state governments over hospital rates – which they could alter after they had been negotiated between the insurance funds and hospital owners.

The pressure for state intervention to curb rising costs re-emerged in the wake of the 1974–5 economic crisis. After the 1976 elections, the Social–Liberal coalition pushed through a package of cost-containing measures, the most significant of which, in terms of regulatory implications, laid down tighter guidelines for fees negotiations between the doctors' associations and insurance funds and created a new organ, the Concerted Action in the Health System, which was to meet twice yearly and bring together representatives of federal and state governments, the sickness insurance funds and the various producers' and service-providers' organizations to deliberate on health policy issues and especially to agree recommendations for expenditure growth. The Concerted Action remains the most visible manifestation of the corporatist regulation of German health care, although the non-binding character of its decisions means that it has little impact on actual developments in the health sector.

3. The Background to the Health Insurance Reform Debate in the 1980s

At the programmatic level, the parties in the Christian–Liberal coalition which came to office in Bonn in 1982 shared an antipathy to state intervention in the health care as well as in other sectors. However, it did not possess anything like a blue-print for the reform of statutory health insurance. Even the 'Lambsdorff Paper' of the then Liberal Economics Minister – which had precipitated the collapse of the old coalition – was very thin on concrete proposals for reforming health care. The most controversial proposal mooted in the coalition's first years in office was a cut in sick pay – which the trade unions and the Labour Minister from the union wing of the Christian Democratic Union successfully resisted. The coalition's first full term produced nothing more than a half-hearted and heavily-diluted reorganization of hospital financing.

Not the international resurgence of economic liberalism as such, but rather the renewed acceleration of health care expenditure growth in the mid-1980s motivated the coalition's decision to attempt a broad reform of the health insurance. There was a consensus in the government that rising contributions were harmful to German firms' international competitiveness and to employment and threatened to counteract the government's tax reduction programme. The debate over the health insurance reform that began in the middle of the 1980s, culminating in the reform's adoption in 1988, provided a forum for those forces which favoured a more or less radical overhaul of the German system.

4. The Health Sector 'Deregulators'

The most striking characteristics of the groups advocating a radical privatization or liberalization of German health care are their small numbers and size and political marginality. Support for such strategies is limited predominantly to groups of professional economists which have relatively tenuous links with, and exercise relatively little influence on, the corporate actors in the health sector or, indeed, on the federal government.

Three such groups participated in the health insurance reform debate. One, the *Kronberger Kreis,* consists of eight economics professors and regularly publishes policy recommendations on current political issues. It produced a comprehensive list of proposals for reforming the health insurance, most of which aimed at reducing its solidaristic character and the extent of the services and expenses provided and covered by the health insurance funds, but which also sought to stimulate competition between

214 The Politics of German Regulation

private-practising doctors and hospitals and make it possible for insurance funds to negotiate contracts with individual doctors and, hence, play the latter off against each other as had been possible in the era before the establishment of the compulsory insurance doctors' associations.

A second group constituted itself *ad hoc* to formulate health insurance reform proposals and was made up of eight health economists. Although it, too, recommended the strengthening of market mechanisms and incentives in the health system, its reform programme was not as radical as that of the *Kronberger Kreis*. A number of its proposals had the goal of expanding the rights of insurance funds to negotiate prices of goods and services with suppliers. Like the *Kronberger Kreis,* it wanted insurance funds to have the right to negotiate contracts with individual doctors or competing doctors' associations. The compulsory doctors' associations' ambulatory care monopoly should be abolished.

The third group, the Council of Economic Experts, the body created by the federal government in the 1960s to advise it on economic policy issues, pleaded for similar reforms to those espoused by the *Kronberger Kreis* – for a greater privatization of the costs of illness and for greater competition between insurance funds and between suppliers, such as private-practising doctors.

Less sweeping proposals, mainly focused on privatizing a greater part of the costs of health care, emanated from the employers' organizations and the business lobbies attached to the Christian Democratic Union, the Economics Council (*Wirtschaftsrat*), which is dominated by big business, and the Association for Small and Medium-sized Business (*Mittelstandsvereinigung*). These organizations' programmes could be distinguished from those of the economists not only by their generally less radical nature, but also by the fact that they contained fewer proposals designed to intensify competition among health care providers. In any event, the weight of business-orientated groupings in the Christian Democratic Union and the coalition as a whole was offset by the party's labour wing, from which came the Labour and Social Affairs Minister who bore primary responsibility for the reform. The liberal Free Democratic Party, lacking a social basis in the manual working class, was less constrained from pressing demands for health care privatization and deregulation. But, like the other aforementioned groups, it, too, stopped short of pleading for regulatory reforms which would have impinged upon suppliers. The Free Democrats' reform proposals also centred heavily on the reduction of benefits and increases in direct patients' charges.

The fundamental decision against attempting to carry out a radical health insurance reform appears to have been taken well before the debate over the reform began in earnest. The Labour Minister pledged that market mechanisms and incentives would not be introduced indiscriminately in the health insurance and also that the existing division of labour between the state and the collective self-administration would not be challenged. 'Intensive talks' would be held with the interest groups while the reform was being drafted (quoted in Webber, 1989, p. 270). The major interest groups – the health insurance funds and the health-care providers' associations, including those of the doctors – were resolutely opposed to far-reaching reforms, market-orientated or otherwise. The Labour Minister let the private-practising doctors be told that a reform 'against' the doctors was neither desirable nor necessary and would not therefore take place (KBV, 1987, p. 52). Out of fear of a repetition of the failed reform efforts of the early 1960s, the government chose consciously at the outset to try to avoid a confrontation with the doctors' lobby. Early decisions were also taken to postpone any attempts to reform the health insurance funds and the hospital sector until after the 1990 federal elections. The health insurance reform remained a politically explosive issue, but by the time the Labour Ministry published its proposals, it could be discerned that the reform would be incremental rather than radical.

5. Regulatory Changes through the Health Insurance Reform

The regulation of health care, like that of other goods and services, may aim at influencing a number of variables. One such variable is that of *market entry*. Through such measures as putting ceilings on the number of doctors establishing private practices, steering the capacity of medical schools or changing the length of medical training, governments may attempt to regulate the number of doctors as a whole, the number of private-practising doctors and/or the number of private-practising doctors licensed to treat members of statutory health insurance funds. A second variable is that of *quality* or *safety*. All modern states have laid down more or less explicit and detailed rules concerning the procedures which must be followed, and the criteria which must be met, before new drugs may be introduced on to the market. Similarly, the nature of the occupational qualifications which must be obtained before a person can supply medical care is typically laid down by law. A third variable is that of *quantity of provision*. Apart from regulating market entry, rules may be adopted and enforced to try to influence the *per capita* or overall volume of services supplied, for example, by private-practising doctors. A further variable is that of *prices*. Governments frequently regulate doctors' and hospital fees or the prices of prescription drugs – or, as in the German case, they may lay down procedures which provide for their regulation by non-governmental actors.

The Christian–Liberal health insurance reform strengthened the role of market mechanisms in the regulation of the health care only at the margin. By increasing the direct charges for some medical services or limiting the extent of their coverage by the health insurance funds, the government reverted to market incentives to try to dampen the consumption of medical care. For the most part, however, these measures did not go very far, and hardship clauses for consumers on low incomes cushioned their potential impact. On balance, the effect of the health insurance reform was to strengthen and expand the scope of *collective self-regulation,* of the regulation of health care through collective agreements negotiated by the organizations of the health insurance funds and the health-care providers. Overall, the degree of regulation of health care provision increased rather than reduced.

These conclusions can be derived from a summary assessment of the measures affecting ambulatory and hospital care and prescription drugs (three subsectors of health-care, which together account for roughly two-thirds of West German statutory health insurance expenditure). By and large, the reform confirmed the existing regulations pertaining to the provision of ambulatory care by private-practising doctors. Doctors' fees – the relative value of different types of consultation and treatment – were to be negotiated, as in the past, by the health insurance funds' and doctors' associations. Similarly, the same two groups of associations were to continue to negotiate the total budget available for the remuneration of private-practising doctors. The negotiation of an annual ceiling on doctors' remuneration means that when the volume of services provided at pre-existing prices (fees) would cost more than the agreed ceiling, the prices per service are, in effect, reduced retrospectively so that the ceiling is not exceeded.

Three reform proposals provoked protests and opposition among the private-practising doctors' pressure groups. One aimed to enable hospitals to diagnose patients before, and treat them temporarily after, hospital stays. This was seen by the private practitioners as an inroad into their monopoly of the provision of ambulatory care. The other two implied an increase in the regulation of doctors' behaviour. The government proposed to revitalize the increasingly moribund medical advisory service attached to the health (and pension) insurance funds and to create various preconditions to enable the funds to detect excessive or fraudulent doctors' fees claims. All three proposals reached the statute book, but in forms much weaker than the Labour Ministry had envisaged in its original draft bill. For our purposes, the most interesting aspect of these measures is that the details of two of them (those relating to outpatient treatment by hospitals and the scrutinization of doctors' fees claims) were not specified in the government's bill, but were left to be negotiated between the doctors', health insurance funds' and, in the former case, hospitals' associations. The government tried by legislation to impose the goal of negotiations and stipulated between whom they were to take place. The substantive decisions, however, were to be reached in collective bargaining between the corporate actors representing health care financers and suppliers.

The hospital sector – as mentioned above – was barely affected by the health insurance reform. Although the government had already reformed hospital financing in 1984, it had not successfully tackled what was commonly diagnosed to be the chief cause of excessive bed capacity – the 'dual system' of financing, according to which state governments financed hospital building and modernization and the health insurance funds, through the daily rates paid to the proprietors, the hospitals' operating costs. The health insurance reform gave the health insurance funds the right to rescind hospitals' rights to treat fund members, but simultaneously granted the state governments a veto power over such decisions. In this sector also, the government's ambition was to expand the decision-making powers of the actors at the level of the collective self-administration. That this ambition could be realized only at the margins, and that the state governments retained a powerful regulatory role in the hospital sector, is a consequence of Germany's federal constitution and the state governments' electorally motivated concern to prevent a reduction of hospital services (see below).

The principal innovation in the reform package affected prescription drugs. Traditionally, prescription drug prices in Germany – in contrast to the dominant practice in the other European Community member states – had not been subjected to any form of regulation other than that of the market. The German market was reputed by some observers to be the 'last paradise' of the pharmaceuticals multinationals (quoted in Webber, 1989, p. 279). Following the failure of 'voluntary' price self-restraint by pharmaceuticals manufacturers to contain growing prescription drugs expenditure in the mid-1980s, the government now decided to lay the foundations for the introduction of a system of fixed or reference prices for prescription drugs. If manufacturers failed to adjust drug prices to the level of the reference prices and doctors none the less prescribed them, the consumer would have to pay the difference out of his own pocket. The reform aimed to stimulate price competition in the pharmaceuticals industry and use it to reduce prescription drugs spending. Once again, the government refrained from trying to set reference prices itself. The health reform law obliged the health insurance funds' and doctors' associations to group prescription drugs in categories for which the same reference price would apply and empowered the funds then to set the price. In addition, the legislation called on the health insurance funds' and doctors' associations to negotiate guidelines for the volume of prescription drugs prescribed by doctors.

The Christian–Liberal health insurance reform thus conformed to the predominant overall trend in the history of German health sector regulation. It brought about an increase in procedural regulation by the state and in substantive regulation by collective bargaining between the health insurance funds and organized service-providers. The substantive regulatory powers of this joint self-administration were increased at the expense both of the state governments (marginally) in the hospital sector and of the market in the prescription drugs sector. The government's strategy was recognizably to try to transplant the regulatory model which already structured relations between the insurance funds and the private-practising doctors into other sectors – except that, in the case of prescription drugs, the insurance funds were to negotiate over their comparability with the doctors' associations rather than with the pharmaceuticals manufacturers and to set the prices unilaterally.

This strategy had a dual motivation. One may be characterized as a 'problem-solving' motivation. In the past, the regulatory arrangements in the ambulatory care sector had proven to be more effective in terms of cost containment than those in other sectors. Thus, in the decade preceding the health insurance reform, no increases in health insurance contributions – in fact they rose on average from 11.4 to 12.6 per cent of wages and salaries – would have been necessary if cost increases in other sectors had been as low as those for doctors' fees (Rosewitz and Webber, 1990, pp. 230–1). However, beyond the issue of cost-containment, the problem-solving record of the joint self-administration in the ambulatory care, as well as other sectors, had been extremely chequered. Often enough, negotiations between the parties in the self-administration over the implementation of legal provisions had collapsed, leaving the law, in effect, a dead letter.

The second, and more important, motive for the government's predilection for delegating policy implementation to the self-administration was that of political expediency. By making the self-administration responsible for deciding policy details, it sought to avert conflicts with powerful interest-organizations, with voters, within the governing parties or between the coalition parties in the government (Webber, 1991). The anti-statist slogan, 'priority for the self-administration', which is commonly evoked in relation to health care in Germany, is often nothing other than a camouflage for the pursuit of a strategy of political conflict-avoidance.

6.   Obstacles to Regulatory Change in the Health Sector

The other alternative to substantive health care regulation by the state, of course, would have been to expand the scope for regulation by market mechanisms and incentives. But, apart from some measures which privatized part or all of the costs of some kinds of medical (especially dental) treatment and one which gave a small group of high-income-earning manual workers the same freedom to opt for private health insurance already enjoyed by high-income-earning white-collar workers, there was little in the health insurance reform which could have enthused proponents of a radical 'de-regulation' or privatization of health care.

Why, also in international comparison (see below), were the regulatory changes implemented or pursued by the Christian–Liberal coalition not more radical? Partly, this phenomenon can be explained in terms of specific prop-erties of the health, as opposed to numerous other, sectors. In other states, too, regulatory reforms in the health sector have been more limited than in others (cf. Lehmbruch, Singer, Grande and Döhler, 1988). The 'objective constraints' or 'pressures' (*Sachzwänge*) militating towards regulatory re-forms in health care are less compelling in so far as there is no international competition (and only limited *potential* for such competition) in most health care sub-sectors, so that national suppliers must not fear losses of market shares if their services are comparatively expensive. There have been no technological changes in the health sector akin to those in such sectors as telecommunications and broadcasting making some degree of regulatory reforms arguably unavoidable. Only indirectly, to the extent that rising health care spending may increase wage-related costs, is international competition a force for cost-saving regulatory reforms of health care. This fear – of declining industrial competitiveness and a loss of employment in exposed industrial sectors – was one of the factors which spurred the Christian–Liberal coalition's attempt to reform the health insurance.

A second factor contributing to the timidity of government 'deregula-tion' strategies in the health, as compared with other, sectors – not only in Germany, but also in Britain – is the continued strong public support for the collective provision of health care. This support, as demonstrated regularly by opinion polls, is so strong and broadly-based that even centre-right or Rightist governments must fear voters' reprisals if they lay themselves too open to charges that they are dismantling this edifice of the post-war West European welfare states. In Germany, increases in direct charges for health-care consumers, for example, are deeply unpopular (Webber, 1989, pp. 262–3 and p. 272). They can be legitimated only by imposing burdens simultaneously on suppliers' groups. The fact that, of the latter, the phar-maceuticals industry was the least popular undoubtedly helps to explain why the government tried to implement more radical measures concerning prescription drugs than against the doctors.

If the above factors account for the comparatively limited extent of regulatory reforms in the health sector in comparison with other *sectors*, they do not, however, explain the greater degree of continuity in regulatory arrangements in the *German* health sector, compared with that observable in the health sector in other countries governed during the same period by right-of-centre governments, such as Britain and the United States (Döhler 1990a and 1990b). The explanation for the particular path taken by German policy – which is idiosyncratic only when compared with the experience of the Anglo–Saxon parliamentary democracies with their first-past-the-post electoral systems and predominantly single-party governments – is primarily *institutional*. It is located in the specific organization of the German political – governmental, party and interest representation – system, which breeds three *logics*, the combined effect of which is to impose relatively tight constraints on radical policy changes.

The first of these logics is that of *coalition government*. Thanks to the electoral system of proportional representation, federal governments in Bonn, with the exception of a single parliamentary period from 1957 to 1961, have always been coalition governments. In coalition governments, policy decisions cannot be made on the basis of the majority principle, but rather require the consent of all the coalition partners – at least, if the coalition is to be stable. Moreover, the co-existence of socio-economic and confessional cleavages, making it difficult for the Social Democrats to mobilize a large section of the manual working class, namely the Catholic or practising Christian part, and for the Christian Democrats to mobilize a sizeable portion of the middle classes, that is, the Protestant or secularized middle classes, means that, in any conceivable federal government, the range of socio-economic interests represented is likely to be very broad and the task of mobilizing consensus around radical policy innovations extremely difficult.

In the Christian–Liberal coalition, the scope for radical health care 'de-regulation' was limited by the labour wing of the CDU, all the more so since its former head, Norbert Blüm, occupied the post of Labour and Social Affairs Minister and was in charge of drafting the reform. Blüm and the CDU labour wing were strictly opposed to a far-reaching privatization of medical care and insisted on compensating measures (for example, the introduction of benefits for caring for the elderly disabled) and sacrifices from service-providers as a *quid pro quo* for their acquiescence in benefit cuts and direct charges for patients (Webber, 1989, pp. 274–80). The position of the bureaucracy in the Federal Labour and Social Affairs Ministry, which had been controlled right through the Weimar Republic and then for the first two decades of the post-war period by the labour wing of the CDU and was a traditional stronghold of Social Catholicism, corresponded largely to that of the CDU left. Its initial draft bill was rather more *dirigiste* than the bill ultimately adopted by the government.

The *dirigiste* tendencies in the reform plans were combated, in turn, by the Free Democrats, who have long maintained close, clientelistic relations with the lobbies of the free medical professions – which opposed any encroachment by the state on their existing prerogatives, as well as, in their majority, market-orientated reform strategies (Rosewitz and Webber, 1990, pp. 301–5). Doctors' leaders attributed 'decisive improvements' in the reform on its way through the legislative process to the efforts of the Liberals (quoted in Webber, 1989, p. 287). Between the labour wing of the CDU, on the one hand, and the Free Democrats, on the other, collective self-regulation represented practically the equilibrium position – as well as helping to deflect (actual or potential) conflicts within the coalition into the ranks of the health insurance funds and organized health-care providers (see above).

The second logic militating against radical policy changes is that of (German) *federalism*. Since the foundation of the Federal Republic there has been an increasing centralization of decision-making powers, but the states have generally traded concessions to the centre against a stronger role in the federal legislative process, so that nowadays over a half of federal legislation requires the consent of the Bundesrat. While, during the 1970s, the CDU/CSU held the majority in the Bundesrat, it was thus able to exercise a strong influence on the policies of the then Social–Liberal coalition. In contrast to its predecessor, the Christian–Liberal coalition was backed by a majority in the Bundesrat throughout the 1980s. The pressure, in the interests of party loyalty, to support the federal government undoubtedly weakened the influence of the states on federal policy. None the less, the fact that federal government legislation never failed on the opposition of the Bundesrat cannot be interpreted as meaning that the Bundesrat majority no longer exercised any veto power. Conflicts between the federal government and the CDU- or CSU-led states were rather mediated in the organs of the CDU or in talks between federal and state government politicians and officials. In particular, the threat by one or the other CDU-led states to coalesce with the SPD in the Bundesrat to defeat a government bill could give it considerable bargaining power and force the government to grant it concessions then incorporated in government bills before they went to the Parliament.

The health insurance reform provided abundant potential for conflict between the federal and state governments – conflict potential which was rooted in the federal and state governments' responsibility for different aspects of health care policy to different electorates and was most manifest in the hospital sector. Whilst the federal government, given its competence for the statutory health insurance as a whole, had an interest in containing rising costs and health insurance contributions, the state governments, being primarily responsible for hospital planning and policy (but not for financing their operating costs), were reluctant to reduce the number of hospitals or hospital beds and wanted to keep the power to make decisions for themselves rather than forfeit them to the health insurance funds. For, 'Not the federation, but the state governments are the scapegoats if a hospital somewhere is closed or the number of beds cut back' (state government minister quoted in Webber, 1988, p. 65). Since the provisions of the health insurance reform relating to the hospital sector required the consent of the Bundesrat, the state governments could veto those proposals which they found unacceptable.

The opposition – across party lines – of the state governments to hospital sector reforms which would have reduced their regulatory powers explains why the coalition agreed at a very early stage to postpone any attempt at major hospital sector reforms. Most of those which were retained were either voted down or substantially amended on their way through the Bundesrat. The FDP's threat to block those provisions of the reform which benefited the states if the latter did not acquiesce in cost-containing hospital reforms had little impact, for none of the former was as attractive to the state governments as the prospect of a loss of control over hospital policy was threatening. As in previous federal–state conflicts over hospital policy, the states' coalition was led by the Bavarian CSU, whose leader, Franz-Josef Strauß, was extremely sensitive to the electoral implications of reduced hospital services.[1] The resistance of numerous state governments to an interstate redistribution of insurance contribution revenues also formed a major obstacle to a reform of the health insurance funds – which was also 'postponed'.

The third logic which constrains the scope for radical changes in regulatory policy for the German health sector is that of *sectoral self-regulation*. Sectoral self-regulation – the joint exercise of substantive regulatory powers by the organizations of producer, supplier or financer interests – is commonplace in the Federal Republic. It is the predominant mode of regulation, for example, of the stock exchanges and of wages and working conditions (see Chapters 6 and 10). In the health care sector, the ideology and practice of sectoral self-regulation have deep historical roots (see above). As intense as their conflicts over other, distributional issues may be, the health insurance funds' associations and the organized health care suppliers generally build a common front to oppose any attempts by the state to usurp their joint regulatory powers.

It is not only against encroachment by the state that the corporate actors composing the 'self-administration' of the health insurance tend to mobilize to defend sectoral self-regulation. Generally, they also resist regulation by market mechanisms and incentives. The health insurance funds reject proposals to give health insurees greater freedom to choose to which fund they want to belong. The doctors' associations oppose the notion that insurance funds be empowered to negotiate fees with individual practitioners on the grounds that the funds could then play doctors off against each other. The chemists' associations oppose reforms aimed at increasing price competition between pharmacies. Both doctors' and chemists' organizations defend existing regulations which prohibit doctors and chemists from employing their respective professional colleagues, purporting thereby to uphold the independent status of private-practising medical professionals.

The wall of defence erected around the system of sectoral self-regulation by its participants is difficult for any government to penetrate. Before the government makes such an attempt, it must have calculated that it can mobilize more public support than can its opponents in the self-administration. In the case of the Christian–Liberal health insurance reform, Blüm may have sought a conflict with the (unpopular) pharmaceuticals industry to give the reform the appearance of social equity which the Labour Ministry thought was vital if it was to be politically feasible (Webber, 1989, pp. 271–2). However, intimidated by the memory of the failed reforms of the early 1960s, the coalition tried deliberately – although without complete success – to avoid a confrontation with the doctors (see above). This inevitably meant foregoing any attempt to 'deregulate' the supply side of the market for ambulatory medical care.

The opposition of the organized sectoral interests may make the implementation of radical regulatory reforms in the German health sector politically difficult, if not impossible. At the same time, the organizational structure of these interests may facilitate indirect governmental regulation of health care, reducing the need for overt state intervention. Successive governments have used the threat of state intervention – albeit with variable success – to try to persuade sectoral interest organizations to exercise 'voluntary' self-restraint (Webber, 1991). Such threats have proven most effective in controlling expenditure on doctors' fees. The structure and powers of the associations of health insurance doctors – which doctors wishing to treat health insurance members are obliged to join, which possess a legally backed monopoly on ambulatory medical care, which alone are empowered to negotiate fees for individual services and the overall budget for doctors' fees, and which remunerate doctors for the services they have performed – enable them to deliver bargains struck with the government and health insurance funds. This capacity, in addition to the doctors' perceived capacity to mobilize public opinion against the reform, helped them to stay out of the political 'firing line' and avert legislation which would have imposed tighter restrictions on their fee-bargaining autonomy with the insurance funds (cf. Rosewitz and Webber, 1990, pp. 285–8). The government could abstain from regulating doctors' remuneration more closely itself because, under the threat that it would do so, the doctors' associations acquiesced in collective agreements which were compatible with the government's goal of stabilizing health insurance contributions.

7. Regulatory Reforms in Health Care: An Anglo–German Comparison

Health care reform was a constantly recurring topic on the political agenda of many West European states during the 1980s. On the one hand, especially in the first half of the 1980s, the economic conjuncture – low growth and high unemployment – depressed tax and social security contribution revenues, creating pressures either to cut health care spending or increase taxes or contributions. On the other, demographic trends alone – the growing proportion of elderly persons in the population – tended to raise demand for health care and health care costs. In addition to these factors, which were operative to a greater or lesser extent across most OECD states, centre-right or right-wing governments were elected to office in numerous states with the proclaimed goal of reducing the role of the state in economy and society and enlarging the scope for regulation by market mechanisms and incentives. At the level of political rhetoric, this applied to the Kohl government in the Federal Republic as well, of course, as to the Thatcher government in Britain.

The Thatcher government's neo-liberal crusade produced fewer far-reaching regulatory reforms in the health care sector than in many others. None the less, apart from privatizing health care costs at the margin through, as in the Federal Republic, increasing various direct charges to consumers, the Thatcher government undertook at least two initiatives which were more radical than any sponsored by the Christian–Liberal coalition. One of these was the creation of a new body of administrators, that is to say, regulators, the general managers, at all levels of the NHS (National Health Service). The new general managers were equipped with broad decision-making powers and subordinated to closer central control than the management organs which they replaced. The general managers introduced a new style of management to the NHS – one much less strongly orientated than hitherto towards achieving consensus with the organized interests in health care (Klein, 1989, pp. 208–12). The other was the plan – the implementation of which began in 1991 – to create internal markets, especially competition between hospitals, in the NHS. The government committed itself to retaining the NHS but, within its walls, tried to strengthen the role of market mechanisms and incentives as regulatory instruments.

An Anglo–German comparison of health policies and politics in the 1980s reveals striking differences not only in respect of the *content and scope* of regulatory changes, but also, and more so, in respect of the *processes* by which these changes were decided and implemented and the *modes of decision-making* which the changes aimed to promote. Whereas the Christian–Liberal coalition strove to integrate the organized sectoral interests into the policy-making process and promoted substantive regulation by negotiation and collective bargaining between health care providers and the health insurance funds, the British Conservative government preferred to exclude the trade unions and supplier lobbies, such as the British Medical Association, from the policy-making process and promoted unilateral decision-making by the new general managers at the expense of seeking consensus with the health service professions. Whilst the corporate actors in the NHS were marginalized, the kind of academic think-tanks that were kept on the political margins in the Federal Republic exercised strong influence on the British government's reform projects (cf. Döhler, 1990a, pp 24–28).

The greater radicalism of the British Conservative government's regulatory reforms, measured both by purpose and by adopted legislation, may be attributed to differences in political will and differences in the institutionally determined scope for the translation of central government programmes into political practice. The greater radicalism of the Conservative programme reflects the different ideological and socio-economic character and organizational structure of the Conservatives and the German Christian Democrats. Despite the adoption of a neo-liberal ideological discourse by some factions in the CDU/CSU (Strauß referred to himself in 1979–80 as the 'German Thatcher'), the political centre of gravity of the Christian Democrats remained closer to the middle ground than that of the British Conservatives right through the 1980s. In part, this is attributable to the existence of a labour wing in the CDU – which occupied the Labour and Social Affairs Ministry and dominated the party's health policy-making organs. The greater moderation of the CDU programme also reflects the more decentralized and fragmented structure of the CDU. This ensures that such intra-party groupings cannot be isolated and marginalized in the same way as Margaret Thatcher was long able to neutralize more moderate currents in the Conservative party and also allows some groupings to exercise disproportionately strong influence over party policy in certain issues – such as the labour wing over health care policy.

It is also important, when comparing the respective programmes of the two governments, to bear in mind that the state-owned and controlled NHS, the creation of the post-war Labour government, was a greater thorn in the ideological flesh of the British Conservatives than was the German health insurance in that of the German Christian Democrats who, in 1982, essentially reinherited the system which they had (re-)created in the early years of the Federal Republic – one which was 'collectively self-regulated' and dominated by private service provision. Even if the two parties had shared the same ideological tenets – which they did not – one might have expected the Conservatives to want to make a more radical break with the *status quo* than the Christian Democrats. (Paradoxically, however, the Conservative reforms, on balance, far from 'deregulating' British health care, brought about more highly centralized state control of the health sector.)

The Thatcher government could better translate its reform projects into political practice because the organization of the British governmental, party and interest representation systems imposes fewer constraints on the governmental leadership to negotiate policy with other actors, either within or beyond the government. Unlike Helmut Kohl, Margaret Thatcher had no labour wing to contend with in her party and government. Unlike Kohl, she was not confronted by any state governments with a constitutionally protected right of veto over hospital reforms. Unlike Kohl and his Labour and Social Affairs Minister, she and her government, through the NHS, were equipped from the outset with a strong capacity for health care intervention, rather than being confronted by a self-administration of highly organized health care suppliers and health insurance funds united in the desire to prevent the state from usurping their regulatory powers and encroaching on their autonomy.

8.   Health Sector Regulation and the Single European Market

The contrasting structures of health care financing, delivery, and regulation in Britain and the Federal Republic are characteristic of the diversity of such structures within the European Community. Levels of health-care provision also vary widely, especially as between the Northern and Southern European member states. The extent of the differences in health care structures and provision levels and the recognition of the political obstacles to eroding them have so far prevented the comprehensive harmonization of health care legislation becoming an issue on the Community's political agenda. The upward harmonization of provision levels would be too costly for the poorer member states or, if it were to be financed through the Community, for the richer member states. Downward harmonization – 'social dumping' – would provoke such massive political opposition in the Community countries with high levels of welfare provision that governments in these states are hardly prepared to contemplate such a project. Moreover, as the Rome treaties make no provision for Community action on social, including health, insurance, the legal scope for initiatives by the

Community organs (Commission, Parliament and Court of Justice), which might otherwise like to expand Community regulatory powers into this policy sector, is extremely limited. On general issues of social policy, the scope for Community action is constrained by the unanimity requirement for social policy legislation contained in the Single European Act. The Social Charter adopted by the European Council in 1989 contained no detailed proposals on health care issues and did not, in any case, bind the member states to implement them.

Structures and levels of health care financing, delivery and regulation will thus continue to vary widely in the Community after '1992'. However, the implications of the 1992 project – the dismantlement of remaining, above all non-tariff, barriers to the free movements of goods, services, capital and labour between the Community states – will vary between the financiers and suppliers of medical services, on the one hand, and the manufacturers and suppliers of medical goods or products, on the other. It is the latter group, which includes manufacturers of 'high-tech' medical equipment and pharmaceuticals, for which the dismantlement of non-tariff trade barriers, such as technical and safety standards, has the most far-reaching implications.

Hitherto, the pharmaceuticals market in the EC has been severely fragmented, especially by conflicting procedures and criteria for licensing drugs. To harmonize these procedures and criteria or to ensure their mutual recognition is one of the EC's '1992' projects. The 'Europeanization' of pharmaceuticals regulation is welcomed by the strong German industry, which can expect to increase its penetration of other Community markets as they become less protected, but which also hopes that EC regulations will be more 'industry-friendly' than those in Germany, especially since the Christian–Liberal health insurance reform. It would like, via Brussels, to dismantle the new system of reference prices for prescription drugs and to secure longer patent protection than it currently enjoys in the Federal Republic. However, the process of the 'Europeanization' of pharmaceuticals regulation – which has already been in progress for 25 years – will last well beyond 1992. According to one observer, 'it will be well into next century before all the regulatory barriers are removed' (Cookson, 1991).

Legal barriers to the free movement of members of the medical professions between the EC states, such as the non-recognition of university degrees, have already been abolished. However, this has not led to any significant increase in the inter-EC mobility of doctors and dentists or in the number of nationals of other EC states working in the medical professions in the Federal Republic – despite the high incomes of German doctors, compared with those of their colleagues elsewhere in the EC (cf. Alber, 1988). The greatest fear of the German medical professions is that the

Brussels competition directorate may try to overturn some fundamental German regulations pertaining to the medical professions on the grounds that they are 'anti-competitive' or restrain free trade within the EC. Such regulations could include the doctors' fees schedules negotiated between the insurance doctors' associations and the health insurance funds, restraints on advertising, and prohibitions on medical practitioners employing other members of the profession – which makes the establishment of chains of doctors' practices or of pharmacies in the Federal Republic illegal. The abolition of such regulations would indeed rock some of the existing foundations of the German health care system. However, there are no signs that the Commission is seriously contemplating launching an assault on German regulations in these areas.

9.   Health Sector Regulation and German Reunification

Compared with European integration, the infinitely more rapid and dramatic process of German reunification had potentially extremely radical implications for existing structures of health care financing, delivery *and* regulation in West Germany. The health care system which had been established in East Germany after the Second World War differed in most respects fundamentally from the West German. Health care was financed by a single social insurance fund run by the state-controlled trade union federation; it was delivered largely either by state-owned hospitals or company- or state-run health centres (*Polikliniken, Ambulatorien*); it was regulated by the state.

All those participants in the West German health care system which had a vested interest in the maintenance of a multiplicity of competing health insurance funds, private health care provision and regulation by collective bargaining or through the market were bound to push for the rapid transformation of the East German system according to the West German model. Their goal was not only to expand into a new market, but also to crush as far as possible the seeds of health policy cross-fertilization, as a result of which elements of East Germany could have been imported into the old Federal Republic. The radically different structure of health care delivery, however, set limits to the short-term realization of such aims. Of some 20 000 doctors supplying ambulatory care in East Germany, only some 500, in many cases elderly, had a private practice. The necessity of avoiding a collapse of ambulatory health care provision made its very rapid privatization impossible.

The conflict in the old Federal Republic concerning the unification of the East and West German systems was reminiscent of that which had taken place in the early post-war period and which had ended in victory for the protagonists of the *status quo*. These were favoured again in the current conflict by the existence of a centre-right coalition in Bonn. However, the political situation was complicated by the fact that, as in the case of the Christian–Liberal health insurance reform, wide differences of opinion existed between, on the one hand, the Federal Labour and Social Affairs Ministry, the head of whose health insurance division opposed the complete transformation of the East German system along West German lines, and, on the other, those currents in the coalition parties, especially the FDP, which wanted such a transformation to be implemented as rapidly as possible.[2] Moreover, the terms of health care unification could not be decided unilaterally by the Bonn government, but had to be *negotiated* with the government in East Berlin.

The victory of the CDU-led conservative alliance in the March 1990 elections in East Germany strengthened the position of the forces pushing for the rapid transformation of the East German system and the conservation of the West German – the health insurance funds, except for the local insurance funds, which initially sensed an opportunity to establish a monopoly in East Germany; the West German health care providers' organizations; the employers' organizations; the FDP and the majority of the CDU/CSU. But it did not pre-decide the issue, as the East German SPD, which wanted to defend some elements of the East German system, was also represented in the Grand Coalition government formed after the elections and even the East German CDU was opposed to the wholesale takeover of West German structures.

The unification process in the health sector turned out none the less to be one in which the influence of the forces advocating the retention of elements of the East German system was rapidly eroded and these forces themselves politically marginalized. In their coalition agreement, the parties in the East Berlin government had stated their wish to establish, at least initially, a single health insurance fund, to retain the company-based and other health centres as the main pillar for ambulatory health care, and to limit the range of prescription drugs (Manow-Borgwardt, 1991, p. 23). The Bonn Labour Ministry sympathized with some of these demands. However, following interventions by the white-collar employees' health insurance funds and unions and by business associations, Chancellor Kohl ruled that the Bonn negotiators should insist on the East Germans' taking over West German health insurance without any modifications (ibid., pp. 22–23).

The only concession which the East Berlin government could obtain from Bonn in the negotiations over the first treaty between the two governments was that the treaty obliged East Berlin to 'adapt' East German health insurance law to West German law rather than take it all over at once and left open the date by which this process should be completed. The Social

Democrats' influence on the health care provisions of the treaty was reduced by the fact that the responsibility for health insurance legislation in the East German government had meanwhile been allocated by the (CDU) prime minister to a Christian Democrat – one who was less sympathetic to demands for the conservation of elements of the East German system than other currents in his party – and by the plan for the rapid introduction of the Deutsche Mark in the GDR. Given the massive demand for the Deutsche Mark's introduction in East Germany, the SPD could hardly have wanted to run the risk of being blamed for its postponement by holding out for more palatable health care provisions in the intergovernmental treaty (ibid., pp. 26–27, 29–31).

The concretization of the treaty's provisions and the modalities of the introduction of West German health insurance law in East Germany still offered considerable potential for conflict. This indeed erupted over the provisions in the corresponding bills – which, although the East German Health Ministry was formally responsible for them and they had to be passed by the East German Parliament, were actually drafted by the Labour and Social Affairs Ministry in Bonn. Some of the provisions, in particular those relating to the respective participation of private-practising doctors and the state-run health centres in ambulatory care, provoked a storm of outrage among the West German health care providers' interest groups and in the FDP. The doctors' associations, which the Labour Ministry had largely excluded from the consultation process, appealed to Kohl to intervene on their behalf. This appeal was spectacularly successful. The bills' original provisions foreseeing controls on the establishment of private doctors' practices in East Germany, setting no limits on the life of state- and company-run health centres, and permitting the centres to take part directly in the provision of ambulatory care to health insurance members were subsequently turned on their head. No controls were imposed on the setting-up of private practices, the life-span of the state- and company-run health centres was limited to five years, then to be subject to review, and the doctors employed in the centres were incorporated in the insurance doctors' associations rather than the centres being granted the right of direct participation in ambulatory care provision.

In respect of health care financing, delivery and regulation, German unification has thus taken place predominantly on West German terms. The traditional West German structures for financing, providing and regulating health care were, despite initial fears among protagonists of the *status quo* that the unification process may be exploited to reform the West German system, reaffirmed. Health care will be financed throughout the united Germany by competing insurance funds. Procedurally, it will be regulated by the state, substantively however by the joint self-administration of the funds and health care providers. Only in terms of the structure of ambulatory care delivery will the health care system in the former GDR continue to differ from the West German, and this difference will have proven only temporary if, in 1995, the East German health centres are indeed closed down.

Whether the closure of the health centres takes place as the unification legislation foresees will depend on the rate at which private doctors' practices are set up in the former GDR – which in turn will be determined by such factors as the relative rate of increase of private doctors' incomes and the preparedness of banks to grant doctors credits for investing in practice infrastructure. If the number of private practices does not expand sufficiently quickly for self-employed doctors to be able to assume the role currently performed by health centres, the latters' life will have to be extended and the issue of whether centres may be established in the old Federal Republic is bound then to resurface. To this extent, the outcome of the conflicts over health care reunification in 1990 may prove to be provisional.

10. Conclusions

The overwhelming impression that emerges from an analysis of the politics of (West) German health care is of the system's extraordinary durability over a period embracing 60 years. Of course, there have been great changes in levels of provision during this period. The statutory health insurance now provides far more services and benefits to a far bigger proportion of the population than it did in the 1930s. But the underlying *structures* of health care financing, delivery and regulation have displayed enormous robustness and longevity. The basic pattern of collective financing through a plurality of health insurance funds, private service delivery and sectoral self-regulation within an overarching and comprehensive framework of law has survived the Nazi dictatorship, the Second World War and the post-war Allied occupation and the reform debates and conflicts of the 1960s, 1970s and late 1980s. Neither the European integration nor the German reunification process has yet led to its erosion or transformation.

After the abortive attempts to privatize a considerable portion of the costs of health care in the early 1960s, no subsequent Bonn government has tried to implement a sweeping health care privatization or 'deregulation'. The Christian–Liberal reform of 1988 certainly went further in this direction than any other in the interim period. However, it privatized costs only at the margin and did little or nothing to 'deregulate' the system. The predominantly intellectual protagonists of a health care strategy of 'deregulation' were kept on or relegated to the political sidelines. The political alternative to the dominant mode of substantive regulation – sectoral self-regulation – in Federal German health care has more often been 'more state' than 'more market'. Increased state regulation, however, has been more evident at the procedural than at the substantive level.

At the latter, the dominance of the traditional paradigm of sectoral self-regulation has survived all changes in ideological, political and economic conjunctures since the middle of the 1970s. State intervention, motivated typically by cost-containment, rather than ideological, goals, has generally amounted to a pragmatic search for instruments to make sectoral self-regulation 'work better'. There has been a transformation of neither the goals nor the instruments of regulation, but rather a series of attempts to refine and extend these instruments. The most common thrust of these attempts has been to extend the range of issues regulated by collective bargaining and thus to strengthen the capacity of the health insurance funds to control costs. The political conflicts over health care in the Federal Republic during this period have culminated in the traditionally dominant mode of substantive regulation in the sector being reinforced rather than eroded.

Often, however, the federal government's appeal to the self-administration to undertake regulatory action has been coupled with the threat that if it does not act, the government will itself intervene. This strategy of indirect state regulation has met with growing resistance in the self-administration, some of the actors in which complain of a growing loss of autonomy *vis-à-vis* the state. It also threatens to erode the legitimacy of the organs of the self-administration – for example, the insurance doctors' associations – among their respective members. The principal manifestation of a growing legitimacy crisis of the self-administration is the rise of an 'anti-systemic' opposition among private-practising doctors and dentists (Webber, 1991).

It is less the grand projects of European integration and German reunification with their manifold implications or, indeed, an unlikely rebellion by doctors and dentists against their respective associations that threatens the character of the regulatory structures in German health care than the creeping practical erosion of the autonomy of the sectoral self-regulators through government cost-containment strategies, which consist as much in threats of intervention as in acts of legislation. For this reason, the most relevant parameter in assessing the future probability of regulatory reforms in German health care is the evolution of expenditure. None of the cost-containment packages of the last 15 years has succeeded in dampening growing costs more than temporarily and there is no reason to think that the Christian–Liberal reform of 1988 will have a greater impact on expenditure trends than its predecessors. The next political battle over health care cost containment and regulation is therefore preprogrammed.

The array of participants in the next political conflicts over health care regulation will, however, be different from that in previous conflicts. Following the 1990 elections, Chancellor Kohl removed the competence for health insurance policy-making from the Federal Labour and Social Affairs and gave it to a newly-created Health Ministry. This step indicated Kohl's displeasure at the role played by the ministry both in the health insurance reform and in the process of German health care reunification, in particular at its conflictual relations with the health care providers' lobbies. By appointing to the top civil service post in the new ministry the official who had advised him on health and social policy issues in the Chancellor's Office and who had been his 'troubleshooter' for resolving conflicts with the pharmaceuticals industry, Kohl also indicated that he wanted harmony restored in the government's relations with the health care providers. Unlike the Labour Ministry, the new Health Ministry will not be embedded in a tight network of relations with the trade unions and employers' organizations (and the local health insurance funds which they jointly manage), so that in the longer term the ministry may develop into an intra-governmental 'lobby' for the doctors and pharmaceuticals industry.[3] It is always possible to change the *regulators* instead of the *regulations*. This change of regulators may prove advantageous for health care providers in future health care policy conflicts and militate against major changes in the existing regulatory framework.

Notes

1 Strauß wrote in his memoirs: 'For the citizens, the hospital sector is one of the most important problems, because it affects, or can affect, everyone. I find in conversations with local government politicians that 40 per cent or more of the points they raise have to do with local hospital problems. I have the same experience at election rallies.... The first question everywhere after my speech is mostly about the hospital' (Strauß, 1989, p. 541).
2 The head of the ministry's health insurance division said, referring to the coalition's plan to reform the health insurance funds in the next Parliament: 'It would be nonsense to force our system on to the GDR without any changes, only then to reform it later' (quoted in Hoffmann, 1990).
3 The former health insurance expert in the FDP Parliamentary Party, Hansheinrich Schmidt-Kempten, quoted in *Der Spiegel*, no. 6, 4 February 1991, p. 105.

References

Alber, Jens (1988), *Die Gesundheitssysteme der OECD-Länder im Vergleich* (MPIFG Discussion Paper 88/2), Cologne: Max-Planck-Institut für Gesellschaftsforschung.

Cookson, Clive (1991), 'In search of harmony to cure Europe's ills', *Financial Times*, 11 March.

Döhler, Marian (1990a), *Policy Networks, Opportunity Structures and Neo-conservative Reform Strategies in Health Policy* (paper presented at the International Sociological Association XIIth World Congress of Sociology, 9–13 July, Madrid, Spain).

Döhler, Marian (1990b), *Gesundheitspolitik nach der 'Wende': Policy-Netzwerke und ordnungspolitischer Strategiewechsel in Großbritannien, den USA und der Bundesrepublik Deutschland,* Berlin: Edition Sigma.

Hoffmann, Wolfgang (1990), 'Von einem Extrem ins andere?', *Die Zeit*, no. 28, 6 July.

KBV (Kassenärztliche Bundesvereinigung) (1987), *Tätigkeitsbericht der Kassenärztlichen Bundesvereinigung,* Cologne: DeutscherÄrzteverlag.

Klein, Rudolf (1989), *The Politics of the National Health Service,* 2nd edition. London/New York: Longman.

Lehmbruch, Gerhard, Singer, Otto, Grande, Edgar, Döhler, Marian (1988), 'Institutionelle Bedingungen ordnungspolitischen Strategiewechsels im internationalen Vergleich', in Manfred Schmidt (ed.), *Staatstätigkeit: International und historisch vergleichende Analysen,* Opladen: Westdeutscher Verlag.

Manow-Borgwardt, Philip (1991), *Strategien gesundheitspolitischer Akteure im Prozeß der deutschen Vereinigung* (unpublished paper), Cologne: Max-Planck-Institut für Gesellschaftsforschung.

Rosewitz, Bernd and Webber, Douglas (1990), *Reformversuche und Reformblockaden im deutschen Gesundheitswesen,* Frankfurt-am-Main/New York: Campus.

Strauß, Franz-Josef (1989), *Die Erinnerungen,* Berlin: Seidler.

Webber, Douglas (1988), 'Krankheit, Geld und Politik: Zur Geschichte der Gesundheitsreformen in Deutschland', *Leviathan,* 16:1, July.

Webber, Douglas (1989), 'Zur Geschichte der Gesundheitsreformen in Deutschland - II. Teil: Norbert Blüms Gesundheitsreform und die Lobby', *Leviathan,* 17:2, July, pp. 262–300.

Webber, Douglas (1991), *Die kassenärztlichen Vereinigungen zwischen Mitgliederinteressen und dem Gemeinwohl* (manuscript to be published by the Bertelsmann Foundation, Gütersloh).

10 Regulatory Reform and German Industrial Relations

Karl Koch

There is little dispute that the German system of industrial relations made a significant contribution to the initial post-war economic recovery of West Germany and continued to play a crucial role in establishing Germany as a leading economic nation. The stability of the West German industrial relations system is well illustrated by the relative low incidence of industrial conflict in comparison with other European countries (Table 10.1). A further aspect of this stability is a continuity of policies in the industrial relations arena. Explanation of the degree of stability of West German industrial relations has tended to focus around the thesis that the German system can be described as a cooperative model, based on a high degree of juridification. Juridification is in turn regarded as one of the central features

Table 10.1 Lost Industrial Working Days per 1 000 Workers

Country	1980 – 87
Netherlands	22
Federal Republic of Germany	39
France	150
Portugal	195
Denmark	195
Ireland	514
United Kingdom	863
Italy	1 053

Source: Eurostat, *Employment and Unemployment*, 1989

of the German industrial relations system. At the heart of German industrial relations lies a complex and refined legal system that regulates the relations of interest between capital and labour.

During the periods of strong economic growth, particularly between 1950 and the first oil crisis of 1973, trade unions were in a position to press for regulatory measures which enhanced the conditions of employment for their constituents and guarded them against the vagaries of the independent wage-earner's existence. In Germany this last aspect is founded on a long historical tradition and ideological predispositions going back to the extensive social benefits legislated for by Bismarck in the nineteenth century.

However, the beginning of the 1980s witnessed a German economy with declining growth rates and new levels of high and persistent unemployment. In this context the Christian Democratic–Liberal coalition of Helmut Kohl came to power in 1982. The consequence of this economic trend was an increasing pressure on the new government, from the employers, to deregulate in the industrial relations field so that employers could benefit from a greater degree of flexibility. The deregulation approach of the German government in the industrial relations area was further encouraged by the need of the economy to become more competitive on the world markets, more innovative and more responsive because of the proposed Single European Market in the European Community by the end of 1992. The dramatic events of November 1989 and the subsequent political and economic unification of Germany have reinforced domestic arguments for the need of flexibility and hence the continuation of deregulation policy. These arguments have been powerfully supported by such lobbies as the Federation of German Industry (*Bundesverband der Deutschen Industrie*) and the employers' associations (*Arbeitgeberverbände*).

The Kohl government developed its economic policy in terms of neoclassical economic theory, arguing for less state involvement, more market freedoms, dismantling of rigidities in economic regulations and an increase in flexibility of labour markets. It was true that after 1986 there was a real upturn in the economy (Table 10.2), but it was weak and did not address fundamental issues of industrial restructuring or German technology lagging behind countries such as Japan. With the exception of the policy of budgetary constraint, which was escalated after 1983, the Conservative–Liberal coalition did not bring about a marked change; the economic *Wende* proved to be a modest affair.

In West Germany the permanent unemployment figures, around 7 per cent to 9 per cent, placed considerable pressures on the trade union and employers' relationship, as well as the industrial relations system as a whole. It also engendered a critical attitude towards the German 'social partner' ethos. The concept of *Sozialpartnerschaft*, which emphasizes the

Table 10.2   Unemployment, GNP and Productivity in the FRG (Percentage Annual Change)

Year	Unemployment	GNP	Productivity
1984	9.3	2.8	2.9
1985	9.4	2.0	2.0
1986	9.0	2.3	2.2
1987	8.9	1.8	1.8
1988	8.9	3.7	3.1
1989	8.0	3.4	3.4
1990	8.8	3.5	3.5

Source: Calculated from *Sachverständigenrat*, 1990–1.

common, rather than the conflictual, goals between trade unions and employers' associations was, therefore, subject to reassessment.

This chapter addresses the question of what regulatory changes have taken place and what the consequences have been in a key area of German industrial relations. The central focus of the analysis is the important issue of collective agreements on working hours. The shift to destandardized and flexible working hours was seen by many as a state deregulation policy in favour of employers. Interpretations of this development can focus on the aspect of labour market, that is 'economic regulation', or on 'social regulation', to use the classification of regulation proposed by Button and Swann.[1] Deregulation may have been stimulated by the economic requirements of the labour market and the issue of the cost of labour in a climate of reduced economic growth. But at the same time the social consequences for the actors in the industrial relations field are obvious and important, and a central characteristic of German regulation has been its concern with social issues and goals. The traditional methods of regulation in the post-war period, in industrial relations, have been the negotiations, conducted by the parties to collective agreements, at regional or industry level. The state had in the early years of the Federal Republic only occasionally intervened directly in this 'dynamic process by which production and social demand adapt'.[2]

1.   Context of Regulatory Reform

The labour market has long been regarded as a distinct market from that of goods and services; the necessity of minimum employment conditions and wages through legal regulation and collective agreements has been a basic tenet of trade union policy. Thus unions have seen part of their function in extending these provisions to cover the entire complex range of employer–employee relations. The German trade unions argue that this has resulted in a complex system of regulations: the Works Constitution Act, co-determination legislation, Collective Bargaining Act and the complex matrix of labour, health and social legislation. From the trade union perspective the goal of this regulatory network has been to curtail the structural superiority of employers in the labour market.

Conversely, the employers have regarded this regulatory framework as restrictive and adding to labour costs in an increasingly competitive market. They have, accordingly, pressed for deregulation of the labour market. This demand for deregulatory policies was readily supported by the Christian–Liberal government of Kohl, and a number of deregulatory laws were indeed passed; the Ordinance on Working Hours, first legislated in 1938, (*Arbeitszeitordnung*), was modified in the autumn of 1984. The changes to Article 116 of the Employment Promotion Act (*Arbeitsförderungsgesetz, 1969*) was a second example. The Employment Promotion Act (*Beschäftigungsförderungsgesetz, 1985*) was, perhaps, the most overt example of the government's deregulatory measures. It facilitated a greater use of subcontract labour and part-time work, granted small firms the right to use workers on fixed-term contracts and extended the use of fixed-term contracts for unemployed persons by allowing such contracts to be concluded for up to an 18 months' period without any need for justification. That this loosening of labour contracts was regarded as a successful regulatory reform of labour market conditions, by the employers, was amply shown by the government's willingness to extend the original period of validity, which was to cease in 1989, to 1995. Early empirical assessment showed that within two years 7.2 per cent of all employees had a limited labour contract; in absolute terms this was an increase of between 800 000 and 900 000 persons.[3] The immediate effect of the legislation is evident from Table 10.3. The first step towards a 'neo-conservative system change' had commenced.[4]

At the end of 1987 the government appointed a Deregulation Commission to examine and report on measures required to dismantle regulations inhibiting the competitive, free market economy as originally conceived by Ludwig Erhard, as Federal Economics Minister 1949–63, and his adviser Alfred Müller-Armack. The Commission, which had failed to present its

Table 10.3   Percentage Temporary/Total Employees, 1984–6

Employees	1984	1985	April 1986	November 1986
All	4.2	6.8	7.2	8.0
Male	4.2	7.0	7.3	9.0
Female	4.1	6.4	7.1	9.0
Part-time	7.6	8.9	9.2	10.0
Full-time	3.6	6.4	6.9	8.0
Under 25 yrs	9.5	16.7	19.3	22.0

Source: W. Adamy, *WSI Mitteilungen*, Nr. 8, 1988, p. 476.

second report dealing with labour market issues by the December 1990 date of the first all-German elections, submitted this report to the Federal Minister of Economics in April 1991. Critics suggested that the report was delayed because of political considerations and the desire, by the government, to intensify its deregulation programme.[5] The Commission was chaired by Professor Jürgen Donges, former Vice-President of the World Economic Institute at Kiel, a prominent liberal, and was deemed, by the trade unions, to be dominated by representatives from the liberal capitalist faction. This view was strengthened by the fact that the Deregulation Commission emphasized the significance of the Single European Market resulting in a sharpening of competition and the consequent necessity for deregulation. Indeed the title of its final report, *Revitalization of the Market Economy*,[6] indicated its priority to encouraging deregulatory policies. Included were proposals which would facilitate dismissals, reduce redundancy costs and promote wages below collective agreement levels. In the case of redundancy provisions (*Sozialpläne*), for example, the deregulation proposals of the Deregulation Commission would have serious repercussions in the five new federal states where closures of plants has steadily increased since unification in 1990.

The report recommends that compensation payments for mass redundancies are not placed purely on employers, but be carried by employers, employees and a number of social institutions. The report proposes abolition of legal norms whereby collective agreements lay down minimum standards of the terms and conditions of employment relationships. The present arrangement, which allows the Minister of Labour to declare a collective agreement binding for all employees (*Allgemeinverbin-*

lichkeitserklärung) in industries where collective bargaining is weak, should be restricted. These proposals, if implemented, would certainly lead to a deregulated labour market compounding the problems for employees in the five new federal states. The Commission's findings not only attracted severe criticism from the German trade unions but also from the Christian Democrats and their influential Social Committees (*Sozialausschüsse*).

If international competitiveness was a significant argument for the reform of economic regulation, technological change can also be seen as providing a vital impulse for deregulatory developments in industrial relations. Technological innovation has a dramatic impact on production processes, work practices and consequently employment structures.[7] This development will be illustrated in this chapter by focusing on the increasing deregulation of working conditions which found its genesis in the implementation of differentiated working hours in German industry. The advent of the demand by the trade unions, since 1984, to reduce the standard working hours to 35 per week had profound repercussions on the German system of industrial relations in general and collective bargaining in particular. A central issue was the reshaping of regulatory policy through the dismantling of legislative regulations which were in favour of employers and the related protective collective agreement structures.

Deregulation, which in the context of German employment conditions is synonymous with the concept of flexibility, has been an important instrument of the government to relocate the locus of power between trade unions and employers. Thus the Annual Economic Report of the government in 1988 states: 'It is imperative that private enterprise has more freedom for initiatives, more favourable conditions for innovation and capital formation as well as more flexibility for enterprise within the Federal Republic of Germany'.[8] This is a clear statement concerning the primacy of a regulatory 'free' social market economy inclusive of the labour market.

2.   Juridification

The German concept of *Verrechtlichung* has been subject to a great many interpretations. In industrial relations the term has become associated with the idea of a complex network of legal categories and procedures by which the industrial relations actors are constrained. In this interpretation industrial relations is seen as subject to a ramified and extensive network of legislation, labour court decisions and legally recognized national and regional collective agreements.[9] Some German commentators argue that this 'legalized' system is peculiar to Germany: 'The West German system of industrial relations has – in comparison with, for example, the British – a strong and comprehensive tendency towards juridification'.[10] However, Spiros Simitis demonstrates that juridification is not a concept restricted to Germany; the evidence suggests that it is a universal feature of all democratic societies.[11] What is peculiar to the German system of industrial relations, though, is the degree of juridification which is undoubtedly more substantial than in many other western democratic societies.

The explanation for the predominance of a legalized industrial relations system are partly to be found in the late, rapid and all-embracing process of the German industrial revolution in the nineteenth century. The state regarded this process as beneficial and was an active participant in it, understanding that the dramatic economic and social consequences required a reappraisal of social and legal regulations. In particular the new emerging relationship between employers and the vast army of the 'proletariat' led to new legislative provisions. The state sought to influence the employee–employer relationship by protecting those most affected by the negative effects of the Industrial Revolution. The long evolution to a 'social state' commences with this development, and the role of the state as a third party in the system of industrial relations begins to play a crucial role. Initial legislation, in the nineteenth century, providing laws for limits on child labour, basic safety regulations, minimum wages and maximum working times accelerated the creation of a corpus of labour law. At the same time labour relations became the object of juridification. This process clearly shows the state's changing perception of its function. The contemplative state gave way to the 'activist state' and thus to a 'law-driven society'.[12]

What is suggested is that labour law was harnessed by the state to 'steer' social and economic behaviour in a particular direction: 'Juridification is thus tied irrevocably to state intervention.'[13] For industrial relations the inference, drawn by Voigt, is that juridification refers to all forms of state intervention that 'reduce the freedom of action of employees and employers in shaping relations at work.'[14] In Germany, therefore, regulatory processes are generated as much by formal labour law as by indirect steering mechanisms, exemplified by the state guaranteeing the autonomous nature of the collective bargaining procedure and a consequent high degree of self-regulation. It is the autonomous aspect of collective bargaining (*Tarifautonomie*) that has been a central issue in the debate on regulatory policies in German industrial relations.

A further aspect of juridification in Germany is the extent of its coverage and the categorization of labour law into distinct legal sections. Over and above the health and safety provisions, dismissal legislation and labour agreement rights there is an extensive co-determination legislation, regulating not only employee participation at plant and enterprise level but also the details of plant-level industrial relations. Indeed, the German system makes a clear distinction between plant-level industrial relations, as defined by the provisions of the Works Constitution Act (*Betriebsverfassungsgesetz*, 1972), and those which prescribe the procedures between the parties to bargaining about wage, salary and employment conditions at industry or regional level.

Within these regulatory frameworks parties may follow their objectives and interests. But should the system become destabilized, the state can and does intervene, either directly by changing, modifying or extending relevant labour legislation, or by curtailing the highly regarded autonomy of the bargaining partners. Juridification is, therefore, a dynamic social and political process which has contributed to the shaping of the specific form that industrial relations has taken in Germany.

The German state has continued to ensure, and recognize, the autonomous method of regulating collective bargaining that has evolved between employers and trade unions. At the same time economic and social pressures have, since the beginning of the 1980s, led to a 'reduction in the regulatory jurisdiction of the collective bargaining parties.'[15]

3.   Collective Bargaining

A number of essential characteristics of collective bargaining and the German industrial relations system are significant for an understanding of regulatory changes. The historical continuity of German industrial relations, and especially of the labour movement, was severely disrupted by the years of National Socialism, which introduced the 'leadership' principle and destroyed the democratic trade union movement of the Weimar Republic. The bitter lessons learned by the destruction of the trade union movement were reflected in the determination of those responsible for restructuring Germany after 1945 to avoid the mistakes of the Weimar period. The multi-unionism of Weimar, with over 200 trade unions based on political or ideological premises, was firmly rejected and in its place the industrial unions, which now dominate Germany, were created. The industrial unions are, however, not the only representatives of organized labour. The German White-Collar Union (*Deutsche Angestelltengewerkschaft*), the German Civil Service Federation (*Deutscher Beamtenbund*) and smaller organizations, such as the Christian Trade Union (*Christlicher Gewerkschaftsbund*) have a role, if a minor one, in industrial relations.

The 16 industrial unions established in Germany adhere to the principle that an industrial union will, through agreement, organize a demarcated industrial sector, such as metal-working or chemicals. Employees, whether blue collar, white collar or civil servants, will belong to the union identified for that industrial sector. The consequence is the central characteristic of German industrial unions: for every plant there shall be only one trade union. The political and ideological criteria of the past are excluded. Industrial unions are also autonomous in regulating their financial affairs and have the right to engage in collective bargaining. The internal organizational structure of the trade unions allows for a centralized bargaining procedure, with a high degree of coordination, to be instituted. The industrial unions are gathered under the umbrella organization of the German Trade Union Federation (*Deutscher Gewerkschaftsbund*), whose function it is to synchronize broad political, social and economic strategies for the union movement, but not to engage in collective bargaining.

This centralization of the collective bargaining process is supported by the organizational structure of the employers; employers are organized on a regional basis according to industrial sectors. The Confederation of German Employers (*Bundesverband der Deutschen Arbeitgeberverbände*), representing 80 per cent of all enterprises, has 11 federal state members in west Germany and is expanding this principle to the new federal states in the east. Because of this organizational structure the employers are able to achieve a high degree of coordination in their bargaining strategy and to relate their bargaining units to the regional structures of the trade unions. The result is that there are significant sized collective bargaining regions which determine wage and salary levels for employees in specific industrial sectors. Company agreements do exist, Volkswagen being an example, but are relatively unimportant in macro-economic terms. Collective agreements at federal state or state level, when they do occur, are predominantly framework agreements.

This central characteristic of the German system has determined the pattern of collective bargaining which itself is based on legislative provisions arising out of the Basic Law of 1949. The autonomy of collective bargaining is derived from Article 9 of the Basic Law and guarantees the right to found associations, in particular trade unions or employers' associations. In this way the state has accepted that wages and employment conditions are, within the context of the appropriate laws, not regulated directly by the state but are the prerogative of employers' associations and trade unions. In this respect Germany, unlike the United Kingdom, belongs to the group of countries deriving their legal systems from the concept of Roman codification, where social rights are guaranteed by constitutional and statutory laws.

A further sharp contrast between British and German industrial relations is that the process of collective bargaining in Germany is regulated by a Collective Agreement Act.[16] The Act specifies that only trade unions and employers' associations, or trade unions and individual employers, can make a collective agreement; this agreement can be declared to be generally binding (*Allgemeinverbindlichkeitserklärung*). Consequently those who are not members of a trade union reap the advantages from these agreements. In practice in 1989 around 540 out of 32 000, collective agreements were subject to the latter provision; around four million employees were covered.

According to the Collective Agreement Act the collective bargaining parties are, during the period of validity of a collective agreement, subject to an obligation to maintain the peace (*Friedenspflicht*). Neither trade unions nor employers' associations may engage in an industrial conflict over matters covered by the agreement. The peace obligation finds a further application in arbitration agreements: almost 70 per cent of agreements include an arbitration provision on a voluntary basis between the bargaining parties. This norm contributes to the stability of the German industrial relations system in as much as it places constraints in the way of initiating legitimate industrial conflicts: the strike or lockout.

A final pertinent clause of the Collective Agreement Act states that the collective agreements, outcome of the collective bargaining autonomy, have primacy over the Works Constitution Act which regulates industrial relations at plant-level. It is precisely this relationship that has been the subject of the most dramatic effects of the changes in regulatory policies affecting industrial relations. At the same time the preservation of the principle of the autonomy of collective bargaining has been supported by the legislators. Otto Kissel, President of the Federal Labour Court, has argued that it has been universally accepted as contributing to the stability of the political order in Germany and that it is an essential element of the stable social and economic framework of that country.[17]

This network of norms, partly legal and partly based on voluntary agreements between the parties, determines the bargaining process, arbitration and the institutionalized forms of industrial conflict in Germany. The process and practice of juridification finds a precise example in this area.

4.   Plant-Level Industrial Relations

The dichotomy between collective bargaining at regional, or industry level and plant-level industrial relations is illustrated by the Works Constitution Act of 1972 (*Betriebsverfassungsgesetz*). This key item of labour legislation has had a long evolutionary path from the Weimar Republic to its present form. The Works Council Law (*Betriebsrätegesetz*) of 1920 had its origins in the demand for industrial democracy as a supplement to the Weimar political democracy. It did not make a great impact under the economic and political conditions prevalent during the Weimar Republic, and the first Works Constitution Act of 1952 did not find the immediate cooperation of the trade union movement in post-war West Germany either. However, the potential significance of works councils as instruments of trade union power at plant-level converted unions towards taking an active and participatory role in them. Works councils provide the framework for the relationship between employees and management at plant-level and are probably the most characteristic feature of the German industrial relations system. They certainly have no direct parallel in Britain, although, of course, they are a feature of many continental European countries.

The Works Constitution Act stipulates that every firm employing five or more employees may have a works council. Such a works council is elected by all employees in that firm; trade union membership is not a criterion. The elected works council (elections taking place every three years) will vary in size according to the number of employees in a firm; a firm with up to 600 employees will have nine works council members while a company of 9 000 will have 31. The works council negotiates with management over a range of industrial relations issues, carefully defined and categorized by the law, and formulates plant agreements (*Betriebsvereinbarungen*) once negotiations have been concluded. However, as has been previously pointed out, the works council cannot negotiate over those issues that have been subject to collective agreement by the collective bargaining parties. The works council is further constrained by an obligation to maintain peace (*Friedenspflicht*); it is charged by the law to work harmoniously with management and is not to be able to initiate industrial conflict. Both parties are, therefore, obliged to exhaust all measures to find a resolution of differences. In this sense the Act is an aspect of the propensity in Germany for institutionalizing conflict in the arena of industrial relations.

The rights of the works council are categorized into information, consultation and codetermination rights. Only codetermination rights, which include the determination of daily working time, can be strictly enforced through a form of compulsory arbitration by third-party intervention. The bargaining power of the works council does, however, depend not only on the legislative stipulations but even more on the size of the firm, type of ownership, technology, workforce structure, history of workplace relations, policy of the works council and, crucially, on the trade union density.[18] Where a firm has a high trade union density, and three-quarters of all works councils in west Germany are dominated by a union affiliated to the German Trade Union Federation, it has a substantially stronger power base *vis-à-vis* management.

In some industries, such as metal-working, 82 per cent of all works councillors belong to the Metal Workers Union (compared to 1.6 per cent of seats held, for example, by the German White-Collar Union). *De facto* their works councils can be regarded as trade union organs, particularly as frequently there are intimate connections to the local trade union organization. In the 1990 works council elections the Metal Workers Union voted 64 962 members into office, a significant coverage for these employee representatives. Theoretically, the local union office should link in primarily with the trade union representatives, representing union interests at plant-level; in practice all works council members also exercise this function. Additionally, the trade unions, especially in metal-working and chemicals, have deliberately evolved a structure at plant-level which has linked the two representative bodies into a symbiotic relationship. Organizational structures have evolved allowing a formal flow of information between trade union representatives and works council. This situation gives rise to a degree of dualism of representation at plant-level but has so far not had a serious destabilizing effect, even though there have been instances, such as the illegal September strikes in the metal-working industry in 1969, where centripetal political and social forces put pressure on the relationship. On the contrary, the works councils have established themselves as the main negotiating and grievance-handling body on behalf of their constituents. In practice they have dealt with central issues, such as supplementary wage bargaining, employment decisions and working hours and have contributed to the low level of overt conflict at plant-level. Related to this was the comparatively low number of plant agreements that had been signed between works councils and management up to 1984.

The major problem that derives from the schism between plant-level industrial relations and the regional, or industry, predominance of collective agreements was, and remains, that specific plant issues, conditions and demands cannot be met by agreements that apply to such large industrial sectors or regions. Since the 1970s technological change has increased the need for plant specific regulations and has acted as a driving force towards an opening of the previously so rigorously defined boundaries. 'What is asked for is a flexibilization of labour law – away from the (relative) rigid regulations at industry-wide level of the respective branch of industry – to the 'made-to-measure' solution of the individual plant.'[19] The trade unions regard this attitude as undermining the established, and hard-fought, rights of employees which have been codified in the matrix of laws, agreements and regulations contributing to the German concept of *Verrechtlichung*. Changes that have located an increasing bargaining function at plant-level are consequently interpreted as deregulatory tendencies.

5.   Regulatory Change of Working Conditions

The trade union movement had pressed for a reduction in working hours since the end of the 1970s. A pace-setting role was played by the Metal Workers Union which agreed at its 1977 congress, against the recommendation of its executive committee, to place the demand for a 35-hour week on the agenda. The steel industry, which had seen a steady decline of its labour force because of world market trends, was the first industry to strike over the demand. In the winter of 1978/79 40 000 employees in the industry carried through a 44-day strike, albeit with a very modest, and finally mediated, result. The issue became more urgent during the early 1980s. Because of the permanently high unemployment figures in West Germany the unions coupled the demand for shorter working hours to the creation of greater employment opportunities. In 1982 the German Trade Union Federation agreed to coordinate the industrial unions in a common strategy to achieve the goal of a 35-hour week. By 1983 the Metal Workers Union had been joined by the unions organizing wood, printing and paper, postal workers and commerce in demanding a 35-hour working week. A momentum had by now been established in the West German trade union movement behind this demand. The emphasis on the issue of shorter working hours also reflected a shift from quantitative collective bargaining goals to qualitative ones. This shift was in line with the German economy which had allowed unions in 1982 and 1983 to achieve only moderate wage increases. In the metal-working industry, the pace-setter for wage agreements in Germany, an average increase of 4.2 per cent had been achieved in 1982 and only 3.2 per cent in 1983. The low wage increases were related to the slowing down of economic growth rates in Germany and to union policy which increasingly linked its collective bargaining aims to broader objectives: democratization of the economy, security of jobs, security of pensions and the maintenance of the German social net. But the central thrust of union strategy in 1984 was the demand for a reduction of working hours per week to 35.

In 1984 the Metal Workers Union initiated a coordinated campaign on the basis of this demand in a selective number of bargaining regions. The negotiations between the union and the Metal Trades Employers' Association (*Gesamtmetall*) soon broke down and led to the biggest industrial conflict (strikes, lock-outs and lay-offs) in German post-war history. The consequences of this strike were to be profound in terms of future bargaining trends as well as of regulatory changes by the government. The Christian–Liberal coalition of Chancellor Kohl had argued not only that there was no support for the 35-hour working week from the union membership but also that the Metal Workers Union's claim that unemployment would be reduced by 1.5 million by 1986 was not realistic. The dispute over benefit payments to employees laid off as a consequence of the industrial conflict ultimately led to changes in the Employment Promotion Act and thus curtailing the unions' ability to strike.

The employers, and the Kohl government, argued that such a reduction in working hours would lead to an increase of at least 18 per cent in manufacturing costs, and hence there would be no increase in productivity. The line taken was that in order to remain competitive in changing world markets companies required greater flexibility to adapt to new production methods and to respond speedily. The central proposal in the 1984 negotiations by the employers was for an increase in managerial flexibility on the structuring of working hours, that is, in particular of working time and part-time work.

As the trade unions and employers were unable to overcome their differences the parties resorted to arbitration and a compromise solution was arrived at by Georg Leber, a former SPD minister, as the arbitrator. The so-called 'Leber Compromise' was unusual as it awarded an agreement that combined both the trade unions' and employers' demand. The resulting collective agreement reduced the working week to 38.5 hours but laid down a more flexible arrangement for working hours. Specifically, for the first time working time could, for the individual regular workweek hours, vary between 37 and 40 hours per week. A clause in the agreement made it possible for these hours to be distributed evenly or unevenly over the five-day working week with compensation at the end of two months. This opened up the possibility of varied arrangements of working time and, therefore, an increase in complex agreements at plant-level. The crucial statement of the 'Leber Compromise' was that plant agreements, an instrument of the Works Constitution Act, were to be the agent of implementation.

The 'Leber Compromise' relocated the locus of collective bargaining to a considerable degree to plant-level, created a multitude of different working conditions and fragmented the collective bargaining system that had been based on significant regional, or industry, bargaining units. It immediately generated the fear that the collective bargaining parties would find their role and authority diminished: 'The expansion of plant agreements to the classic area of collective regulation must lead to a loss of authority of the collective bargaining parties....'[20] Regulatory reform was understood, in this case, as seriously disturbing a central pillar contributing to the social partnership ethos which had evolved between trade unions and employers associations.

Despite grave reservations about this new development, which suggested a serious disruption of what had been seen as a successful two-tier bargaining system, the trends towards both pressing for the 35-hour week by the trade unions and the increase in flexibility demanded by the employers continued. In 1987 the Bad Homburg collective agreement for the entire metal-working industry set the working week at 37.5 hours, to be implemented on 1 April 1988, finally to be reduced to 37 hours as of 1 April 1989 with a range of 36.5 and 39 hours. Agreed working times were to be negotiated at plant-level, thus confirming the principle agreed on in the earlier arbitrated collective agreement of 1984. The Metal Trades Employers' Association continued to achieve success on the flexibility issue by raising the implementation period from two to six months; this allowed management to plan for seasonal fluctuations through the application of flexible working hours.

> Hence, theoretically in a period with few orders, employees could, for example, be required to work only 34 hours a week for 3 months, but during seasonal peak periods, 41 hours a week for 3 months – over 6 months this would produce the required average of 37.5 hours a week. The limits to these flexible working hour models, embedded as they are in collective bargaining agreements, are found only in the standards set by the 'Ordinance on Working Hours'; this well illustrates the common direction of state deregulation policies and the flexibility strategy of the employers in the Federal Republic.[21]

What had no precedent at the time of the 'Leber Compromise', that is the move away from the collective agreement to the plant agreement, had become accepted, if heavily criticized by the trade unions and the influential legal lobby. The 1990 collective agreement in the metal- and electro-industries continued to achieve agreements that balanced reduction of working hours with the flexibility that the employers sought. The 'Göppinger Model', agreed in May 1990, shortened the working week as of April 1 1993 from 37 to 36 hours and, at last, in October 1995 the working week will be 35 hours. However, the economic and political climate of the unified Germany, and the approaching Single European Market in 1992, led to the caveat that either party could hold discussions over the practicability of implementation three months prior to these dates.

The 'Göppinger Model' had clear elements of greater flexibility. It was agreed 'that immediately 18 per cent of the employees of a plant (inclusive of leading white-collar employees and white-collar employees not covered by collective agreements) could have the freedom of choice to work up to 40 hours per week and would in return receive time in compensation within 24 months or additional pay.'[22] The year 1990 established the decoupling of wage collective agreements from those concerned with working times, a manifest consequence of the regulatory changes that had begun with the collective agreement of 1984. The trade union establishment has seen in this persistent trend a move towards decentralization of the German collective bargaining structure. They interpret this trend as a disadvantage for them and their constituents.

However, the works councils have under certain circumstances taken a broader view. Rapid technology innovations have led to technology agreements which are plant specific and where the collective agreements, negotiated at regional level, only display a limited value. A proliferation of plant agreements has been the consequence; a major car manufacturer in West Germany, for example, had around 200 individual plant agreements in operation in 1990.[23] Works councils and managements have, as a direct consequence of the shift in the locus of bargaining, extended the range of substantive and procedural issues at plant-level. Trade union dominated works councils have in the process been reinforcing their power base. As a result the informal dimension of workplace industrial relations, a distinctive but not completely recognized feature of German industrial relations, has become more central.

6.   Regulatory Reform and Economic Change

For industrial relations the key development, from the early 1980s to the beginning of the 1990s, was the shift of bargaining to the plant-level and the new fexibility that was thereby triggered off for the German industrial relations system. The major factors responsible for this development were major economic changes which, from 1974 onwards, included rising levels of unemployment. The fact that economic indicators did improve, so that by 1989 economic growth rates were around 4 per cent, that inflation was controlled and the German balance of trade figures still showed a healthy surplus, did not diminish the unemployment problem. As Germany moved into 1991 the old federal states continued to have strong output performances, industry was working to full capacity and costs were still kept at manageable levels. However, the full price, in economic, political and social terms, of German unification became increasingly obvious as unemployment in east Germany accelerated towards estimates of 50 per cent of the working population by the end of 1991. The regulatory changes that had so far taken place were now regarded as advantageous in resolving the mounting problems; more deregulation and not reregulation was the proposed response from government and employers. The new economic landscape threatened to change the German idea of the 'normal' employment relationship (*Normalarbeitsverhältnis*); that is, the relationship which existed prior to the permanent unemployment problem and which had established acceptable norms for the conduct of industrial relations. What 'normal' means in this new context is subject to a continuing and mounting debate amongst German labour lawyers.

The pressure to liberalize markets, including the labour market, will increase not least with the European Community's '1992' programme. Given the increasing interdependence of markets, political decisions and employment policies, it is certain that EC regulatory measures will exercise an influence on German labour market dynamics. German employers do not expect a positive employment situation for the German labour market in the period 1993–6. They expect that the Single European Market will substantially increase productivity, and that there will be an increase in exports and direct investments outside Germany, rather than additional inland investments, with a resultant increase in employment abroad. If differences in industrial sectors and regional variations, including the uncertainty of the industrial regeneration of east Germany, are taken into consideration, then the conclusion is that employment in critical industries and sectors will develop negatively.[24]

Employment levels in individual EC-countries will depend on a complex mix of factors, including labour cost factors, which will determine decisions concerning the location of investments and companies. Economies

Table 10.4   Authorized Annual Working Times in Manufacturing, 1989

	Average Weekly Hours	Holidays, Free Days, etc. Days	Annual Hours
West Germany	37.9	40	1668
Denmark	37.5	33	1699
Belgium	38	31	1740
Netherlands	38	29	1756
France	39	34.5	1759
Italy	40	40	1760
United Kingdom	39	33	1771
Luxembourg	40	37	1784
Spain	40	36	1792
Greece	40	31	1832
Ireland	40	28	1856
Portugal	45	36	2016

Source: Calculated from *Der Arbeitgeber*, Sonderausgabe, März 1990.

of scale and competitiveness are other crucial factors. In this connection the different labour norms, collective bargaining regulations and procedures, and the contribution of working times to total manufacturing costs will play a significant role. In 1989 the latter factor showed marked differences in the EC. According to the figures in Table 10.4, Germany had the least authorized annual working hours in the manufacturing sector.

The pertinent question is whether the regulatory matrix is denser in Germany than in other EC states and if regulatory provisions inhibit a flexible operation of the labour market. The employers' answer is that present regulations do inhibit a prompt and efficient response to the structural changes taking place in the economies of the EC countries. The trade unions recognize the need for response but reject the dismantling of protective labour legislation to achieve this. The employers' notion of flexibility collides in this instance with the trade unions' insistence on societal protection of the less advantaged.

7. Conclusions

From the mid-1970s economists in West Germany began to criticize specific regulations as inhibiting economic growth and, in the labour market, as increasing costs. The forces underlying regulatory reform have been well summarized by Libecap, who presents five propositions: 'i) dissatisfied incumbent firms join with consumers in lobbying for deregulation and seek to capture quasi rents during the transition to a more competitive environment; ii) stockholders, dismayed at poor firm performance, pressure management to jettison regulation; iii) management chafes at government restrictions; iv) regulators lose enthusiasm for regulatory controls; and v) exogenous forces, such as changes in regulatory policies in other jurisdictions, force adoption of more competitive arrangements.'[25]

For industrial relations many of these forces have had an impact, albeit in diverse ways contingent on the level of the system. At the level of state policies there have been, as we have seen, regulatory reforms. The traditional legal framework regulating industrial relations in Germany did not emerge from a predetermined pattern but was the consequence of historically conditioned attitudes and a consequent consensus between trade unions, employers and the state. It was seen as an indivisible part of 'Model Germany' whose central characteristic was a stable framework and order for economic development and stability. 'Model Germany', and in particular the regulatory paradigm underpinning it in industrial relations, was not swept away by the regulatory changes of the 1980s. The legal changes have acted as a social steering mechanism but have had a moderate effect on reforming the labour market. In the case of the Employment Promotion Act Keller concludes: 'Development trends in labour markets can, through specific forms of deregulation, be influenced but never generated. It is not the labour norms, which are regarded so highly by legislators and legal experts, which are relevant for employment changes but economic factors such as economic returns and profits.'[26] The pace of regulatory reform has in general been slow, in comparison to the USA and the United Kingdom, and the impact on industrial relations has been of a specific nature.

This chapter has argued that, at the collective bargaining level, where the bargaining partners determine regulations within a legal framework, significant change has taken place. There were two aspects to the transformation. Firstly, the essential institution of collective bargaining autonomy was seen as being threatened and eroded through the increase in bargaining activity at plant-level. Secondly, there was a related attack on the protective legislation and measures that formed the accepted and complex juridified corpus of German labour law. Discussion and debate of the consequences have thrown up new cleavages and interest conflicts within employers' associations and between trade unions and employers.

In practice the trend to flexibility, the price the trade unions paid for the reduction of the working week to 35 hours, has both increased the activity and power of the works councils as well as intensifying plant-level industrial relations. In Germany a distinction has traditionally been made between disputes over rights (*Rechtsstreitigkeiten*) and disputes over interests (*Regelungsstreitigkeiten*). The former are subject to labour court rulings, while the latter may be resolved on an intra plant basis. Regulatory reform has meant an extension of the number of issues arising from disputes over interests, forcing the parties at the plant-level to modify and adjust their relationships.

At regional level the industrial unions have, since the advent of the Conservative–Liberal government in 1982, seen a reduction of their influence and power in favour of the employers. Although at the same time the framework of labour protection, guaranteed by the state, has been reduced, and deregulation policies have caused further pressures, the industrial relations institutional framework has prevailed.

The forces driving these changes have gained their momentum from economic impulses and, in particular, the unacceptable levels of high unemployment since the end of the 1970s. Regulatory reform in the industrial relations sphere has been 'a child of permanent unemployment'.[27] The economics of German unification, with its spiralling costs at the beginning of 1991, seem likely, on that basis, to support those social and political elements pressing for further reforms. The scope of regulation in industrial relations has expanded; it promulgated rules aimed at stabilizing the labour market. The extent to which regulation has achieved the objectives for which it was destined is not altogether clear and requires further empirical research. For Germany, however, it did have a substantial impact on the practice of industrial relations, above all at plant-level.

Acknowledgements

The University of Surrey is to be thanked for the award of a Minor Awards Grant towards this study and the Institute of Sociology, University of Hamburg, for providing a base. All translations of German sources by the author.

Notes

1   K. Button and D. Swann, *The Age of Regulatory Reform*, Clarendon Press, Oxford, 1989, p. 4–6.
2   R. Boyes (ed.), *The Search for Labour Market Flexibility*, Clarendon Press, Oxford, 1988, p. 8.
3   W. Adamy, 'Deregulierung des Arbeitsmarktes', in *WSI Mitteilungen*, Heft 8, 1988, p. 476.
4   R. Hickel, 'Deregulierung and Flexibilisierung als gesellschaftspolitische und ökonomische Gesamtstrategie', in *Menschliche Arbeitszeiten – geschützte Abeitsverhältnisse*, Union Druckerei, Frankfurt, 1988, p. 44.
5   See R. Hickel, 'Wirtschaft', in M. Kittner, *Gewerkschaftsjahrbuch 1990*, Bund V., Köln, 1990, p. 170.
6   'Abschlussgutachten der Deregulierungskommission', *Revitalisierung der Marktwirtschaft*, Wirtschaftsministerium, Bonn, 1991.
7   See R. Henn (ed.), *Technologie, Wachstum und Beschäftigung*, Springer V., Berlin/Heidelberg, 1987.
8   *Jahreswirtschaftsbericht 1988 der Bundesregierung*, Ziff.17.
9   R. Erd, *Die Verrechtlichung industrieller Konflikte*, Campus V., Frankfurt, 1978.
10   W. Müller-Jentsch, *Soziologie der industriellen Beziehungen*, Campus V., Frankfurt, 1986, p. 251.
11   S. Simitis, 'Zur Verrechtlichung der Arbeitsbeziehungen', in F. Kübler (ed.), *Verrechtlichung von Wirtschaft, Arbeit und sozialer Solidarität*, Nomos V., Baden-Baden, 1984.
12   S. Simitis, op. cit., p. 74.
13   J. Clark, 'The juridification of industrial relations', a review article', *The Industrial Law Journal*, **14**, (2), June 1985, p. 71.
14   R. Voigt quoted in J. Clark, op. cit., p. 71.
15   R. Voigt (ed.), 'Gegentendenzen zur Verrechtlichung', *Jahrbuch für Rechtssoziologie und Rechtstheorie*, **9**, 1983, p. 155.
16   *Tarifvertragsgesetz*, 9.4.1949, version of 25.8.1969.
17   O. Kissel, 'Die Entwicklung der Tarifautonomie im 20 Jahrhundert', in Bertelsmann Stiftung (ed.), *Zwischen Konflikt und Kooperation: Der Beitrag der Tarifparteien zur Entwicklung der Gesellschaft*, Gütersloh, 1989, p. 38.
18   See H. Kotthoff, *Betriebsräte und Betriebliche Herrschaft*, Campus V., Frankfurt, 1981.

19 G.v. Hoyningen-Huene and U. Meier-Krenz, 'Flexibilisierung des Arbeitsrechts durch Verlagerung tariflicher Regelungskompetenzen auf den Betrieb', *Zeitschrift für Arbeitsrecht*, **19**, Jhr., Heft 3/1988, p. 294.
20 O. Kissel, 'Das Spannungsfeld zwischen Betriebsvereinbarung und Tarifvertrag', *Neue Zeitschrift für Arbeits- und Sozialrecht*, **3**, 1986, p. 78.
21 R. Schmidt and R. Trinczek, *Standardized and Differentiated Working Hours in the Context of an Increasing Deregulation of Working Conditions – The West German Experience*, unpublished paper given at the International Workshop on the Redesign of Working Time, Arnoldshain, March, 1988, pp. 8–9.
22 *Sachverständigenrat, Jahresgutachten 1990/91*, 1990, p. 117.
23 Interview with IG-Metall Regional Officer, Munich, February 1990.
24 See *Regelungsprobleme des Arbeitsmarktes im Zusammenhang mit dem EG-Binnenmarkt*, Projekt im Auftrag des Ministers für Arbeit, Gesundheit und Soziales des Landes Nordrhein-Westfalen, Düsseldorf, December 1990. Unpublished.
25 G.D. Libecap, 'Deregulation as an instrument in industrial policy', *Journal of Institutional and Theoretical Economics*, **142**, 1986, p. 72.
26 B. Keller, 'Ein Irrweg der Deregulierung: Das Beschäftigungsförderungsgesetz', in *WSI Mitteilungen*, 42 Jhr., **5**, 1989, p. 282.
27 R. Hickel, 'Deregulierung der Arbeitsmärkte: Grundlagen, Wirkungen und Kritik', in *Gewerkschaftliche Monatshefte*, Nr.2, February 1989, p. 96.

11 Regulatory Culture and Regulatory Change: Some Conclusions

Kenneth Dyson

At the heart of this volume has been the relationship between regulatory change at the micro level of sectors and the opportunities for, and constraints on, regulatory change created by international and by macro-level national factors (that is, by regulatory culture and institutional structures). A regular theme has been the way in which, in Germany, a firm framework of regulatory culture and institutional structures has shaped processes of regulatory learning at the sectoral level. Generally speaking, the case studies reveal how a broad and powerful regulatory culture, with deep historical roots, has provided the central and — till the 1980s — stable context within which regulation has operated and regulatory learning occurred. Regulatory paradigms at the sectoral level have, in other words, tended to reflect this cultural imprint. The result has been a pervasive pattern of *Ordnungspolitik*, limiting the exercise of political discretion and favouring the pursuit of long-term objectives that are characteristically both enshrined in a firm legal matrix and established and realized in a framework of consultation with powerful organized interests.

At the same time regulatory paradigms have also been part and parcel of a broader learning process about the scope and methods of regulation. This regulatory learning process draws attention to the nature of sectoral policy coalitions and the changes, notably international, technological and economic, that are affecting actors in these coalitions. The question that arises is whether new processes of regulatory learning, unleashed by international, technological and economic changes, are threatening the enduring strength and resilience of the inherited regulatory culture and the institutions that support and reflect that culture. The power of processes of internationalization was, for instance, evident in the 1989 reform of the German securities exchanges. In broadcasting, telecommunications and financial services increasingly intense international competition is providing the environment within which legislators and regulatory authorities are making their tactical choices. It is not at all obvious, however, that it is determining the substance of those choices.

A configuration of three interwoven sets of factors has emerged: the complex of new international, economic and technological changes that are affecting policy coalitions at the sectoral level, through a process of redefinition of interests, and thereby creating pressures for change in regulation; the specific character of German regulatory culture, endowing regulation there with a bias towards a particular form and style rooted in the independence of public law; and the individual institutional and ideological configurations of different policy networks, and the policy coalitions that they include, underpinning the diversity of experience of regulatory learning and change across sectors. The resulting pattern of pressures for regulatory change has been far from clear-cut and one-dimensional. Whilst analysis has properly tended to focus on economic and technological forces as catalysts for change in the direction of liberalization other dimensions of change have also been apparent, for instance in environmental regulation and aspects of financial service regulation. Legal codification and control has been strengthened in some areas, in the wake of EC harmonization (for example, insider dealing), of events like the Chernobyl nuclear accident and nuclear scandals, and of wider cultural changes, themselves prompted by the adverse or threatening implications of economic and technological changes for public health and security. In health policy, too, escalating cost-containment problems have reinforced rather than reduced substantive regulation.

The chapters in this volume have underlined the importance of the sectoral specifics of regulatory learning and change. The implication is that explanation in terms of macro-level institutions and culture alone cannot do justice to the variety and different potentialities for regulatory change in Germany. Regulatory culture is by no means able to provide a single, simple explanatory framework for regulatory change. At one extreme, a firmly embedded regulatory culture is suggested by the scope and rigour of regulation and the processes of heightened regulation in nuclear energy. At another extreme, banking seems to illustrate the weakness of a regulatory culture. In the latter case regulation, or the lack of it, reflects the sectoral power of the universal banks inherited from the nineteenth century. Meanwhile, somewhere in the middle, as in telecommunications and insurance, market forces have persistently pushed for liberalization. One is reminded that the fragmentation and decentralization of political authority has had its own dynamic effects on regulation. Consequent effects have been felt not only on the institutional capacity for central, macro-level steering of regulatory development but also, sometimes, on the capacity for coordinated direction at the sectoral level, as in nuclear policy and in implications of compartmentalism in environmental regulation for the effectiveness of policy.

Detailed case studies of the type contained in this volume are useful means of exposing the complexities and ambiguities of regulatory policies. In the process they help to avoid the danger of treating the concept of regulatory culture as a monolith. Analysis is rather sensitized to the distinctive characteristics of policy sectors, to different modes of implementation and to the importance of political expediency and timing. Yet, despite these important qualifications, the impression remains of the strength and durability of the German regulatory culture. It faces significant challenges, above all from the fast-changing circumstances induced by the EC Single European Market Programme ('1992') and by German unification. The result is accumulating stresses and strains but, by early 1991, no clear signal that the German regulatory tradition had lost its grip on policy. Still typical was a style of cooperative regulation, exhibited in a preference for sectoral self-regulation (as in health and in industrial relations) and a tendency for change to be informally negotiated with the main organized interests (as in insurance, environmental pollution and commercial broadcasting).

1. The Nature of German Regulatory Culture

In order to grasp the nature and power of German regulatory culture it is essential to recognize it as the outcome of two reinforcing traditions, the state tradition (Dyson, 1980) and the industrial culture that was produced by the specific characteristics of German industrialization in the nineteenth century (Dyson, 1983). The state tradition refers to a complex of attitudes towards public authority that give priority to the principles of order, consistency, predictability and integration as the basis of institutional life. Consistent with these principles, with their tendency to codify social relationships in legal form, is a pronounced respect for the norm of objectivity and for technical argument rather than the adversarial procedure of contest. The concept of good citizenship emphasizes the precedence of public obligations over the private concerns of 'selfish' individuals. Assumptions about the need for legal regulation of economic and social relationships are interwoven into a tradition of thought about public authority that focuses on state and community. In addition, the nature of regulatory culture was profoundly influenced by the terms of Germany's industrialization. Germany entered the path of industrialization at a time when the capital and skill requirements were higher than for the earlier industrializers like Britain. From the outset German industrialization was seen to depend on the institutional capacity to mobilize capital and skills. In short, institutional reforms established intermarried principles of 'self-help' and collaboration within industry. German industrialization neither reflected nor spawned a 'market society'. 'Self-organization' became its central characteristic, with regulation as the embodiment of public requirements of responsibility within capitalism. This background of industrial culture and of a state tradition makes for the marked difference between regulation in Germany and regulation in the Anglo–American politico-legal tradition. In the German regulatory tradition there is much less hostility to the concept of firms or other social and economic organizations as enmeshed within a web of institutional interests. German regulatory culture gives priority to a 'public' conception of the firm as interlocked with a network of institutional interests over a 'private' conception of the self-sufficient firm. One result is that in Germany, unlike in Britain, there is no open market for corporate control. The legal environment of company law fosters widespread long-term commitment to companies, not least by financial institutions and employees, and inhibits mergers and acquisitions by difficult rules for changing the supervisory board of a company (Woolcock, Hodges and Schreiber, 1991, p. 14).

The specific character of German regulatory culture derives from the disposition to debate regulation in legal terms, to focus on the 'public interest' rather than 'market failure' basis of regulation, and to marshal a strongly constitutional case for constraints on the exercise of discretionary power. In these respects the language in which regulation is debated tends to differ from the markedly more economic approach to regulation in Anglo–Saxon countries. Regulation has been traditionally seen as the application of constitutional principles, regulatory issues and conflicts as about the interpretation of these principles. Hence a distinctive characteristic of German public policy has been an elaborate and formalistic legal framework of regulation and the extent to which bargaining takes place within that framework (Hancher and Ruete, 1987). The corollary of this regulatory culture is that in Germany the political problems of relaxing or reducing regulation appear to be politically more difficult than in most other countries, and certainly more difficult than tightening them or developing new regulation. As we have seen, the strength and character of German regulatory culture makes for the presence of powerful regulatory paradigms at the sectoral level. The consequences for regulatory learning have been profound, most notably a strongly-held preference for orderly and consensual change.

In order to further unravel the nature of German regulatory culture, it is important to note how public ideology has conspired with party structure to impede the practical impact of ideas of radical reform of regulation. At the ideological level there has been a close affinity and overlap of such central ideas as the 'social market economy', 'social partnership', 'social peace' and the 'self-government of the economy'. In effect, the social content of the 'social market economy' has been substantially filled in by the other three concepts; and, since its Bad Godesberg Programme of 1959 when the SPD accepted the 'social market economy', this concept has formed the bedrock of a powerful domestic political consensus about the proper relationship between state and economy. 'Social partnership' and 'social peace' have found support across party boundaries, taking in not just the SPD but also the *Sozialausschüsse* of the CDU. In essence, these twin concepts legitimate a significant role for employee interests and for regulation, for instance of industrial relations and health insurance, to secure these interests through mechanisms of social partnership. From this perspective regulation is needed to mitigate social conflicts, to broaden the basis of commitment to the market system and to ensure the role of 'social peace' as a productive factor in the economy.

The concept of 'self-government of the economy' finds its strongest support from employer interests close to the CDU. In this case legitimation is provided for an independent role of the chambers (of trade and industry and of crafts) in establishing, interpreting and monitoring standards, for instance of occupational qualification and entry into markets. From this perspective regulation is about maintaining quality, reliability and predictability in the market economy. The emphasis on the value of integrated action within the private sector means not only a substantial autonomy of the state but also a role for regulation as a defensive mechanism against competitors, notably through barriers to entry.

Taken together, these concepts form a complex bridgehead against radical reform of regulation. They have ensured that the 'social market economy' has proved compatible with a high level of regulation. The bridgehead is certainly not unchallenged: the SPD is critical of the rigidities induced by the power of the chambers; and the FDP and sections of the CDU are critical of the rigidities produced by 'social partnership' and 'social peace'. Yet, overall, the party system has provided a powerful reinforcement for the regulatory tradition. With the main exception of the FDP neither of the main political parties can be easily mobilized for radical reform, a point emphasized in Lehmbruch's chapter. The difficulties of mobilizing radical action have deeper roots than simply the party system. They relate to the complex, balancing institutional characteristics of the Federal Republic and the cultural context in which they are embedded (see Dyson's introductory chapter). The consequence is that the beneficiaries of regulation – like powerful business associations and firms – are built into relatively cohesive and well-integrated policy networks, exerting politically effective resistance to 'deregulation'. This point emerges again and again in the sectoral case studies of this volume.

A distinctive feature of German regulatory culture is the high valuation that politicians and bureaucrats tend to place on the 'public interest' rationale for regulation, compared to arguments about the social and economic costs of regulation. This type of rationale has figured most prominently in the debate in all policy sectors, for instance:

maintaining 'social peace' in industrial relations;

regional and distributional objectives (for example, broadcasting, financial services and telecommunications);

securing reliable and/or safe network structures (for example, nuclear energy and telecommunications);

protecting the public from technological risks (for example, nuclear energy and environment);

protecting the interests of depositors, insurance policyholders or patients from professional incompetence or malpractice (for example, financial services and health);

and ensuring professional/occupational standards (for example, craft trades and the liberal professions).

These 'public interest' arguments lay behind the heated arguments in the 1980s about the partial relaxation of labour market regulations, the reorganization of the Bundespost and some deregulation of telecommunications, and the limited liberalization of shopping times. Particularly sensitive have been issues of labour market liberalization, as Koch shows. There is a strong resistance to the idea that the functioning of labour markets can be compared with that of markets for goods and services.

Continuity is a striking characteristic of German regulation, leading Donges and Schatz (1986) to conclude that only half the West German economy operated according to market principles. Regulation tends, as in the past, to be most heavily focused on price controls or on entry barriers, or both. After 1945 many regulations were taken over, for instance those in the insurance industry from early this century (1901 and 1908) and, from the 1930s, those in the energy sector, haulage and the craft trades. Thus, for instance, whilst the chambers of crafts and their function of occupational training are regulated under the 1953 *Gesetz zur Ordnung des Handwerks,* this post-war legislation draws heavily on the *Handwerkerschutzgesetz* of 1897 (creating the chambers of crafts as public-law institutions) and subsequent legislation of 1908 and 1935 dealing with the organization of training. New regulations actually proliferated in the 'social market economy'. Examples include the restrictive statutory requirements governing many liberal professions; strict closing hours in the retail sector; and, in the labour market, nationwide mandatory minimum wages, strong protection of workers against dismissal and provision for high levels of redundancy pay (Donges, 1986). As Koch's chapter underlines, regulation is especially strong in the labour market, with its very complex system of collective wage-setting, labour market laws and jurisdiction by the labour courts (Soltwedel, 1988). A notable exception to the regulatory trend appeared to be the anti-trust law of 1957, establishing the general principle of the prohibition of cartels and other competition-limiting agreements. However, some very significant exceptions were explicitly made: agriculture and forestry, banking, coalmining, insurance, iron and steel, public utilities, telecommunications and transport (Krakowski, 1988). With the expansion of the service sector, the overall weight of regulatory restrictions has been increasingly felt.

2. The Deregulation Debate: The Case of the Commission on Deregulation

'Deregulation' is a word that has with difficulty been imported into Germany. In fact, it appears to have first been used in a report produced by Soltwedel (1986) for the Federal Economics Ministry. It was adopted in the title of the Commission on Deregulation (*Deregulierungskommission*), appointed by the federal government in December 1987. In German the key words have been 'liberalization' (*Liberalisierung*) and 'opening of the market' (*Marktöffnung*). This difficulty of assimilating a new international term reflected the character and strength of the German regulatory culture. *Deregulierung* appeared to undermine the supreme function of regulation as a necessary framework of order, without which there would be a descent to chaos. In this respect, it is interesting to note that, in its first report, the Commission on Deregulation (1990) states that 'there is, of course, no justification for deregulation from principle'. It is understood to refer to 'every well-justified change of the rules that serve economic freedom.' This statement heralds a pragmatic and cautious approach. Nevertheless, enormous opposition was aroused.

The beginnings of the debate about the need for an overhaul of German regulation can be dated back principally to 1982, the year in which, following the Free Democrats' statement of opposition to the economic approach of their coalition partners, the Social Democrats, the new federal government of Helmut Kohl assumed power. Central to the so-called *Wende* ('turning point') was the idea of 'rolling back the state'. In the first full legislative period (1983–87) this idea was given a fiscal emphasis. Priority was given to budget consolidation in the form of large reductions of public expenditure to radically reduce the budget deficit and create scope for tax reductions. From 1984 onwards the need to act on the issue of regulation was increasingly recognized by the Federal Economics Ministry, not least prompted by the implications of the new EC commitment to complete the Single European Market. In particular, this new integrated European market would involve freedom of movement of services, a direct challenge to the regulatory barriers surrounding the German service industries. In very large part, the new 'deregulation' debate was a reaction to changes at the EC level. These changes highlighted the fact that the Single Market struck at areas that, under the anti-trust law of 1957, were exceptions: like insurance, transport and energy. The word 'deregulation' was used in the new governmental declaration of 1987, the government committing itself to establish a Commission on Deregulation. It should not be forgotten that political pressure from the FDP was a significant factor in this development. Also, in a number of reports two prestigious public bodies gave increased ventilation to concern about the impact of regulatory burdens on the competitiveness of German industry – the Council of Economic Experts (*Sachverständigenrat*, 1987, 1988 and 1989) and the Monopolies Commission (*Monopolkommission*, 1988 and 1990). In the process 'deregulation' was being given a new respectability.

The very composition of the Commission on Deregulation was destined to evoke opposition, notably its chairmanship by Professor Jürgen Donges and the heavy weighting to employers and market-orientated economists. In its brief the Commission was asked to pay particular attention to the economic costs of regulation, especially in the service sector, and to the macro-economic effects of 'rolling back the state'. Otherwise, it was free to establish its own priorities. In practice, these priorities were heavily influenced by the likely implications of the Single European Market and the fact that the Uruguay round of trade negotiations under GATT were focusing in particular on services. From 1989 onwards, and especially in its second report (1991), the issues raised by German unification came to overshadow the work of the Commission. The Commission also paid a great deal of attention to overseas experience, especially the United States and the United Kingdom.

In its first report (1990), the Commission reviewed two sectors, applying a series of principles designed to maximize the scope for competition – the private insurance sector and the transport sector. The proposals were radical. In insurance they included liberalization of premiums (except private health insurance) and policy conditions; elimination of monopoly rights for public insurance companies; and repeal of anti-trust immunity (again with the exception of private health insurance). In transport the main recommendations involved splitting the Deutsche Bundesbahn into two companies, the railway system operator and the carrier; open access for new carriers; removal of the Bundesbahn's universal service obligation; elimination of lorry licensing on domestic routes and of all price regulations; repeal of the anti-trust immunity for domestic aviation; liberalization of entry into domestic air routes and of air fares; removal of local taxi licensing and liberalization of fares; and liberalization of long-distance bus routes.

The proposals of the first report of the Commission on Deregulation enjoyed some significant political support, not least from the Federation of German Industry (*Bundesverband der Deutschen Industrie,* BDI) and the *Deutscher Industrie- und Handelstag* (the national association of the chambers of industry and commerce). In particular, support was strong for deregulation of transport in order to reduce the high costs of road and rail haulage. This powerful support coincided with the pressures exerted by changes at the EC level to open up new scope for regulatory change (see Bulmer's chapter). Even so, as Lehmbruch's chapter shows, under Article 65 of the Basic Law the responsible Bonn ministries would be the real agencies of regulatory reform, and they had deep vested interests in resisting change. The Transport Ministry, for instance, entered considerable reservations about the proposals. Resistance to further proposals to be presented in 1991 by the Commission was made clear in advance, particularly in relationship to the labour market, craft training and certain professional groups like tax lawyers and solicitors. The Central Association of German Crafts (*Zentralverband des deutschen Handwerks*) reacted so strongly that Chancellor Kohl gave his personal assurance, in advance of the publication of the second report, that the craft apprenticeship system would be protected. It was clear that a reinforcement of political pressure from the FDP, with a more determined FDP Economics Minister, was a precondition for significant 'deregulation'. However, this precondition, assisted by the improved position of the FDP in the first all-German federal elections of December 1990, proved not to be sufficient.

German unification in 1990 appeared to create another powerful incentive to reconsider the regulatory legacy. The former German Democratic Republic (GDR) was itself bound to experience an unprecedented scope and depth of 'deregulation' as it was transformed from a centrally planned, socialist economy. The wider question was whether the critical need to radically improve productivity and attract new investment to the five new

Bundesländer would create formidable internal pressures to reduce German regulation as a whole. Would the limited administrative capacity of these new states in confronting such major problems of economic and social transformation lead to a radical redefinition of the scope and goals of regulation? In short, would 'deregulation' be part of the price of German unity? New pressures arose to consider a new role for private providers of telecommunications, for tackling the huge financial problems of the East German Reichsbahn by injecting competition, and for labour market deregulation and reform of craft training to make inward investment in the east more attractive. The prospect of a combination of EC pressures with the problems of German unification seemed, in the estimate of the Commission, to create new prospects for 'deregulation' in the 1990s. In practice, as the reaction to the Commission's second report (1991) revealed, German unification did not prove to be the catalyst for wide-ranging reforms of, for instance, labour relations and craft training. The high level of regulation associated with the old West Germany was seen as a guarantor of high product and labour market standards during a period of painful transition. In the context of German unification, and of the pressures that it unleashed, the 'public interest' arguments for regulation seemed politically more rather than less appealing. As Lehmbruch suggests, German unification did as much to undermine as strengthen the case for 'deregulation'.

3.   Lessons from the Sectoral Case Studies

The case studies in this volume have underlined significant differences in the intensity and timing of regulatory reform across sectors: from, for instance, the period of intense reform of broadcasting regulation in the early and middle 1980s to the more limited and protracted reform of health and telecommunications regulation. At first sight the impact of international forces might be expected to be profound. In certain sectors where international forces were most strongly at work – like broadcasting, financial markets, labour relations and telecommunications – and where EC action was potentially important, they were indeed significant in stimulating domestic debate about regulatory change and the emergence and activism of coalitions for regulatory reform. Except through the direct action of the EC, and then usually only in very general terms, international forces did not determine the contents or degree of regulatory change. Their prime importance was in altering the contextual conditions of regulatory action. In other words, the presence and dynamism of international forces represented a significant factor in explaining general differences in the pressures for regulatory change, not in accounting for the specific nature and degree of regulatory reform.

As the chapters have demonstrated, the interaction of two political factors – cultural and institutional legacies and policy coalitions – have had a more pervasive and a deeper influence on the definition of regulatory goals and the use of regulatory instruments. These political factors have defined the terms of regulatory learning and the extent of paradigm change at the sectoral level. The particular contribution of German regulatory culture was as a force for integration at the sectoral level, establishing similarities of regulatory action in such otherwise disparate areas as environmental, industrial relations and broadcasting regulation. At the same time policy actors at the sectoral level have served as a source of distinctive interests from those embedded in the regulatory culture and institutional structures of Germany. As we have seen, for instance in the chapters on broadcasting and financial markets, they are able to formulate, choose and pursue regulatory ideas, characteristically through coalition activity. Regulatory agencies themselves could play an important role as organizers or opponents of coalitions for reform, demonstrating that agency politics could be a key factor. Institutional philosophy and self-interest might suggest opposing 'deregulation', as in the case of the Federal Supervisory Office for Insurance (which was protecting its jurisdictional territory), or promoting it, as in the case of the Federal Cartel Office (which stood to gain jurisdictional territory as exemptions to competition law were removed).

In order to understand the detailed content and the degree of regulatory change in Germany it is necessary to focus on the specific configurations of political forces, resulting from the interaction of cultural and institutional legacies at the macro national level with policy coalitions at the sectoral level. In effect, analysis needs to draw on the cultural-, institutional- and coalition-centred approaches outlined in the introductory chapter. Two political characteristics emerge as of central importance to an explanation of regulatory change.

1. The availability of a 'reform' coalition to provide the agenda, direction and will for regulatory reform. Emergence of an effective 'reform' coalition will in turn depend on the ideological commitment and self-interests of the actors in question, their access to power and the levers of power, and their capacity to mobilize support in other related policy sectors. The chapters on financial services, telecommunications and broadcasting provide contrasting pictures of the potential and limitations on the emergence of such 'reform' coalitions.

2.   The institutional capacity for regulatory reform, in particular the de-
     gree of centralization and concentration of power in the policy process
     and the extent to which institutional arrangements facilitate unilateral
     action by one or more actors. Potential for reform will be influenced
     by the nature of constitutional and legal constraints, the organization
     of the policy process and the nature of the cultural assumptions under-
     pinning the network of actors involved.

In the case of German regulatory policies, federalism and the departmental principle enshrined in Article 65 of the Basic Law have combined to
create a highly decentralized and fragmented policy process. When these
characteristics are added to the legalistic and collectivist ethos of German
regulatory culture, it becomes clear that the institutional capacity for regulatory reform has been, on the whole, limited. Regulation has been caught
up in the interdependence and complex dynamics between the interest and
will displayed by policy actors in the pursuit of regulatory reform and the
cultural and institutional framework within which they operate. These dynamics are by no means clear-cut, as these case studies demonstrate. On the
one hand, as telecommunications and health care regulation show, the
manifest impact of cultural and institutional factors on the capacity to
implement a programme of radical regulatory reform shapes the interest in,
and will to initiate, such reform. On the other hand, the will to reform,
fuelled by international pressures, ideological commitment and redefined
self-interest, can initiate an interest in cultural and institutional change,
revealed for instance in the chapters on broadcasting and financial service
regulation.

Ultimately, the will for regulatory reform is closely interdependent with
the cultural and institutional potential for reform. This volume demonstrates
all too clearly that, in the case of Germany, cultural legacies and institutional
structures did not offer the same opportunities and incentives to radical
regulatory reform as were to be found in the United Kingdom. It also
shows that, despite the powerful institutional obstacles to creating and
mobilizing coalitions for regulatory reform, one should not underestimate
the considerable regulatory changes of the 1980s: from the more activist
approach to nuclear energy regulation to the shift in the centre of gravity of
industrial relations regulation. The catalysts were not always the same:
scandals, as in nuclear energy in 1987; market changes, as in the redefinition
of self-interest by actors within the system of self-regulation in industrial
relations; and, in the case of health, the huge problem of cost containment
and, of environment, the problem of *Waldsterben* and the fears unleashed
by Chernobyl. Whatever their specific nature, such catalysts served to
galvanize and mobilize support for change and to set off new opportunistic

behaviour patterns. Change was apparent not just in regulation but in the regulators: the 1990 federal election was followed by the creation of a new Federal Health Ministry; 1986 saw the establishment of the new Federal Environment Ministry; whilst new *Landesmedienanstalten* gained importance in broadcasting. Such institutional reforms promised important long-term consequences.

4. Conclusions

The 1980s was a decade of fierce and mounting controversies about regulation, of mounting uncertainties about the inheritance of regulatory culture and of search for new solutions to emerging regulatory problems, not least with a more assertive role for the EC in harmonizing regulation. Underlying this new climate of uncertainty and questioning were perceptions of policy failure, a widening of the cast of actors in regulation, redefinitions of institutional self-interest, a new corporate opportunism and, consequently, a greater disposition to experiment in regulation. New coalitions for regulatory reform began to make their presence felt. These characteristics were apparent across such sectors as broadcasting, financial services, health, industrial relations and telecommunication. In this new context debate focused increasingly on the appropriateness not just of existing regulatory instruments and the way in which they were operated but also of regulatory goals. New ideas began to inform regulation: for instance, the 'precautionary' principle (*Vorsorgeprinzip*) and 'ecological modernization' in environmental regulation, and 'external pluralism' (*Aussenpluralismus*) and the 'dual broadcasting order' in broadcasting. As the respective chapters on environment and broadcasting by Weale and Dyson indicate, however, the broad trend was for existing regulatory paradigms to be supplemented, rather than supplanted, by these ideas. In other sectors the grip of traditional regulatory ideas remained firm and unyielding: of the *Schutzpflicht* of the state in nuclear energy, of 'social peace' in industrial relations and of *Selbstverwaltung* in health policy, for instance.

The picture of the direction and the magnitude of the regulatory changes that emerges from these sectoral studies is complex and varied. In terms of the direction of change, policy outcomes have been the result of a varying mix of different dimensions of change – of liberalization, of increased legal codification and control, and of international harmonization. The general conclusion is that, given the fragmentation of authority, no one institution or actor has been able to dominate in any single policy area, let alone across policy areas. This combination of different dimensions of regulatory change with the complexity of institutional arrangements has also affected

the magnitude of change. Overall, the general conclusion must be that
Germany has not witnessed a radical, wholesale change in the hierarchy of
regulatory goals and instruments. In significant part because of the diffusion
of authority, produced by Germany's complex institutional arrangements,
and because of the absence of an economic shock, regulatory paradigms
were not radically challenged and replaced. Even so, in an increasing
number of sectors, regulatory issues became embroiled in an intensifying
society-wide debate and conflict. Whilst these changes raised the prospect
of radical regulatory reform, they lacked either the catalyst of economic
shock or a structure of authority that opened up opportunities for major
'deregulation'. In this respect the combination of '1992' and German unity
promised to be significant. However, '1992' seemed unlikely to administer
an economic shock, given the strength of the German economy within the
EC. It did, at least, shift the location of authority and open up avenues for
new ideas, for instance the introduction of 'insider-dealing' regulation and
liberalization of road haulage. The general impression was, nevertheless, of
'systemic congruence' between Germany and the EC in the general style of
regulation (see Bulmer's chapter and Weale's chapter on environmental
regulation). German unification, by contrast, created the real possibility of
economic shock and consequent political pressures to radically reconsider
the regulatory inheritance. As Lehmbruch's chapter indicates, the immediate
casualty of the shock administered by German unification seemed to be the
neo-liberalism of the federal coalition government rather than the regulatory
inheritance. The overwhelming trend remained that of accelerated regulatory
learning continuing to be largely embraced within a remarkably resilient
regulatory culture and a powerful institutional matrix.

References

Deregulierungskommission (Commission on Deregulation) (1990), *Marktöffnung
und Wettbewerb,* Bonn: Wirtschaftsministerium.
Deregulierungskommission (1991), *Marktöffnung und Wettbewerb: Zweiter Bericht,*
Bonn: Wirtschaftsministerium.
Donges, J. (1990), 'Wieviel Deregulierung brauchen wir für den EG-Binnenmarkt?',
Beihefte der Konjunkturpolitik, **36**, 169–87.
Donges, J. and Schatz, K.-W. (1986), 'Staatliche Intervention in der Bundesrepublik
Deutschland–Umfang, Struktur, Wirkungen', *Kiel Discussion Papers,* 119/20.
Dyson, K (1980), *The State Tradition in Western Europe,* Oxford: Martin Robertson.
Dyson, K. (1983), 'The Cultural, Ideological and Structural Context', in Dyson,
K. and Wilks, S. (eds), *Industrial Crisis: A Comparative Study of the State and
Industry,* Oxford: Basil Blackwell.

Hancher, L. and Ruete, M. (1987), 'Legal Culture, Product Licensing, and the Drug Industry', in Wilks, S. and Wright, M. (eds), *Comparative Government–Industry Relations,* Oxford: Clarendon Press, pp. 148–80.

Krakowski, M. (ed.) (1988), *Regulierung in der Bundesrepublik Deutschland – Die Ausnahmebereiche des Gesetzes gegen Wettbewerbsbeschränkungen,* Hamburg: Verlag Weltarchiv.

Monopolkommission (Monopolies Commission) (1988), *Die Wettbewerbsordnung erweitern,* Baden-Baden: Nomos.

Monopolkommission (1990), *Wettbewerbspolitik vor neuen Herausforderungen,* Baden-Baden: Nomos.

Sachverständigenrat (Council of Economic Experts) (1987), *Vorrang für die Wachstumspolitik,* Stuttgart, Mainz: Kohlhammer.

Sachverständigenrat (1988), *Arbeitsplätze im Wettbewerb,* Stuttgart, Mainz: Kohlhammer.

Sachverständigenrat (1989), *Weichenstellungen für die neunziger Jahre,* Stuttgart: Metzler-Poeschel.

Soltwedel, R. et al. (1986), *Deregulierungspotentiale in der Bundesrepublik,* Tübingen: Mohr.

Woolcock, S., Hodges, M. and Schreiber, K. (1991), *Britain, Germany and 1992: The Limits of Regulation,* London: Pinter.

Index